The Book That Takes Q's and Kicks A's

MAIL CALL

By R. Lee Ermey

HYPERION

Copyright © 2005 A&E Television Networks

The History Channel, the **"h" logo**, *Mail Call*, and "Takes Q's and Kicks A's"
are trademarks of A&E Television Networks. All rights reserved.

Library of Congress Control Number: 2004116382

ISBN 1-4013-0779-5

Hyperion books are available for special promotions and premiums.
For details contact Michael Rentas, Manager, Inventory and Premium Sales,
Hyperion, 77 West 66th Street, 11th floor, New York, New York 10023, or
call 212-456-0133.

Produced by Print Matters, Inc.
Design and page make-up by A Good Thing, Inc.

First Edition
10   9   8   7   6   5   4   3   2   1

CONTENTS

PART 3: GRUNTS • 105

"Whether you're
crazed Viking, a Ninja
warrior, or
a tank driver in
Baghdad- you're still
a grunt!"

PART 4:
AIRPLANES • 133

"Butts down and ears
up, maggots- we're
headed for the wild
blue yonder!"

PART 5: SHIPS • 175

"Hey, who let you
pukes on this
seagoing vessel? Stow
that sandwich and
start scrubbing!"

PART 6:
VEHICLES • 207

"Nobody dismissed you
yet! Oohrah! Let's
take these
babies for a spin!"

Now, listen up, puke, 'cause I'm only gonna say this once! I've got the best damn job in the whole world. That's right, as host of The History Channel's *Mail Call*, I get to drive the tanks, fly the airplanes, blow up the watermelons, shoot all kinds of weapons—and I don't even have to clean 'em!

As you can tell, hosting *Mail Call* makes the Gunny very happy. So when the idea came up of doing a book based on the show, I said, "Hell, why not?" Well, here it is, folks. Everything you ever wanted to know about military technology— past, present, and future— plus tons of great pictures.

Now, before I begin, let me just say, I ain't that big on introductions—I like to get right to the main event, if you know what I mean. But be patient. We'll get into the thick of it in just a moment. In the meantime, here are a few thoughts I put together. **And pay attention! There'll be a pop quiz later.**

The Famous Gunny

Even before *Mail Call* came along, people would often recognize me from my movies. I've been in a lot of films over the years, but the one that folks seemed to remember me most from is *Full Metal Jacket*. Fellas used to come up to me when I was walking through the airport and shout, "Hey, Gunny, *Full Metal Jacket* rules!"

But now an interesting thing has happened. When I walk through the airports of America these days—and I'm on at least four airplanes a week going coast to coast—I can't seem to take ten steps without someone yelling, **"Yo, Gunny, Mail Call rules!" Oohrah!** It's a beautiful thing.

How It All Got Started

I was up in Canada shooting this movie, *Saving Silverman*, when my longtime manager Bill Rogin got a call from a guy named Rob Lihani. Rob, along with his partner, Rob Kirk, run's this production company, Digital Ranch. They make a lot of shows for The History Channel and they wanted to know if I would like to give them an interview for a show they were making called *Sarge!*

Now, any of my fans with half a brain knows that the Gunny here was a real Marine Corps Drill Instructor from '65 through '67. So I can tell you a thing or two about what makes a good sergeant.

I told Rob, "Hell yes!"

Well, no surprise to me, the show was a hit! The next thing I knew, the two Robs and Beth Dietrich-Segarra, an executive producer over at The History Channel, came to me with a totally new kind of show hosted by yours truly. And that was the origin of *Mail Call*.

The idea was that I'd answer questions that viewers had e-mailed in about military technology on everything from the latest high-tech firepower to Civil War chow. Lihani and Susan Michaels, the writer, sort through hundreds of thousands of e-mails and pick out the most interesting questions to use on the show.

Of course, I don't know all the answers off the top of my head, but we have a staff of researchers who have not been wrong yet. I tell 'em, "Whenever you guys screw up, I'm gonna have to own up to it and do push-ups on national television. And if I have to do push-ups on air because you guys screwed up . . . well, crap rolls downhill, folks!"

A Day in Gunny's Life

A typical day for me begins with reading a book in my bathtub. That's right, Gunny reads in the bath—got a problem with that, moron? The books I read are usually about the Marines or by a Marine author. Today, for example, I'm reading *Ace*, an autobiography by R. Bruce Porter, who was a Marine fighter pilot in World War II and lives not far from me out here in California. Reading stuff like this in the morning helps me start focused and ready to attack the day.

I generally arrive on the set at about 0700 . . . that's 7 o'clock in the morning for you civilian pukes! We shoot our show not too far from my house at a ranch used for making movies. To get there I drive my truck down all these old gravel and dirt roads. By the time I arrive, the boys and girls are putting the finishing touches on the *Mail Call* tent—my canvas mansion in the woods.

I grab a cup of black coffee right off the bat, and go over the script with Susan and Rob. Our cameraman is busy lighting the set. He's a real hard-charger named Brian Callahan. But we call him "Shooter" ever since he got to play jet jockey in an F-15 when we did a story on fighter jets. Scott Harvey is our audio engineer and he makes sure everything the Gunny says can be heard loud and clear. Beats the hell out of me how Scottie ain't deaf, since he has heard more of my yelling than just about anybody. When my sweet little jeep arrives, we are good to go, and Rob yells, "Roll tape!"

Now, the ranch is where we film my little introductions and closes that appear at the beginning and the end of each segment of the show. Sometimes we also film segments where I demonstrate something like the crossbow, or a samurai sword, an antique machine gun, or cavalry horse saddle. For the really fun stuff, like anti-tank rockets or high explosive demolitions, we head off to a military base.

We spend a lot of time out in the field with the Marines at Camp Pendleton and 29 Palms or with the soldiers at Fort Irwin. I'm proud of how we've developed a damn good rapport with the military. They were a bit skeptical when the show first started, but now, five seasons later, units all over the world call us asking, "Hey, how about us?" It's great . . . we've really won their trust. Answering viewer e-mails gives us a chance to promote the military, and show Americans how sharp they are.

Gunny and the Ladies

I do lots of personal appearances at some really first-class custom car shows. At these events, there are thousands of cars in the convention center or football stadium. And tons of people. But the most incredible thing for me is to see these folks line up for hours to meet the Gunny! It's beautiful. I take time to talk to everybody, answer questions, sign autographs, you name it.

And you should see how many kids line up. And how many women! You'd be surprised—women love *Mail Call*. At last count I had twenty-six e-mailed proposals of marriage. Now, don't get me wrong, I'm happily married already, and my wife—for some strange reason—won't let me marry anyone else. But the point is, women are watching the show. Why? Chances are many of them couldn't care less about 155 howitzers, M1 Abrams tanks, or 81mm mortars. But what they do like is a good laugh.

You see, the truth is that a lot of women watch the show because the ol' Gunny makes 'em laugh. The ladies hug me and say, "I think you're funny, Gunny." And that's just fine by me. When I was first hired to do *Mail Call*, I told everyone I wasn't going to be a serious Ollie North type. Now, I respect Ollie for what he does, but that's just not me. I wanted the show to be not only informative, but also colorful and off-the-wall.

Take the infamous crossbow episode, for example. That crossbow we had was an absolute piece of crap. If I was stuck with that crossbow in a combat situation, I would use it as a club instead. It was useless! And the Robin Hood–looking guy who was featured on that segment had never fired the crossbow before—he'd borrowed it from a friend. Neither he nor I could hit the broad side of a barn with that thing. After taping this segment, I thought if there was ever a sequence we wouldn't be able to use, it was this one. But the *Mail Call* videotape editors, Stephen Pomerantz and Joey Barasch, managed to cut that sucker into a really funny story, and it actually became one of the audience's favorite episodes. The way I look at it, a little humor never hurts.

Watermelons

People always ask me about the watermelons. The first show we did was a segment on samurai swords. First the reenactor and I talked about the history of these swords, the time period in which they were made, and all that good stuff. But then, when it came time to demonstrate how to use one of the damn things, it struck us—what was I supposed to do with the sword, chop down a tree? And just at that moment, an idea came to us. We remembered the watermelons that we had eaten with lunch that day. `"Hey," I said. "Have we got any of those left?" So the watermelons were brought out, and we chopped 'em up with the samurai sword.`

Well, ever since that day, we have never been without watermelons. It just caught on. Now, whenever we want to demonstrate a Tommy gun or a medievail battle-ax or whatever, we roll out the watermelons. And after we blow them up, we get to eat them! Not to mention, it's cool to see how far we can hurl 'em with a trebuchet. Watermelons just seem to fit right into our little show.

My Philosophy

We went to Iraq with *Mail Call* in May and July 2003. After we'd finished taping the show, I stayed on with my friend Keith Guinto, the *Mail Call* Coordinating Producer, and we crisscrossed the country in two CH-46 helicopters from the First Marine Air Wing. It was an amazing experience, my trip to Iraq. I gave a speech to thirty-two different Marine units all over the country. It felt great to lend my support to America's fighting men and women, and this is also one of the most important reasons that I do the show.

I constantly hear from my old Marine comrades. I was in the Marine Corps for eleven years. You'd be surprised how many of the old privates I trained still come to see me. They bring their platoon yearbook and I sign it for them. And I've met some of the Marine greats. Chesty Puller. Carlos Hathcock. "One Shot One Kill Hathcock" they called him, the great Vietnam-era Marine sniper. He's one of my heroes—I even got him to autograph a copy of his book for me.

I've also had ROTC colonels come up to me and say that *Mail Call* is mandatory viewing for their cadets, and they all discuss the show at their meetings. Three times, I've had commanders bring their junior ROTC units to see me.

There's not a single family in America that doesn't know someone in the military—be it a daughter, son, nephew, niece, husband, wife, friend, whoever—and they're interested in learning about what these people do. The equipment they use, the training they've had, their motivation. In this sense, not only is *Mail Call* pretty damn entertaining—I believe it also provides a valuable service.

Are you falling asleep, puke? Want to get right to the action? Well, you know what—so does the Gunny!

Semper fi.
Carry on.
Turn the page! Now!

R. Lee Ermey
Gunnery Sergeant
USMC/VA (very active)

CREDITS

I'm obliged to salute these fine folks for all their work in making my show and this here book a big hit:

Glen Ash
David Aykens
Joey Barasch
David Barsky
Rob Beemer
Mel Berger
John Binninger
Hal Buell
Brian Callahan
Mark Chait
Jane Comins
David Connelly
Drew Cook
Scott Corburn
Tara Craig
Caley Cronin
Joseph Cummins
Beth Dietrich-Segarra
Arthur Drooker
Matt Duclos
Allan Duffin
Jeremy Evans
Yvonne Fannon
Harlan Glenn
Keith Guinto
Ann Hackett
Gary Harper
Scott Harvey
Lou Hirsch
David Hodge
Marc Honorof
Derek Hunt
Garry James

Tom Jennings
Tom Jones
Laura Jorstad
David Kingery
Rob Kirk
Rob Lihani
Jim Lindsay
Tony Long
David Lott
Charlie Maday
Mike Matus
Susan Michaels
Bob Miller
Chris Mortensen
Andy Papadopoulos
Howard Petlack
Steve Pomerantz
Sean Quinn
Erich Randolph
Keith Reiner
Bill Rogin
Richard Rothschild
Abe Scheuermann
Valarie Sheldon
Martha Sloan
Matt Stevenson
Rob Stone
Greg Taylor
Amy Thomas-Rogin
Carrie Trimmer
Mike Twardy
Mike Vincenti
Morgan Worth

Now quit patting yourself on the back and get back to work!

PART ONE: WEAPONS

"From crossbows
to lasers,
a whole lotta
whup-ass!"

THE ROMANS' NASTY LITTLE SURPRISE

The gladius.

"What were the secret weapons of the ancient Romans?"
—Craig, Kennesaw, Georgia

Good question, Craig, because the Romans were pretty darn creative in coming up with new ways to aim 'em and maim 'em. They used all types of weapons to build their empire . . . daggers, swords, spears—they really liked sharp stuff.

First, let's talk about some of their not-so-secret weapons—like the gladius, their double-edged short sword, designed to thrust. Then there was a longer weapon called a spatha, which was what the horse troopers used. It had a longer reach so you could attack a guy on the ground. And those pesky Romans also carried the pugia, which is a kidney dagger. Ouch!

But listen up, barbarians: Even if you dodged the swords, the Romans still had a nasty little surprise waiting for you. The pilum was the secret weapon of the Roman Empire. And believe me, it was a lot more than a stick with a sharp point. This was the weapon that revolutionized Roman warfare. Each of the Roman legionnaires carried two of them. They would throw these—javelin style—right into the ranks of an enemy force as it charged toward them.

• **Caius Man, Roman reenactor:** One advantage of the pilum is that it will fly a great distance, because of its sleek shape and convenient grip.

"The pilum: nothing to mess around with!"

Other advantages are the sharp, pointing tip and the long, thin shaft, which allows it to penetrate very deeply through an opponent's shield. If I'm a Roman soldier and I get a good throw on this thing, even if my opponent's arm is all the way out, the pilum will go right through into his belly, causing him some serious grief. The final advantage is that the iron shaft was designed to bend or break upon impact—which made it impossible for the enemy to chuck it back. •

So there's your look at the secret weapon that devastated the enemies of Rome. Julius Caesar coined the Latin phrase *Veni, vidi, vici* . . . I came, I saw, I conquered.

That's not bad, but I got a better description. It doesn't need a translation:

Slice 'em, dice 'em, kill 'em.

THE MYSTERY OF GREEK FIRE

Back in seventh century A.D. Greece, a lot of battles were being fought on the sea, and you had to get pretty darn close to your enemy to do any damage. So along came a Syrian engineer named Callinicus who thought up something called liquid fire. Basically, he cooked up a concoction that got shot through a hose and burst into flames. It was called "Greek fire" because the Greeks first used it at the siege of Constantinople around A.D. 670. It was nearly impossible to extinguish and wreaked a lot of havoc. Greek fire sounds kinda like the ancient version of napalm: It sticks to everything and burns like hell. Now, napalm is basically jellied gasoline . . . but to this day the exact ingredients in Greek fire remain a mystery.

"Ermey-us Maximus goes in for the kill."

WICKED WEAPONS OF MEDIEVAL TIMES

"What were the most wicked weapons in medieval times?"
— Matt, King Salmon, Alaska

"The defenseless watermelon feels the war hammer's wrath!"

Here's your answer, Matt, and it ain't gonna be pretty.

Warriors in the Middle Ages had all kinds of vicious weapons to choose from when the you-know-what hit the fan. They had the chopping kind, the poking kind, and my very favorite weapon, the crushing kind! We visited Jeffrey Hedgecock, our neighborhood knight from Historic Enterprises in Ramona, California, to help us sort all these weapons out. He started with a lance—talk about a poke in the eye with a sharp stick!

• **Jeffrey Hedgecock:** The lance is basically a longer form of a spear. The knight had the advantage that he could couch the lance under his arm and transmit all of the force of horse and rider to his enemy. And there wasn't very much that could withstand that penetrating power. •

But the lance got plain clumsy in close quarters and hand-to-hand combat. That's when you'd chuck the sucker and grab a war hammer to deliver some "smashing power." The war hammer was used in one hand to deliver crushing blows to enemy armor. It had all its weight concentrated at the head, so it was a very unbalanced weapon. But, man oh man, when you get hit with that—watch out! It also had a spike on the back to deliver a very strong blow.

And if that didn't work, you whipped out the old battle-ax. And I ain't talkin' 'bout my dear mother-in-law, God bless her!

"Each could put a hurtin, big time!"

• **Jeffrey Hedgecock:** As with the war hammer, the battle-ax has all its weight right at the head. It has a spike on it, which is very similar to the one on the war hammer. And that blade could cut through some of the toughest armor of the day. •

But one of the most effective ways to repel an enemy was with a mace. I'm talking about the face-smashing mace! Its major advantage was that it had six flanges—sometimes fewer, sometimes more. But with the flanges facing in all directions, it didn't matter which direction you struck your opponent. The mace had one more advantage, too: Since it didn't have a large blade or a large hook on it, it was less likely to get tangled in your opponent's weaponry.

But what about the poor foot soldier, who got clobbered by knights all day? What did that guy have? Well, the weapon of choice for your basic infantryman was not bad at all. It's called a poll ax, not a pole ax, because *poll* refers to the head of the weapon. It was a sharp blade on the end of a long pole, which was pretty darn good for defending yourself against virtually all types of other soldiers—whether they were on foot or horse, and whether they were masked or not. 'Course when firearms entered the picture, all this went out—but I still wouldn't want to be on the receiving end of one of the medieval world's wicked weapons!

I HEAR YOU KNOCKIN' BUT YOU CAN'T COME IN!

From ancient times up to about the fifteenth century, siege warfare was the name of the game, and if you were on the outside looking in, you had to go over, under, or through the enemy's fortifications. Enter the battering ram. At first, Greeks and Romans got a tree, put a hunk of iron on the head, and had ten or twenty guys batter down the wall. Later on, some smart weapons designer got a bigger tree, suspended it from a beam, and had a hundred or more guys swing it into the wall. They covered the whole thing with armor plating, which worked even better 'cause it protected the grunts inside. They called this contraption a *testudo*, which is Italian for "tortoise," 'cause that's kinda what it looked like!

TEST YOUR MILITARY IQ

How much did the average medieval weapon weigh?

Answer on page 232.

CROSSBOWS

CROSSBOWS

"Just how accurate was a medieval crossbow?"

— Steve, Mobile, Alabama

Steve, the first thing you gotta remember here is when it comes to the medieval crossbow, we're not talking high technology. You've basically got a hunk of wood, a bowed metal spring, some type of trigger gizmo, and flexible animal gut. But back when Richard the Lion-Hearted was waging war during the Crusades, this was the deadliest thing going. It had a lot of pluses. Crossbows were easier to aim than longbows because the crossbowman didn't have to use one hand to pull back the string. The weapon could also be cocked and loaded and carried that way, for immediate use, if need be. And you didn't have to be as all-fired strong to shoot the

"The medieval crossbow: the deadliest thing going!"

damn thing as you did with the longbow, which needed lots of pull.

Our pal Tim Pickles, the medieval weapons expert, filled us in on more.

• **Tim Pickles, crossbow expert:** The crossbow was a way of breaking through stronger armor that would stop the swords and arrows that were being used at the time. Crossbows did it by ramping up the thrust. With a hardened metal spring creating up to two hundred pounds of tension, the weapon had to be cocked with a special hook and lots of leg strength. Lay in an arrow—they called them bolts—and you've got a projectile with the same speed as a ball fired from a musket. •

So even at the peak of medieval armor technology, when a breastplate would protect its owner from any weapon, it would not stop a crossbow bolt. The arrow would burst right through the armor. If there was chain mail underneath that, the bolt could split the rings apart. Then it would pierce the padding, and flesh and bone had no chance whatsoever.

To answer Steve's question about accuracy: The crossbow could certainly outperform any longbow in terms of distance—using an actual medieval crossbow, for instance, one modern British shooter sent a bolt 490 yards. However, the crossbow was pretty inefficient when it came to accuracy. The draw length of the bow was so short (compared to that of the longbow) that the bolt, while powerful, was erratic in flight.

We here at *Mail Call* wanted to test one of these babies for ourselves, but since we'd never fired a crossbow before, we decided to make things a little easier on ourselves. We set up our breastplate target just thirty yards away—a piece of cake . . . or so we thought. After repeated attempts, it turned out none of us could hit a barn door with the damn thing!

So, Steve, the crossbow lesson for today is: Get up close before you fire!

That's why, in medieval times, they put laws on the books prohibiting ownership of these crossbows. They

ASSASSINS AND CROSSBOWS

Just as Lee Harvey Oswald had a particular weapon in mind before he committed his nefarious deed, assassins loved crossbows—the smaller-sized bows in particular. They were easy to carry and conceal, they were light in comparison to other bows, and if you could get close enough, you could put a big-time hurtin' on some king or nobleman before his bodyguards even knew it.

were highly expensive, in any event, and your average peasant didn't have the cash to go out and buy one. But the rich did, so crossbows often found their way into the hands of the medieval era's most deadly assassins.

"Shooting a crossbow is a heckuva lot harder than we thought!"

THE DEADLY LONGBOW

A modern medieval expert tests his mettle.

> "What made the longbow a war winner back in the Middle Ages?"
> —Aaron, St. Mary's, Ohio

The Gunny plays William Tell.

In their heyday six or seven hundred years ago, English bowmen used longbows to win on many a medieval battlefield. Jeffrey Hedgecock, our medieval weapons expert, showed me the power, precision, and rate of fire that made the longbow such a revolutionary weapon. Now, Jeff didn't just pick this thing up at the local sporting goods store; he handmade this bow, so it's as authentic as possible.

• **Jeffrey Hedgecock, medieval weapons expert:** This is a longbow made out of a wood called yew. It used to be grown in England and in Europe, but now most of it comes from the Pacific Northwest states like Oregon and Washington. The string is made out of linen, although sometimes it was made out of hemp. So it's a grass that's processed into fiber and then spun into string. The bowmen used a variety of arrows. There were armor-piercing arrows, with what's called the bodkin point and what's called the barbed broadhead. And finally there was what was called the swallowtail, an arrow used for hunting, but also against horses. If it doesn't kill the horse right away, it can certainly anger the animal and make it useless in a battle formation. •

The biggest advantage in a battle situation with a longbow was that it could be fired quickly. You can shoot probably up to twelve arrows per minute. Now, crossbows were powerful, too, but they were harder to aim, they had a shorter range, and their rate of fire was a lot slower than a longbow. Longbows were about five feet tall, and it took some serious muscle power to draw and fire one accurately. A well-trained archer could penetrate armor at more than 50 yards; he stood a good chance of getting a kill at 100 yards, and could still wound the enemy from 250 yards away. And these guys weren't just sissies, either, firing from the rear.

• **Jeffrey Hedgecock:** They were almost anywhere in a battle formation. Often they were on the flanks. And they would move to the front and fire at the enemy when the enemy was a good distance away. As the enemy got closer they might break back to the flanks and eventually into the rear and fire over their own troops at the enemy. •

Longbows were so effective that these archers often made up more than three-quarters of a total English battlefield force. Other European armies either relied on the crossbow or tried to outnumber the English with heavier forces. But the elite English archers usually cut them down before they got close. It could take ten years of hard training to develop the upper-body strength and keen eye to be a top-notch longbowman. And with that

The medieval longbowman used a variety of sharp-pointed arrows.

kind of investment in each archer, the Brits made sure he had some backup weapons if things got dicey.

• **Jeffrey Hedgecock:** By and large all archers needed to have a secondary weapon other than their bow. And that was a long sword, which had a blade anywhere from two feet to three feet in length and weighed from two to three pounds. And then they might have a dagger . . . which would be a weapon of last resort for close-in fighting. •

Of course, you maggots just know I had to take a shot with this baby after our fiasco with the crossbow, so Jeff gave me some instructions, and then . . . Well, let's just say I turned out to be quite the accomplished bowman. Ten years my ass; I had this down in ten minutes!

TEST YOUR MILITARY IQ

When was the longbow replaced by firearms?

Answer on page 232.

DEADLY NINJA WEAPONS

> **"What kind of weapons did ninjas use?"**
> —Bruce, Eureka Springs, Arkansas

Back in twelfth-century Japan, ninjas were highly disciplined warriors skilled at martial arts and covert operations—kinda like the first Special Forces. They would creep around, spy, gather intelligence, maybe knock off a bad guy or two . . . and then disappear into the night.

In fact, the word *ninja* in Japanese means "one who is disciplined in stealth." But when they had their backs to the wall, ninjas unleashed some nasty little surprises. It was ninja expert Dan King who gave me the dope on the unique fighting weapons of these warriors.

So, Dan, the ninja was basically an ancient Asian version of a CIA, recon-type individual, right?

• **Dan King, ninja expert:** Right. Most of their weapons were defensive in nature, like the *kusarigama*—basically just a farm implement that's got a chain and a weighted ball on the end. Then there are the blades called the *shuriken*, of which there are several different varieties. We have the *kudama shuriken*, which means "wheel shuriken"; the *bo shuriken*, which is the "stick shuriken"; and the *shu shuriken*, or "palm shuriken." •

Boys and girls, *shuriken* means "hand-throwing blade"—it's a blade that's thrown with your hand. That should be obvious, but I just wanna make sure you're listenin', maggot! The throw is overhand, and you're aiming for an enemy's weak spots . . . like the eyes. If you're wondering why I haven't mentioned nunchaku, forget it. Those are a twentieth-century invention strictly for the movies. Even though Bruce Lee used 'em pretty doggone effectively, nunchaku would have been about as familiar to real-life ninjas as a laptop.

Kusarigama and *shuriken*: simple, deadly, and effective.

"Pay attention, you grabasstic snot ball. There's a lot more coming up!"

SAMURAI SWORDS

"What makes samurai swords so dangerous?"
—Sean, Indianapolis, Indiana

An ancient, elegant three-foot-long razor blade.

The word *samurai* means "those who serve." And we're not talkin' lunch here! This elite class of warriors served their Divine Emperor beginning in ninth-century Japan. The samurai's instrument of death was as glorious, spiritual, and powerful as the men who wielded it. Let's talk to historian Dan King again . . .

• **Dan King, historian: The sword consists of three major pieces. There is the handle, called the** *tsuka*, **which is made up of sharkskin and cotton cloth. Then you have the** *tsuba* **or hand guard, and also the** *saya* **or scabbard. The** *tsuba* **could have family history on it, and sometimes it's inlaid in gold or silver. And depending on the smith, sometimes the** *tsuba* **itself can fetch more than the sword. Now, moving on to the sword itself, the samurai sword has basically been called a three-pound razor blade. And the most unique thing about the samurai sword is this wavy pattern called a** *hammon*, **which is beautiful but strictly decorative.** •

So what made this sword so formidable? Dan tells us it was the forging. The swordsmith would first heat the steel; then, with his assistants, he would pound a fold in the metal. This process would be repeated as many as one hundred times to create more than thirty thousand layers. A single sword took months to make. The techniques used to forge a sword were handed down from master to apprentice. The swords have lasted a lot longer than the samurai. The emperor outlawed these warriors after they participated in a failed rebellion in 1876. But when the Japanese military rose to power, the swords found a new home.

There are still a lot of samurai swords out there somewhere. If you need a little kick in the rear to go check out your closets and your attics, keep this in mind: A perfect samurai sword from one of the best makers could today sell for more than a million bucks . . . and that'd even put a smile on this ol' man's face.

"Don't chop through a watermelon as if you're cutting cordwood. You want to slice and pull through."

NASTY PIRATE WEAPONS

"What kind of weapons were used by pirates?"
—Taylor, Carrolton, Texas

W ell, shiver me freakin' timbers, matey, those guys were armed to the teeth. Cannons, cutlasses, guns . . . they had it all. I mean, even if they lost a hand, they just strapped on a hook!

A pirate's arsenal was a hodgepodge of long-range and up-close battle gear. One piece of artillery pirates liked to use was called a swivel cannon. This was a small cannon that mounted easily on the side of the ship, and could be quickly turned and fired at the approaching enemy. Once a pirate ship was inside cannon range, pirates broke out their long-range personal firearms. Pirates were also fans of shorter muskets called musketoons. A really nasty-looking version was called a blunderbuss. It could be loaded with musket balls, nails, or anything sharp, making it basically a garbage disposal with a trigger and a big bang. It's big, it's mean, it's nasty looking—it's the Dirty Harry weapon of the pirate age!

But perhaps the most iconic weapon of the pirate trade was the short sword called the cutlass, with its famous curve. The curve made it handy for slashing enemies and

The tools of any self-respecting pirate's trade.

cutting through rope lines on deck. For intense hand-to-hand combat, pirates favored the sharp steel blade of a dagger, which was great for fighting in close quarters.

My own favorite pirate-fighting tool is a particularly gnarly little piece of steel called a "barefoot barb." It consisted of two pieces of metal bound together, and when it was tossed on the deck of a ship—well, any barefoot enemy was in for a pain like he had never known. But you can count on this—if these boys were caught in a jam and had to break out their weapons to fight, they'd have no problem killing you right there on the spot.

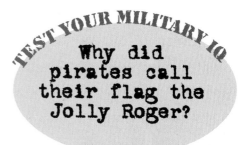

TEST YOUR MILITARY IQ

Why did pirates call their flag the Jolly Roger?

Answer on page 232.

HOW TO MAKE A TOMAHAWK

> **"How did Native Americans make and use tomahawks?"**
> —Ian, Morehead City, North Carolina

The tomahawk was the favorite weapon of many Native American warriors for hand-to-hand combat.

Most people think of a tomahawk as a metal hatchet. But actually the word was first used by Algonquin Indians in the 1600s to describe any wood, stone, or metal club used to strike an opponent. Believe me, those babies could pack a wallop! A skilled warrior would aim for the head, hoping to crack the skull and kill the enemy quickly.

To learn more, we went to the plains of South Dakota and met with expert craftsman Melvin Miner of the Cheyenne River Sioux tribe. Melvin makes tomahawks in the ancient way, using traditional methods and materials . . . a stick, a stone, and some rawhide to bind it all together. The first step is to carve a groove in a stone. The tomahawk handle is a pliable willow stick that's bent around the grooved stone. Then he ties it all with natural rawhide. It can take Melvin all day to make just one high-quality cranium cracker.

Native Americans eventually got their hands on the metal hatchets made by European settlers. These penetrated the flesh a lot easier. With these new sharp metal hatchets, you didn't have to hit your enemy in the skull;

you could hit him in the arm and he'd bleed to death. Back in the day, a well-armed warrior might carry a tomahawk for offense and a shield for defense. The tightly drawn hide could protect warriors from just about anything, except bullets. Bows and arrows were pretty effective when attacking from a distance, but for close-in hand-to-hand combat, nothing topped the tomahawk.

HOW POWERFUL WAS THE ANCIENT SLING?

It may not look like much, but add a rock and a skilled operator and you've got a pretty effective weapon. The sling has been around just about as long as recorded history . . . after all, it was the weapon of choice when David had a little disagreement with Goliath. The theory behind the weapon is simple: Add a rock or a choice chunk of lead, put some muscle into it, and you've got what amounts to a handheld catapult.

The ancient Hawaiians put a nice little twist on this weapon. They made their slings out of the intestines of their enemies. Oohrah!

ROCKETS' RED GLARE

Francis Scott Key

**The Congreve rocket:
a thirty-two-pound fiery love letter.**

**"What kind of rockets were
first used in combat?"**
—Roger, Denver, Colorado

Well, Rog, imagine bottle rockets . . .
on steroids!

To track the flight path of how rockets came to the modern battlefield, you gotta blast back in time to the thirteenth century, about the time the Chinese developed gunpowder. They attached canisters filled with the explosive powder to arrows and fired them into the air. Their enemies called the new weapon "thunder that shakes the heavens."

In the eighteenth century, the armies of India used rockets against British forces—and the Brits soon realized they'd better get their hands on some, too. A British colonel named William Congreve created a long-range rocket that could really decimate an enemy. His creation, which he modestly named the Congreve rocket, was a thirty-two-pound fiery love letter addressed to an enemy up to two thousand yards away. Basically, the rocket consisted of an iron cylinder strapped to a guide stick. It was filled with a gunpowder propellant and tipped with an explosive charge. British rocketeers lit a fuse to ignite the propellant and launch the rocket skyward.

• **Mark Dennis, military historian:**
The idea was that you could deliver a nine-pound charge, which would

Francis Scott Key put it all in the national anthem.

normally take a ton-and-a-half cannon and a hundred yards of road. With a rocket, though—one tube, one launcher, two men. The Congreve rocket got its first test during the Napoleonic wars in the fall of 1806, when a fleet of British warships was anchored outside of Boulogne, France. In just over a half an hour the crews launched two thousand rockets and pummeled the city. •

The most famous use of Congreve rockets came during the British bombardment of Fort McHenry near Baltimore during the War of 1812. A young lawyer named Francis Scott Key witnessed the event. When he saw the

U.S. flag still flying after the battle, he wrote "The Star-Spangled Banner." His line "and the rockets' red glare, the bombs bursting in air" refers to Congreve's rockets.

"I'm in your face, scumbag . . . basic training starts right now!"

But there was an inherent problem in the Congreve. Even though designers adjusted its size for better aerodynamics, it always had trouble flying straight. As powder inside burned, the weight of the rocket changed—along with the weapon's center of gravity.

The solution came in 1843, when a British inventor named William Hale inserted small directional vanes in the exhaust nozzle. These vanes forced the rocket to spin like a bullet, which kept it on a straight flight path. In 1848, the United States purchased twenty thousand of these weapons; the first American rocketeers went into battle during the Mexican-American War.

But rockets had reached their apogee—that means "highest point of development," numb nuts! By the time the Civil War began a decade later, the improved range and accuracy of cannons and artillery left rockets obsolete . . . but by World War II, they were back on the battlefield in a big way!

The British rocket Fort McHenry, 1812.

"What is a bowie knife?"
—Rick, Yuba City, California

"Not bad—almost like my old friend, the K-Bar."

The bowie knife, the kissing cousin to my trusty old Marine K-Bar. When you say bowie *knife*, most people know what you're talking about. It's the biggest, most famous battle blade in American history. It's kind of our version of King Arthur's Excalibur. Some of 'em are more than eighteen inches long, but it's about more than just size. What makes a bowie knife a bowie knife? Author J. R. Edmondson of Fort Worth, Texas, is a nationally recognized authority on the bowie knife.

Jim Bowie, the larger-than-life hero who started it all.

• **Jack Edmondson, bowie knife expert:** There was hardly any task it could not do . . . from marking trees, skinning game, cutting through the bones, or chopping, to whittling. In the era of the single-shot firearm, pistol or rifle, when there was not time to reload, the bowie knife was also a most effective last-ditch defensive weapon. •

The mystique surrounding the bowie knife begins with frontier adventurer Colonel Jim Bowie. Jim first made the knife famous in a bloody 1827 brawl between two rival Louisiana political factions called the Sand Bar fight. Jim Bowie was shot twice and stabbed six times. But he still used his trusty knife to kill one of the fellas who'd jumped him, and he survived to fight another day. Ol' Jim was a hard man to kill!

The Sand Bar fight captivated the country. It made legends out of both James Bowie and his knife. The knife became perhaps the first real American fad. There were southern gentlemen who did not feel properly attired unless they were wearing their ornate bowie knife. Actually, Jim's older brother, Rezin, claimed he invented the famous blade in the form of a hunting knife years earlier—I guess either way you could still call it a bowie knife. Descended from the simple riflemen's butcher knives of the Revolutionary War, the bowie knife's unique design also helped it capture the attention of a nation.

The clipped point, perhaps the most defining feature of a bowie knife today, was according to popular legend ground to create a false edge, an edge for cutting upward, as in a knife fight. The real advantage to a clipped point, however, is that taking out steel provides a finer point and also reduces the weight at the end of the knife. The clipped point is so distinctive that these days, any knife with that feature is generically called a bowie knife. Because the design was so popular, a lot of people made bowie knockoffs in the old days.

Given all the copycat bowies produced back then, finding one that you can prove was made by a real Bowie is now virtually impossible. If you can in fact prove that either Jim or Rezin was somehow involved with your particular knife, though, it'll be worth millions of dollars—and you'd better give some of that to your Gunny, ratboy!

JIM BOWIE AT THE ALAMO

The final chapter in Jim Bowie's colorful story took place in 1836. He and about 180 Texans were holed up in a broken-down mission called the Alamo fighting for Texas independence against General Santa Anna and three thousand troops of the Mexican army. Exact details about his final days are kind of fuzzy, but we do know that Jim Bowie stayed with Davy Crockett and his other buddies even though he was pretty sick—probably with tuberculosis. And when those *soldado*s came into his room, he would have tried one more time to prove that he was a hard man to kill. Jim Bowie died at the Alamo, his bowie knife by his side, on March 6, 1836.

Last stand at the Alamo.

TEST YOUR MILITARY IQ

During the Civil War, soldiers of which army carried the bowie knife?

Answer on page 232.

MR. GATLING AND HIS GUN

"How fast can a Gatling gun fire?"
—Frank, Las Vegas, Nevada

The first machine gun: the rattlin' Gatlin'!

Well, Frank, let's put it this way: When it was first fired in combat, there was nothing faster than a Gatling. If you were a Civil War soldier, it was pretty scary what with all that flying lead around.

And that was exactly the intent of inventor and idealist Dr. Richard Gatling. Back in 1862, he patented his rapid-fire gun in the hope that the weapon would be so intimidating, armies would see the futility of war and solve their differences peacefully. Unfortunately for Gatling, that dream backfired. His invention quickly became the most popular hand-cranked machine gun in the world. Here you had a weapon that wasn't gonna hurt you, wasn't gonna kick you, and wasn't gonna move around; it'd shoot exactly where you pointed it, without any of the sighting problems of a shoulder-fired weapon.

We asked Gary Harper of Harper Haus Weapons Productions to show us just what these babies can do.

• **Gary Harper:** After getting the gun into battery position, you would sight along the right-hand side, just like you would a normal rifle, and adjust with your right hand for elevation into the target. Then select the automatic oscillating device feature, which will swing the muzzles of the gun slightly, producing a spreading effect, at any kind of distance. Or select straight-on firing for direct firing into a set position, call for your first magazine of ammunition, insert that into the weapon, and you're ready to fire at will. •

On paper, the Gatling gun is capable of firing twelve hundred rounds per minute. In actual practice Gary's team can blast only six hundred rounds per minute. But that's still a heckuva lot better than dozens of infantrymen armed with single-shot rifles.

• **Gary Harper:** There's another problem a Gatling gunner has to contend with: All that black powder ammunition generates a huge amount of smoke. A gunner has to rely on a spotter for target adjustments. That slows things down even more. •

So in a real-life combat situation with a spotter, the Gatling gun would fire just about five hundred rounds a minute. Still, even at that rate, the Gatling was considered overkill in its day. Accuracy of fire into large groups of people—which was how armies were maneuvered on the field at the time— was far more important than speed of fire. Trouble was, the fast fire ended up putting ten rounds into one body instead of three or four; it was a waste of ammunition.

The military declared the Gatling obsolete in 1911 after fifty years on the battlefield. But Gatling's invention was given new life decades later when its multibarreled design was used in the automated Vulcan gun. This new-and-improved Gatling can fire anywhere between three and six thousand rounds per minute. I'll bet good old Dr. Gatling never even dreamed of that kind of firepower.

"Knock off the jaw-jacking and pay attention. There's more *Mail Call* coming up!"

Dr. Richard Gatling hoped for peace.

An extraordinary advance in technology.

AIMING CIVIL WAR ARTILLERY

"How did Civil War cannoneers aim their artillery pieces?"
—Andy, Commack, New York

These days, hard-charging Marines put steel on target using global positioning satellites and computerized fire direction control systems. In fact, they can accurately hit an enemy up to fourteen miles away.

But back in 1862, during the Civil War, no artillery crew had it that easy—believe me! A group of Civil War historians known as the Richmond Howitzers, who are just about as crazy as I am, agreed to show me how it was done. I went with a snappy cover and a mustache just to blend in a little bit, and we gathered around a ten-pound Parrott gun, which has a maximum effective range of slightly over a mile.

Maximum effective range: one mile.

• **Ed Mann, reenactor:** The most common sight used on the Parrott gun during the war was the stadia sight. You look through the peep sight at the rear, using the front blade as the front sight, adjusting left or right with the hand spike at the back and the yellow leading screw until you are on target, and then you'd fire. Another way to aim is with a pendulum hausse, and it works on the same principle, with a sight that goes up and down based on the number of degrees of elevation. It's

"Hey, can I hit a bale of hay with this thing?"

got a longer sight radius, the front side being out at the muzzle of the gun, and again it works on the same principle of iron sights. •

With aiming under our belt, we moved on to the firing sequence. Each man on the gunnery crew was known by his number. Number 1 man sponged down the barrel to extinguish any ember. Number 2 took the ammo from number 5 and loaded it into the weapon. Number 1 then rammed it down the barrel. The gunner sighted the weapon, adjusted the elevation, and directed number 3 to move the gun right or left. Number 3 punctured the powder bag, called the prick and prime. Number 4 inserted the primer then, on command, pulled the lanyard.

Now, that's what I call doin' it by the numbers, boys!

The recoil from firing a round kicked the cannon completely out of place, and this whole process had to be started all over again. As much time was spent in relaying the gun as was spent in loading it. A well-trained artillery crew could get off about two rounds a minute.

GRAPESHOT: A LOT MORE THAN SOUR GRAPES!

When you think *Civil War cannon*, you're probably thinking *Civil War cannonball*.

But that wasn't the only thing flying out the muzzle of those old guns. Trust me on this. For real action, cannoneers used something called grapeshot.

Grapeshot's been around since about the time of the Revolutionary War, when it was used to take out the British at close range. An accurate shot from 250 yards or less could tear up a ship's mast and rigging. Basically, grapeshot was a bunch of small iron balls held together with wooden rings and a center bolt, then wrapped in cloth and twine, making it look like a bunch of grapes. When the grapeshot was fired, the wrapping came apart, letting the balls fly—basically turning a cannon into a big-ass shotgun.

Of course, we took a few shots at a bale of hay and it took us quite a while to hit it, but when we finally did, you could see that it could put in a whole lot of hurtin', Civil War style!

DUELING GUNS: SPRINGFIELD VS. ENFIELD

> **"Which rifle was better, the Confederate Enfield or the Union Springfield?"**
> —Sonny, Pendleton, Oregon

What's the difference and which one was better? Let's figure this out.

Both sides in the American Civil War took advantage of the latest technology and firearms. Smooth bores were out. Rifle barrels and percussion caps were in. The U.S. Model 1861 Springfield .58-caliber rifle was used by the Union army. The British-pattern 1853 .577-caliber Enfield saw action on both sides, but mostly with Confederate troops.

Why was the South using British rifles? They didn't have much choice—the Yanks had cornered the market on Springfields, so the Rebs were forced to shop on the other side of the Atlantic for their rifles. But the weapons were almost identical in style. The Enfield was a bit lighter. The Springfield was a little heavier and more robust.

The sights were really where you found the biggest difference between the two rifles. The Enfield had a leaf sight. It flipped up. They were graduated out to a thousand yards and pretty damn accurate at that, as many a pretty, horse-prancing Union general found out to his regret. Now, the Springfield had graduated sights, set at one hundred, two hundred, and three hundred yards. But it could provide a whole lot of hurt at a thousand yards, too.

The two weapons were loaded basically the same way. First you tore open the paper cartridge, poured the powder charge down the barrel, and

Enfield vs. Springfield, a hot debate.

put the bullet into the muzzle. Both rifles fired a bullet called a minié ball. Now, that name makes the minié sound kind of dinky, but it was actually a big slug. After you rammed the bullet home using the rod, you put a percussion cap on what gunsmiths called the nipple . . . hey, rifle-making must have been a lonely business! Anyway, when the hammer struck the cap, it shot the flame down and ignited the black powder that propelled the projectile out the end of the barrel. The invention of the percussion cap made these rifles easier and faster to fire, and a minié ball that expanded to grip the grooves of the barrel made the rifle more accurate than the old smooth-bored flintlocks.

Now, it looks as if the Enfield and the Springfield were about equal. So you know what, boys and girls? I'm thinking it wasn't the weapon, it was the shooter. You may not believe what I'm about to tell you, but it's true so don't give me any crap: The Confederates shot and killed twice as many soldiers as the Yankees did. So even though the weapons were about the same, it looks like Johnny Reb was the better marksman.

Sight alignment . . . trigger squeeze . . . cool nerves. That's what makes the difference when you're talking rifles.

THE BRITISH ARE COMING OVER THE HILL—HOW FAST CAN YOU SHOOT?

Compared to the Springfield and Enfield, the Revolutionary War flintlock was primitive. But just how fast could a minuteman fire his weapon? Let's say you've got redcoats coming up to run a blade through you. Do you wait until you see the whites of their eyes? Not unless you want to be dead quick, puke! Loading a flintlock is a fifteen-movement drill. You tear the cartridge, prime the pan, check the risen, pour the powder down the barrel with your rammer. Ram the cartridge all the way home. Reseat your rammer. Pull the cock. And fire! A trained Revolutionary War soldier in General George Washington's army should have been able to load and fire three aimed shots per minute. Try *that* sometime!

TEST YOUR MILITARY IQ

Who was the minié ball named after? Think, maggots-it ain't Minnié Mouse.

Answer on page 232.

THE CLASSIC COLT .45 AUTOMATIC

"When did the Colt .45 begin its service in the U.S. military, and when did it end its career?"
—Carson, Golden, Colorado

The Colt 45 Automatic.

Hey, Carson, that's a good question. So listen up.

First things first: Proper nomenclature for this weapon is "pistol, Caliber 45, Automatic, M1911."

Invented by our old friend the gun designer John Browning, and built by the Colt Firearms Company, the M1911 is without a doubt one of the most famous military handguns of all time. It's best known as the .45 automatic, or simply the .45.

The 1911 had its official birthday in—not surprisingly—1911, when the government was looking for a reliable enemy-stopper to replace the wimpy .38-caliber pistols then in service. In a shootout between Colt and the Smith & Wesson gun company, a single Colt M1911 shot six thousand rounds without a malfunction and became the handgun of choice for the U.S. Army, Navy, and Marine Corps.

It was loaded in the grip by a detachable seven-round magazine and weighed just shy of two and a half pounds. During World War I, more than 375,000 .45s were issued to our troops. In 1924, the 1911 was modified slightly and redesignated the 1911-A1 . . . and that gun was used starting in World War II and was made by a lot of companies besides Colt to keep up with demand.

Handguns are basically weapons of last resort, but the hefty .45 gave many American fighting men a great feeling of security. The .45 automatic remained on active duty all the way up until the early 1980s, when the Department of Defense decided to switch over to the 9mm Beretta as the standard military-issue sidearm. In 1983, the .45 automatic was officially retired after seventy-two years of loyal service. I feel like saluting!

Perfect for close-up work in the jungle.

DUELING GUNS: LEWIS VS. BROWNING

"What can you tell me about the Lewis gun?"
—Nate, Columbia City, Indiana

"How does a water-cooled machine gun work?"
—John, Haymarket, Virginia

Let's talk about the two big, bad machine guns of World War I.

The Lewis gun was *the* light machine gun of the Great War. Its inventor was U.S. Army colonel Isaac Newton Lewis, and like his namesake, Lewis proved that what goes up must come down . . . because the Lewis gun was the first machine gun ever fired from a plane. The .30-caliber Lewis gun, with its unique round magazine, was also a favorite with the doughboys, and it stuck around long enough to see combat early in World War II. The drum was what made the Lewis gun unique.

When John M. Browning came up with the basic design for the M1917-A1—in 1917, of course—it revolutionized the way all future guns could be fired. In a nutshell, Browning figured out how to use the momentum in the recoil to load ammo automatically off a belt feed. Worked great, but the barrel got red hot from the gun's high rate of fire. So hot it could even melt. So Browning put a big hollow sleeve around the barrel with a small hole on top. Before firing, the crew poured in water from a can to fill the sleeve. But as things heated up, the water turned into steam, which exited through a hose and condensed back into water in the can for reuse. That did the trick, and the Browning company made almost seventy thousand of these weapons for the U.S. military. Browning claimed that if you had enough ammo, new barrels, and kept the water coming, the M1917-A1 could fire ten thousand rounds in an hour.

Now, that's what I call kicking some A!

"Before you shoot your Lewis gun at home, always remember ear protection."

UP CLOSE AND PERSONAL: THE TRENCH SHOTGUN, GREASE GUN, AND STEN

"Does the military ever use shotguns?"
—Darrell, Davis, California

Well, they sure as shot do, Darrell. But how far back do shotguns go in military history? Unofficially, guys have been grabbing their shotguns off the wall since the Revolutionary War. But one of the very first, official purpose-built shotguns was the Mossburg 12 gauge.

See, when we got into World War I, Central Command figured out right quick that our troops needed something special to fight a new kind of trench warfare. In 1917, the War Department ordered Winchester to make a combat version of its Model 1897 pump-action shotgun, one that was capable of mounting a bayonet. The result was a 12-gauge shotgun, officially designated "Trench Gun, Model 1917." Winchester delivered almost twenty thousand of those honeys during World War I, and they all worked damn good. The wide spray of shot was great for close-range trench fighting, but the Model 1917 also saw plenty of action in the Pacific during World War II.

"Why was the M3 submachine gun called the grease gun?"
—Charlie, Columbus, Ohio

Listen up, Charlie, you might learn something!

When the United States got into World War II, American GIs had only one submachine gun that they could turn to: the hard-hitting Thompson. The Thompson was an excellent weapon and very well made. But it wasn't cheap. By 1942, the Army was looking for a slightly less pricey alternative. And on December 24, 1942, the Ordnance Department accepted a new design it dubbed "Submachine Gun, Caliber 45, M-3." Now, the M3 wouldn't have won any beauty contests. It was stubby, crude, and cheap looking. But that was the whole point. The weapon was made from stamped steel, welded together, with no frills and no fancy wooden stock.

M3s cost less than twenty bucks apiece. Compare that to about a hundred bucks for each Thompson and you've got yourself a bargain!

At first the GIs were wary, but once they took the gun into battle, they changed their opinions real quick: The M3 was lighter than the Thompson, and practically foolproof thanks to its simple design. The grease gun fired a .45-caliber cartridge from a 30-round magazine at a rate of about 350 to 400 rounds a minute. That was a bit slower than the tommy gun, but that rate also made it easier to keep the M3 on target, since it didn't buck as much. It had an effective range of about one hundred yards, which was just fine for close combat.

The M3 soldiered on into Korea and even saw some action in Vietnam. But why did the GIs call it a grease gun? Well, take a look at the vintage tool mechanics used to lubricate their vehicles. And take a look at the machine gun. Doesn't take much imagination, does it now?

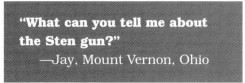

"What can you tell me about the Sten gun?"
—Jay, Mount Vernon, Ohio

The M3 wasn't the only submachine gun made on the cheap with stamped steel. The British had a comparable weapon called the Sten gun. The Sten gun got its name from combining the first letters of the last names of the designers, R. V. Shepherd and H. J. Turpin, and the first two letters of the Enfield Royal Small Arms Factory, where it was manufactured.

The Sten was the first submachine gun to be made with stamped steel parts. It's where we got the idea for our grease gun. The Sten fired nine-millimeter ammunition. It was updated during the war and the later

version, known as the Mark 5, was a favorite with British airborne troops because it was a lightweight weapon that still packed a good punch. And with the thirty-two-round magazine sticking out the side, the Sten gun was easier to shoot from the prone position than any grease gun. Anyway, the Tommies used this baby to good effect all during World War II and after.

The Model 1917 trench shotgun stayed in action right through Vietnam.

How the grease gun got its name.

With its sideways magazine, the Sten was perfect for prone shooting.

GOING TO THE BIRDS: CARRIER PIGEONS

"Fly home to Mama, baby!" Not much to look at, but fast and true.

"How were carrier pigeons used in wartime?"
—Jared, Winchester, Virginia

Well, Jared, during both world wars, pigeons were trained to always return to a particular base no matter what. So if I was on the front lines at Verdun, say, and radio communications were down, I could still get a message to HQ by attaching it to a pigeon's leg and sending him off into the wild blue yonder.

Of course, I'm not that old, ratbag. I'm speaking hypothetically!

After a promising start in World War I, the Signal Corps' U.S. Pigeon Service had more than fifty-four thousand carrier pigeons by World War II. The birds were trained to carry critical dispatches and routine messages from the front lines back to headquarters. They were a vital link when rudimentary telecommunications were always one step behind advancing forces.

The English also perfected the art of carrier pigeon use. Royal Air Force planes leaving England sometimes carried two pigeons on board, which the crew could release if they got into difficulties. Crates of carrier pigeons were also delivered to members of the French Resistance, and they brought back important messages—in fact, folks, it was a carrier pigeon that first brought back news of the D-Day invasion.

These molting messengers could fly up to sixty miles an hour and cover more than six hundred miles in one trip if they had to. Just to be sure, each message was usually written out four times and sent to four different destinations via four birds. One pigeon, named Mary, delivered messages throughout the war even though she was wounded three times, had part of her wing shot off, and was attacked by a hawk—that must've been a German hawk! Many of these brave birds were even buried with full military honors for their service.

Some of these brave birds even won medals.

"You payin' attention, class? Wake up, maggots—there's gonna be a pop quiz!"

TEST YOUR MILITARY IQ
True or false: Okay, birdbrain—was there really a special carrier pigeon Medal of Honor?

Answer on page 232.

CANINES COURAGEOUS

"Me and my Molly, just the way I like it!"

Well, Jason, they're not worth a damn when it comes to paperwork, but neither am I!

Every year, 250 pooches earn their stripes and come on active duty. It takes about three months to train a hopeful military working dog to do two things: Use those pearly whites to catch the bad guys, and use its schnozz to sniff out bombs and drugs.

We've used dogs in the military for all kinds of things. During World War I, both sides had what were called Mercy Dogs, to rescue wounded left on the battlefield. In the Second World War, some lucky dogs were inducted at an early age; the Marines used them in the Pacific to sniff out the enemy.

And by Vietnam, canines were everywhere. They called them sentry dogs, and used them as patrol and attack security. They saved our boys by sounding the alert when bad guys were nearby. The Vietnam Dog Handler Association estimates that ten thousand American lives were saved by dogs during the war.

Today all military dogs are trained at the 341st Training Squadron at Lackland Air Force Base, also known as the Department of Defense Military Working Dog School.

• **Lieutenant Colonel John Probst, commander, Military Working Dog School**: Once you've had a dog in your unit, you realize you probably never want that dog to go away. The squadron procures, trains, and distributes dogs for all branches of the military, as well as the FAA. Typically, they train German shepherds, Belgian Malinois, and Dutch shepherds because their strength and aggression make them good at both patrol and detection duty. Other breeds, such as sporting dogs, are better suited for sniffing duty. •

Rewarding the dogs for positive behavior teaches them they've done the right thing. In patrol training, the dogs are taught to chomp a person anywhere on the body except the neck and head. They're also trained to hold back when the bad guy cries uncle.

• **Master Sergeant Jack Lawson, superintendent of dog training:** We're trying to take the natural instincts of a dog and bring those out to give us a final product for a patrol dog. The primary reward is actually the bite itself. You'll hear verbal rewards—that's to reassure the dog that whatever action it did was the right action. •

There will always be uses for canines on the battlefield . . . dogs can do things that people can't do, like sniffing out bombs. And they're always ready to go! The dog doesn't stop before he does his job to consider, *Well, am I gonna see my family again? Did I pay my bills? You know, I'm so close to retirement, could I wait for backup?* Dogs simply respond because of their training. They're bright, they're energetic, they're loyal, and they run heart-strong all the time!

THE MERCY DOGS OF WORLD WAR I

In World War I, brave canines traveled the no-man's-land between the two stalemated armies to rescue wounded soldiers lying there—these dogs of war actually saved lives!

Sent by the Red Cross of both the Germans and the Allies, these dogs helped only wounded men and were actually trained to ignore dead soldiers. If the wounded man was conscious, he could avail himself of the water or medical supplies strapped to the dog's chest. If unconscious, the dog would return with a cap or helmet, which informed the animal's handlers that a victim had been found.

Trained never to bark in case they drew enemy fire, many of these animals nonetheless lost their lives in no-man's-land.

From World War II to Vietnam and beyond, canines have served and protected faithfully.

SELF-PROPELLED ARTILLERY

"Say your prayers, boys!"

> "If self-propelled artillery is so good, why isn't all artillery self-propelled?"
> —Corporal John Revezzo

John drove some big guns in the anti-aircraft artillery battalion back in the Korean War, and he wants to know more about self-propelled artillery. Well, I'm no cannon cocker, John, but here's what I found out.

Self-propelled guns got their start in World War I, probably about four seconds after some envious artillery guy watched the first tanks chug across the battlefield and realized how much easier that would be than towing and digging an emplacement for his gun. The British and the French were the first to mount artillery guns on trucks and tractors as a way of helping artillery keep up with the new tanks. The U.S. Army tried it, too, but the Army really wasn't hot to trot for self-propelled artillery. I asked Gary Harper of Harper Haus why he thought the U.S. Army of World War I didn't really want self-propelled guns.

• **Gary Harper:** The standard trucks of the World War I period were adequate for highway or road travel, but they had virtually no cross-country capability. Take the tractors that were available at that time—they're very slow vehicles. Even their off-road capability wasn't that great. •

It was the Germans who really got self-propelled artillery going at the beginning of World War II. Their tanks and mobilized infantry were racing across Western Europe, and they needed some fast-moving artillery to keep up. When the U.S. Army found out how well the German mobile guns worked, they kicked out one of their own self-propelled guns.

In 1942, we came up with the M7 Priest. This was our first self-propelled gun of the war. The Priest is basically the tried-and-true 105mm howitzer set on top of a tank chassis. Pretty simple, huh? It was called a Priest because of the anti-aircraft ring mount for the .50-caliber machine gun, which was a round, tower-like structure; when somebody was in there with the gun, it looked like the pulpit in a church.

The Priest was such a hit, we made more self-propelled guns, some with no protection for the gun crew and some with closed crew compartments.

By the mid-1960s, we had settled on the M109 as our standard self-propelled gun. The M109 A6 self-propelled howitzer is known as the Paladin. As soon as the driver hits the brakes, the Paladin's crew of four can select a target, aim the gun, and, as these cannon cockers like to say, "put steel on the target" . . . all in less than sixty seconds.

The crew of the M109 A6 "Paladin" can put steel on target in less than sixty seconds.

MEET GUSTAV!

If you're looking for the artillery piece with the greatest total weight and shell size, then the winner is the eighty-centimeter Gustav gun used by the Germans in World War II.

The Germans first used this behemoth for thirteen days to blast the Russian fortifications at Sevastopol. They used it again two years later to shell Warsaw.

The Gustav fired two kinds of shells—a high-explosive shell weighing nearly five tons, and a seven-ton concrete-piercing shell. One shot reportedly penetrated more than a hundred feet of earth to destroy an underground Soviet ammo dump. So basically we're talking the world's first bunker buster here. It took twenty-five trainloads of equipment and two thousand men to assemble and fire the Gustav. Even though it proved more trouble than it was worth, it still holds the record for the biggest of the big guns.

TEST YOUR MILITARY IQ

Name two other big guns of World War II. Hint: They sound like your grannies, maggots!

Answer on page 232.

THE FAITHFUL M-1

"The greatest battle implement ever devised."

The M1 Garand is the weapon that General George S. Patton called "the greatest battle implement ever devised."

Matter of fact, Phil, it's the first rifle that I ever qualified with in the Marine Corps—expert, too, I might add.

Here's the skinny on the M1. It's a clip-fed gas-operated shoulder weapon that's been around since the late 1930s. It's a .30-caliber semi automatic, which means it fires a round every time you pull the trigger. The M1 weighs just under ten pounds—not a bad weight for a combat infantryman's right arm! *Gas-operated* means that when you fire the weapon, the expanding gas hits the piston, automatically cocking and reloading the weapon. This highly versatile weapon fires eight different kinds of rounds, from the most common (ball ammo) to dummy rounds, armor-piercing ammunition, crimped cartridges—for firing rifle grenades—tracers, and superaccurate match condition rounds.

The history of the M1 goes like this: John C. Garand came to work at the Springfield Armory in Massachusetts in 1919. The thirty-one-year-old Canadian-born engineer set about designing a new rifle to replace the World War I–vintage 1903 Springfield rifle.

The '03 Springfield was a good rifle, but it was a bolt-action weapon—which meant that each time a soldier fired it, he had to manually operate the bolt to load a new cartridge in the chamber. Well, John Garand had the bright idea of building a rifle that would reload itself each time it was fired . . . a so-called semiautomatic rifle.

In the 1920s and early '30s, the Army tested a lot of different designs for semiautomatic rifles. After nearly two decades of work, Garand perfected his design, and on January 9, 1936, Garand's invention officially became "U.S. rifle, Caliber 30, M-1." In the late '30s, with war looming on the horizon, the Springfield Armory cranked up its assembly line and quickly increased its rate of production from a hundred rifles a month to thousands a month. The M1 was the only semi-automatic rifle issued in large numbers to any army during World War II. Nobody else had a rifle this good. And the firepower, accuracy, and the reliability of Garand's rifle no doubt saved the lives of many of our servicemen. By the end of the war, more than four million M1s had come off the Springfield assembly line.

The M1 stayed on active duty through the Korean War until it was replaced in 1957 by the M14 rifle. John Garand died in 1974 . . . but his name lives on, thanks to the immortal M1.

THE MP44 GERMAN ASSAULT RIFLE

The MP44 was the first assault rifle in the world. The Germans dubbed it the *sturmgewehr*. The vast majority of German troops went into combat with the K98, a powerful, accurate bolt-action rifle. But the Germans wanted to combine the accuracy of a rifle with the firepower of a machine gun. Late in the war, they came up with the MP44 assault rifle and a new pint-sized round that had more power and range than a submachine-gun round but less kick than a full-sized rifle cartridge. That did the trick. The secret to this weapon was in the rounds. The Germans figured out how to make 'em small and light—a .30-caliber round with less recoil. The MP44 was a favorite among those German soldiers who could actually get a hold of one.

The .30-caliber, semiautomatic gas-operated M1.

TEST YOUR MILITARY IQ

What's M1 thumb?

Answer on page 232.

DUELING GUNS: MA DEUCE VS. LITTLE .30

"What weapon currently in use by the military has been on active duty the longest?"
—Phil, Acton, California

"What about the .30-caliber light machine gun, .50-caliber Browning's little brother?"
—Randy, Bartelsville, Oklahoma

Phil, let's cut right to the chase. It's the M2 .50-caliber Browning machine gun—what we fondly refer to as Ma Deuce. The M2 .50-caliber Browning has been the large-caliber machine gun of choice for all branches of the military since it first went into active service in 1925.

During World War II, nearly two million M2s were produced by a bunch of different companies, including AC Spark Plug and Frigidaire. And these hulking, heavy front-line weapons wreaked havoc on the ground and in the air, in both Europe and the Pacific. At anywhere between 125 and 500 pounds, the Ma Deuce with its tripod was a behemoth, but what it lacked in portability it more than made up for in massive firepower. The rate of fire is around 450 to 550 rounds per minute, with an effective range of twenty-five hundred yards. This is an awesome shooting machine. And with relatively few modifications, the Ma Deuce of the 1920s is still the standard weapon of its type in the U.S. military today.

That's more than seventy-five years of active service and still going strong.

Randy, here's the skinny on the .30 cal. As early as 1917, John M. Browning was supplying the military with water-cooled .30-caliber automatic weapons. These guns were good, but they were heavy. So in the 1930s, Browning came out with a radically new air-cooled lightweight machine gun called the M1919-A4—the A4, for short. It weighed only about forty pounds with the tripod—less than half the weight of the old water-cooled machine gun—but the Baby Browning could still get off four or five hundred rounds a minute. In World War II, nearly a half a million A4s were produced; it was the bread-and-butter weapon of the ground foundry.

John M. Browning, firearms genius. With his .30 caliber.

The .30-caliber air-cooled, the finest light machine gun of its time.

DUELING GUNS: THOMPSON VS. BURP GUN

"Which is better: the American tommy gun or the German burp gun?"
—William, Tryon, North Carolina

As William indicates, there were two submachine guns that were real popular back in World War II—the American Thompson M1928-A1, better known as the tommy gun, and the German MP40, called the burp gun.

Rate of fire, seven hundred rounds a minute

During the Second World War, the king of German submachine guns was the MP40, what our boys called the burp gun because of its distinctive cracking blasts. The burp gun could put a lot of lead on target pronto. It had a thirty-two-round detachable magazine, weighed about 8.75 pounds, and could fire five hundred rounds a minute.

But we also had a little firepower of our own, the Thompson Model 1928. The tommy gun weighed nearly eleven pounds, had either a thirty- or a twenty-round detachable magazine, and fired seven hundred rounds a minute.

Which of these two weapons was better? Well, they were both pretty reliable. But accuracy-wise, just keep this in mind: The German MP40 had a slightly slower rate of fire than the Thompson. That meant the German gun didn't buck as much as the tommy gun, making it easier for the shooter of an MP40 to keep the

weapon's sights on the target. So you could say the burp gun was more accurate. But the tommy gun fired a heavier slug, so it was more likely to knock down a guy with one hit than the German gun, which fired a smaller round.

Once again it all comes down to who's doing the shooting.

"The Germans insisted the burp gun was better— hey, who won that war, anyway!"

KNIVES OF WORLD WAR II

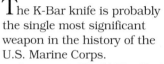

"What makes the K-Bar knife so special?"
—Leroy, Fort Lauderdale, Florida

The K-Bar knife is probably the single most significant weapon in the history of the U.S. Marine Corps.

A year into World War II, the K-Bar Knife Company in Olean, New York, came up with a new general-issue Marine Corps knife design that caught on like wildfire and became the prized possession of all fighting Marines. They depended on them as combat weapons, for mine clearing, and for everyday tasks like opening ration cans and letters. The K-Bar is sharp, stays sharp, and it's easy to sharpen.

Other branches of the service wanted 'em, too, and by the end of the war there were more than a million K-Bars in use. Marines in the Korean War and Vietnam also brandished the K-Bar even though it officially went out of production in 1946. A lot of Marines are still carrying that old K-Bar today.

"What can you tell us about the British Fairbairn Sykes dagger?"
—Brandon, Salt Lake City, Utah

The Fairbairn Sykes dagger was really the first commando knife. It was a real favorite with the British paratroopers in World War II, and for good reason. When it came to close-quarters

combat, this little beauty was a soldier's best friend. The Fairbairn Sykes commando knife was named after its inventors, William Fairbairn and Eric Sykes. In the 1920s and '30s, these guys were police officers in Shanghai—at the time the most dangerous city in the world. Trust me, you had to have eyes in the back of your head! Anyway, these dudes honed their fighting skills on the streets and brought what they learned back to England, where they developed their classic commando knife and then taught soldiers and secret agents how to use it.

"Is the khukuri knife ornamental or is it a real weapon of war?"
—Jake, Coeur d'Alene, Idaho

The answer to your question, Jake, is both.

Sometimes called a kukri knife, the khukuri is carried by the elite British regiments of Nepalese soldiers known as Gurkhas. Nepalese soldiers have been using the khukuri for more than five hundred years and revere it as a magical weapon with supernatural powers. But the real power of the weapon comes from its unique L-shaped design, which makes the knife ten times more effective than a straight blade because you don't have to decelerate at the end of a cut. Gurkhas favored their khukuris for swift and silent attack. They could decapitate an enemy in seconds without a sound.

FLAME-THROWERS

"How does a flamethrower work?"
—Scott, Detroit, Michigan

Well, Scott, it's a lot like what happens when you go camping, and you eat a can of beans, then you light a match. Woo!

The flamethrower was a short-range, portable can o' whup-ass that was most effective against fortified positions like bunkers and gun emplacements. The Germans were the first to use flamethrowers in combat, against the French in World War I. The United States didn't even develop a flamethrower until 1940. I guess somebody should have lit a fire under the R&D guys. We asked Sergeant Tom Williams of the U.S. Marine Corps Historical Company to talk to us a bit about this dangerous weapon.

• **Tom Williams:** The M2-2 flamethrower, as it's officially known, can squirt diesel fuel, straight gasoline, or gel gasoline, better known as napalm. If the operator takes a round in the tanks, whenever there is an opening, that's where you're going to have product coming out and vaporizing. And any ignition source will have a tendency to ignite it. This is what happened with many flamethrower operators that were killed during World War II. •

The weapon was made up of a tank attached to a pack-carrier frame, which came with quick-release straps so you could ditch your weapon in a hurry. It had two triggers. The back trigger controlled the flow of the juice; the front trigger lit it off. Flamethrowers found a welcome home in the hands of the Marines fighting the up-close and personal war in the Pacific. When the Marines landed on Iwo Jima in 1945, some 485 flamethrowers came ashore with them, ready to root out a dug-in and fanatical enemy.

The weapon served again in Korea, and in Vietnam . . . and was finally taken out of service in 1975. By then it was thought that chasing guys out of caves was a thing of the past! Ironic, huh? You understand irony, maggot?

The flamethrower was primarily used against entrenched Japanese on Pacific islands.

THE NOT-SO-MIGHTY SHERMAN?

"What made Sherman tanks such deathtraps?"
—Ken, Mount Tabor, New Jersey

The Sherman M4: the workhorse of the U.S. Armored Division.

The workhorse of the U.S. Armored Division in World War II was the M4 tank. It's the medium tank, better known as the good ol' Sherman tank. You know 'em, you love 'em, but they had some problems. The M4 Sherman possessed a deadly combination of thin skin and a weak main gun. So a lot of times American crews watched their shells bounce off enemy armor while the bad guys sliced right through the Sherman.

• **Bert Close, Third Armored Division:** Every time we got into a tank it was suicide . . . we could have been killed at any time, and we knew it. •

The problems started long before the fighting began. After World War I, America's young tank corps was disbanded. In the 1930s, American tank development was left to the Army's infantry and cavalry units. They came up with light models to suit their own needs for infantry support and scouting. Nothing strong enough to take on another tank.

Then, on September 1, 1939, the Germans unleashed their armored blitzkrieg on Poland, overrunning France in the spring of 1940. American developers suddenly had to play catch-up. In April 1941, they introduced the M3 medium tank. It was basically the earlier infantry tank with a 75mm gun added on the side. The British and American tankers who used them in North Africa were not impressed, since you had to basically turn the whole tank to fire the main gun at the target.

In February 1942, the first M4 Sherman came off the assembly line. The big improvement was that its 75mm cannon was mounted on a fully rotating turret. It was also simple to operate.

• **Fred Ropkey, president, Ropkey Armor Museum:** The Sherman tank was manned by farm boys who had been used to working with tractors and that sort of thing. When they sat down, they weren't at a loss, because mechanics had been a major part of their life. •

But it didn't take long for the boys to figure out that the Sherman had some serious shortcomings. The Germans, with their 88s, could pierce the front armor, travel through the compartment, and right out the back.

Sherman tanks quickly became known in the field as Ronsons—a nickname that came from the American cigarette lighter whose slogan was "It Always Lights the First Time." Besides light armor, poor placement of stored ammo in the crew compartment made the tanks real firetraps.

So if it wasn't the Sherman, what was the best tank in World War II? Well, German Panthers and Tigers were pretty good, but most gearheads think that the Soviet T-34 was by far the best tank of the war. The Russians built ninety thousand of them—so it was a good thing they were on our side back then.

WHY IS SHE CALLED A TANK?

In World War I, the "landship," as the Brits called it, was designed to transport troops between the trench lines on the Western Front, through no-man's-land. But they had to have a code name for the landships, something catchy that wouldn't tip their hat. Since the vehicles were about the same shape and size as military water carriers—especially the very first British tank, Little Willie—they decided to call 'em WCs.

But Albert Stern, secretary of the Admiralty Landships Committee, pointed out that WC was a British term for a toilet, and he wasn't going to have the boys riding around in a toilet. So instead, Stern came up with the code name *tank*, as in *water tank*, and it must have been good enough because the name's stuck ever since. Back then, tanks were called either male or female. The female tanks had side-mounted machine guns. The tanks with the big, proud cannons were the males . . . for obvious reasons.

Fast, maneuverable, but thin-skinned.

THE FREAKING BAZOOKA

"What is the evolution of the bazooka?"
—Brian, Rochester, New York

The powerful modern bazooka.

Brian, basically, you're asking how did we get from the old bazooka to the Marine Corps' latest tank-busting weapon, the kick-ass AT-4.

The AT-4 is officially known as the M136—a recoilless rocket. The whole AT-4 setup weighs less than fifteen pounds, so it's easy for ground-pounders to haul around. And the live rounds pack a wallop, penetrating up to fourteen inches of armor—first shooting out a 9mm tracer round at the target, then letting go a whole lot of whup-ass!

> **" Mail Call is the only show in America where the host has got a bazooka and knows how to use it! Oohrah!"**

The AT-4 has a maximum range of more than two thousand yards, but it's better suited for close-range targets, up to about three hundred yards. The rocket is propelled by a small charge that ignites in the base of the round. At the same time, it creates a big blast out the back of the tube. It's that back blast that prevents any recoil from knocking shooters on their cans. But the blast means that not only do you need to watch where you're aiming the thing, but you'd also better make darn sure that none of your buddies are behind you. The blast can send rocks and junk flying like shrapnel up to a hundred yards behind the launcher.

Now, there's no fancy-shmancy guidance system here. You gotta shoot it the old-fashioned way, like you do a rifle. Sight alignment. Trigger squeeze. A direct hit with this weapon to the troop compartment of an APC, you're gonna have a 100 percent casualty rate. No one is walking out.

The ol' bazooka—first cranked out in 1942—operated on the same principles: Let the exhaust of the rocket shoot out the back so there's no recoil, and use a shaped charge to punch right through the armor. The bazooka went through some improvements during World War II. Even though it couldn't penetrate the heaviest armor, a well-placed round could at least knock the treads off a tank. An improved bazooka, which could cut through eleven inches of armor, saw action in the Korean War and early in Vietnam.

In 1962, grunts got their hands on the LAW, or light anti-tank weapon. It was the first anti-tank weapon made with a lightweight disposable launcher, tube, and rocket all in one. Once you fired it, you just threw the empty tube away. Pretty simple. The LAW stuck around until the mid-1980s, when my new friend the AT-4 showed up.

HOW DID THE BAZOOKA GET ITS NAME?

It wasn't Bazooka Joe and his bubble gum, as many people think—that wasn't invented till the end of World War II.

What happened was this. It sure was a mouthful to say to your buddy, "Hey, hand me that recoilless shoulder-fired anti-tank rocket launcher M1." The guys needed a catchier name, and somebody came up with *bazooka* because the weapon looked a lot like a bizarre musical instrument called the bazooka. Never heard of it? Well, you would have if you were listening to the radio back in the 1930s, 'cause back then one of America's best-loved comedians was a guy named Bob "Bazooka" Burns. Bazooka Bob invented this noisemaking gizmo and was supposedly the only person who could play it.

They could knock the treads off a tank and stop it dead.

Bob "Bazooka" Burns.

Le Maquis: the brave men and women who helped cripple the Nazi war machine.

WEAPONS OF THE FRENCH RESISTANCE

The Liberator.

"What kind of weapons did the French Resistance use against the Germans?"
—Harry, New York City, New York

Back in World War II, the French army was not an army that the Germans feared or revered. Still, these small groups of French civilians gave the Germans one helluva wake-up call when they began waging their very personal war of revenge. During this time, the secret warriors of the Resistance had to be pretty darn creative about how they armed themselves. The Allies came up with one particular little doozie, especially designed for the Resistance fighters. It came to be called the Liberator!

• **Harlan Glenn, World War II author-historian:** The Liberator pistol is a simple and cheaply manufactured weapon. It's one shot. It could be reloaded, but the idea was to drop thousands of these behind the lines that the French Resistance fighters could pick up. •

Another kind of weapon the Allies were able to get into the hands of the Resistance packed a lot more punch—plastic explosives.

Knocking out a bridge or rail line could really wreak havoc on German troop and supply movements. This was especially important leading up to the Allied landings on the beaches of Normandy in June 1944. Once the Resistance knew the Allies were just offshore, they kicked things up a notch. Unfortunately for the Resistance, the Germans had one more opportunity to exact revenge on French civilians. Four days after D-Day, the town of Oradour was still under German control. When the French Resistance attacked and delayed the Second SS Panzer Division, the Nazis burned that village to the ground and killed everyone in it, men, women, and children.

More than six hundred people were murdered that day. But thanks to the sacrifices of the determined Resistance fighters, it took the Second SS Panzer two weeks to get to the front lines. And by the time they finally got there, it was too late to do any good. The tide of battle had swung in the favor of the Allies, and the Germans were tastin' a little bit of their own medicine!

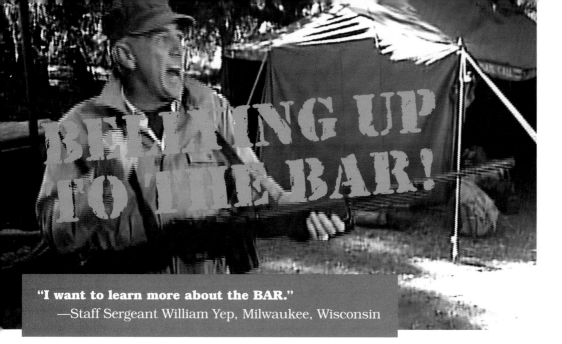

BELLYING UP TO THE BAR!

"I want to learn more about the BAR."
—Staff Sergeant William Yep, Milwaukee, Wisconsin

Well, Sarge, I'm gonna assume that you're not talking about a cocktail party here, but instead the BAR—Browning Automatic Rifle.

The .30-caliber Browning Automatic Rifle, named after its inventor, John Browning, put a lot of firepower in one guy's hands. They started using the BAR in 1918 at the end of World War I. It caused a big sensation at that time 'cause of its quick magazine changes (unlike the Lewis gun, which took a while to change drums). The BAR was kept in service all the way up to Vietnam—some thirty years—and copied in Europe. In fact, the FN MAG machine gun uses the BAR special bolt action virtually without modification—quite a compliment.

"The Gunny loves marching fire."

In combat, the BAR was used in a number of ways. By World War II, it was supplied with a special tripod, but most GIs threw that away because of its extra weight. Instead, they used a little maneuver called marching fire. The guys had a cup attached to a belt that they could seat the rifle in; then it was just full speed ahead. Talk about great suppressing fire! Oohrah!

TEST YOUR MILITARY IQ

Who else besides the military got a lot of use out of the BAR?

Answer on page 232.

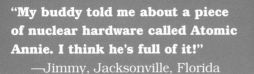
ATOMIC ANNIE AND DAVY CROCKETT

> **"My buddy told me about a piece of nuclear hardware called Atomic Annie. I think he's full of it!"**
> —Jimmy, Jacksonville, Florida

Atomic Annie, 1953: a nuclear cannon.

Well, Jimmy, you've come to the right place, because the Gunny is one guy who's not going to blow smoke up your butt.

In May 1953, the Army rolled out a 280-millimeter cannon for a whole new kind of test firing. This monster fired short-range nuclear warheads. That's right, a nuke on wheels.

They nicknamed this cannon Atomic Annie, and believe me, this is one girl you don't want to tick off. Transported by two huge tractor trucks, Atomic Annie could be set up in less than twenty minutes by a crew of twelve men. Old Annie never fired a round in anger, but when that power rammer went into action and she was loaded for bear, you'd better crawl under your desks, kids.

"You can get out from under your desk now, Nancy. Gunny's coverin' your ass!"

And if you think the Atomic Annie's a crazy-ass weapon, the Army went one step crazier. In the early 1960s,

they developed and tested the Davy Crockett. Believe it or not, that's a nuclear bazooka that could be fired from the back of a jeep!

Hmmm . . . If you fire the Davy Crockett, you better make damn sure the wind is at your back.

All of this brings up a good question:

> **"What the hell was the Army doing in the missile business anyway?"**
> —Stan, Cedar Rapids, Iowa

Here's the answer, Stan:

At the end of World War II, it was the U.S. Army's job to develop our missile program. The folks in the Army knew they had a lot of catching up to do.

The first step was pretty simple. If you can't beat 'em, steal 'em! Our side captured the brains behind Germany's World War II missile program, scientist Wernher von Braun and his research team. We set them up at Fort Bliss,

Texas, in December 1945. With Von Braun's brains and the Army's checkbook, we had a winning combination. The first missile to really take off was our version of the long-range German V2 missile. In December 1946, that rocket traveled twenty-one miles—kinda wimpy, but it was a start.

The Army program was going like gangbusters, so they decided to move the whole thing to the more spacious Redstone Arsenal in Huntsville, Alabama. In October 1949, Von Braun and his boys unveiled the Redstone missile. It was more accurate than the V2 and could be launched from a mobile platform under battlefield conditions. On May 16, 1958, combat-ready soldiers got their first chance to fire a Redstone missile. One month later, the Redstone was added to the arsenal of U.S. troops stationed in Germany.

In addition to long-range nuclear missiles, the Army was developing specialized missiles, like the Nike-Ajax and Nike-Hercules surface-to-air missiles. In November 1951, a Nike-Ajax missile intercepted an unmanned target aircraft flying at thirty-three thousand feet from fifteen miles away. That was the first successful kill of an aerial target by a U.S. guided missile.

But the mother of all long-range missiles has to be the ICBM, or intercontinental ballistic missile. The ICBM has a curved or ballistic trajectory that takes it to the edge of outer space and allows it to go a whole lot faster and farther than missiles that travel through the lower atmosphere.

The Army's Jupiter missile, developed by Von Braun and his team, became America's first successful ICBM. Even though the Jupiter was a success, in November 1956 the Department of Defense decided that the

Army should limit its missiles to a range of two hundred miles for tactical battlefield situations and leave the long-range, strategic stuff to the U.S. Air Force.

Davy Crockett, the world's only nuclear bazooka.

The captured German scientist Wernher von Braun, who led the U.S. missile program after World War II.

DEEP IN A MISSILE SILO

"Can I get a tour of a real missile silo?"
—Floyd, Belton, Missouri

Floyd, old son, if I showed you everything I'd have to kill you, but here's enough to give you a taste of what we've got going on underground.

Well, like I just told you, for forty years—since the early days of the Cold War—we've been arming ourselves with ICBMs, the ultimate "big stick." I'm talkin' now about the Minuteman—a forty-ton rocket armed with a devastating nuclear warhead. Oohrah!

We have hundreds of 'em. And we keep each one in its own little underground launch tube, called a missile silo. These silos—which are unstaffed—and their centralized control centers are grouped into huge complexes that spread over thousands of square miles of remote territory.

One place you'll find a complex like this is at Minot Air Force Base in North Dakota. The guys and gals of the 91st Space Wing keep an arsenal of Minuteman missiles on full alert 24/7, 365 days a year.

• **Lieutenant Colonel Shawn Jansen:** The mission here at Minot Air Force Base is to defend the United States through safe and secure ICBMs immediately ready to put bombs on target. •

A missile complex includes 150 missile silos and fifteen control centers, called missile alert facilities. Each alert facility controls ten silos. Each silo contains a launch tube and rooms for machinery and maintenance work. The launch tube consists of a steel liner, reinforced by six feet of concrete and rebar. It's capped off by a steel closure door that's four feet thick! But it's in the missile alert facilities—the control centers—where the action really takes place. Each facility is partially aboveground and partially below. Topside, a building houses a chef and temporary living quarters for maintenance personnel and security forces.

Underground—protected by sixty-five feet of North Dakota soil—is a launch control capsule. Here a combat crew of two officers, called missileers, keeps watch over a group of ten missiles. These are the folks who would carry out a launch.

But you can rest easy, folks. It's not like a lone missileer can go berserk and bring about Armageddon all on his or her own. A missile cannot be launched without several people agreeing that it's the right thing to do. Just for starters, it requires the physical turning of two launch keys and two control knobs simultaneously.

• **Captain Matt Cantore:** It's impossible for one person to launch, because not only do you not have four hands, but it also requires a second capsule to turn at the exact same time, sending out launch votes from two different sites. And, of course, before you can even turn keys for the missiles to launch, you need to ensure they're enabled. And we don't have the enable codes. The enable codes are passed down from

the chairman of the Joint Chiefs of Staff, and only after the president has authorized the missile launch. •

The official motto of the 91st Space Wing is "Poised for Peace." Well, let's just hope the rest of the world lets 'em keep it that way. I'm glad we have the right stuff operating those nukes, but I hope to hell we never have to ask them to turn those keys for real.

Computer simulation of a missile launch.

On the front line of missile defense.

CLAYMORE: KING OF MINES

"How may watermelons can I blow away with one Claymore mine?"
—Ed, Lockwood, California

"The Claymore is about to put a world of hurt in this evil gourd!"

Great question, Ed—and to answer it I took some of my favorite gourds out to Camp Pendleton, where I learned all about a compact world of hurt called the M18A1 fragmentation antipersonnel mine . . . better known as the Claymore.

Now, this is something the Gunny has a little experience with, since we used a lot of these honeys in Vietnam. In fact, during the most intense part of that war, the factory was pumping out eighty thousand Claymore mines a month.

And these mines have hardly changed at all since they were field-tested back in 1956, after Korea

The M18A1 fragmentation antipersonnel mine—but the guys call 'em Claymores!

taught us that we needed something simple and directional to mow down waves of suicide attackers. And this is one case where size doesn't matter. Every little Claymore has a fifty-yard kill zone and a hundred-yard casualty radius. That means that if you're within a football field in front of this thing, either you're gonna be dead or you're gonna wish you were.

How does it work? Well, basically, you've got a blasting cap attached to a box of seven-hundred-plus steel BBs. And what makes those little bullets fly? A nice-sized wad of plastic explosives.

But what about Ed's question—how many melons can I blow up with a Claymore? Well, what do I look like, a freaking produce manager? I'm not here to make fruit salad . . . but just to satisfy you fruit sadists, we blew one up out at the range and I'll say right now that it went all to pieces!

The deadly Scottish Claymore.

HOW DID THE CLAYMORE MINE GET ITS NAME?

If you think the Claymore mine gets its name from the guy who invented it, think again, rosebud. The mine is actually named after a military sword called the Claymore. The Claymore was the weapon of choice back in Scotland in the eighteenth century. The name *Claymore* is actually used to describe two different Scottish swords. One is the military Claymore, which has a distinctive basket hilt. There's also the sword's bastard grandfather, a sixteenth-century two-handed mother called the *clavemoor*, which is Gaelic for "great sword" . . . and sorta sounds like "Claymore" if you say it fast enough.

The Claymore helped protect our perimeters in Vietnam.

TEST YOUR MILITARY IQ

How much does the M18A1 Claymore weigh?

Answer on page 232.

M16 VS. M14 - THE CONTROVERSY

"Why did the military switch from the reliable M14 to the M16?"

—Dan, Horseheads, New York

"The M14: highly dependable, good range, plenty of firepower."

They've been debating that question for four decades now, Dan—and they still ain't quite got the answer right!

Let's start with the old M14. The M14 was designed to replace the M1 rifle. The good ol' 14 was highly dependable, and had good range and plenty of firepower. The M14 fires a 7.62-millimeter round. It's magazine-fed, designed primarily for semiautomatic fire, and it's gas-operated. And if you read our little bit about the M1, you know what *gas-operated* means!

But in the mid-1960s, the military started phasing out the M14 and replacing it with the M16; by 1968, most grunts were carrying the M16. And let me tell you, not everybody was too happy about it, either.

So what's the big deal about switching rifles? Well, soldier and rifle develop a pretty tight bond in combat. And changing up in the middle of a war, even if the new weapon is better in some ways, caused a real uproar with some folks.

• **Dr. Roger McGrath, author-historian:** The biggest objection to the M16 was that it wasn't as reliable as the M14. The M16 started malfunctioning and jamming. It worked fine in demonstrations and also in environments that were almost pharmaceutically–grade clean. Problem was, in combat there's so much dirt, mud, debris, and muck, and you can't constantly clean the weapon. The other factor that stood out for a lot of people was accuracy. The M14 is accurate up to six, seven hundred yards, and it's effective at that distance as well. But the M16 is a much smaller rifle. It also does not have the accuracy or the killing power at the great distances that the M14 had. It's a much better rifle at a hundred or two hundred yards than it is at four or five hundred. •

So why the hell would the U.S. military adopt a less accurate weapon that jammed a lot? Well, for one, the M16 was a good three to five pounds lighter than the M14; it also had a carrying handle, a convenient pistol grip for those cowboy types, and far less recoil under fully automatic fire. The smaller kick is from the M16's smaller ammo— 5.56 millimeters compared to 7.62 for the M14. Since they were smaller, soldiers could carry more of the M16 rounds. But a lot of grunts worried that they weren't lethal enough.

All of these M16 features, good and bad, were part of a major shift in infantry fighting going on in the Army.

• **Dr. Roger McGrath:** Instead of training their infantry to be expert marksmen, the U.S. Army felt it was easier to train great numbers of soldiers to spray down an area. On the contrary, in the Marine Corps, they always believed in the one-shot kill, which served to demoralize the enemy. This difference in philosophy between the Army and the Marines could be demonstrated in the ratio of rounds expended per enemy kill. During World War II, we expended twenty to twenty-five thousand rounds per enemy kill. In Vietnam, it was two hundred to four hundred thousand rounds per enemy kill. •

The M16 has gone through a lot of improvements over the years, making it a top-notch infantry weapon these days. But the old controversy isn't gonna go away anytime soon.

The M16 became the official infantryman's weapon in Vietnam.

THE VIETCONG BOOBY TRAPS ON THE HO CHI MINH TRAIL

"What kind of booby traps did the Vietcong use?"
—Drew, Orlando, Florida

"How the hell did VC move so much gear along such a crappy dirt path as the Ho Chi Minh Trail?"
—Lionel, Goshay, Mississippi

Well, they had a helluva lot of them, and even though they were primitive and homemade, they were a pain in the butt.

The most famous are probably the punji spikes—sharpened bamboo sticks hidden in pits. Sometimes the Vietcong would smear them with dung so your wounds were more likely to get infected. We had to go through a boot redesign to deal with the punjis. There were also pits topped with metal spikes that trapped your legs; the more you tried to pull yourself out, the worse you'd be injured.

The Vietcong were also pretty good at taking our trash and turning it against us. They'd collect old C-ration cans, then take a grenade, pull the pin, tie a trip wire around it, and slide it back into the can. Some poor unsuspecting soldier would come along, hit the trip wire, and it would explode, probably killing or maiming anything within twenty feet. It was pretty nasty.

Well, Lionel, you obviously weren't there—so let me enlighten you.

The Ho Chi Minh Trail was the main infiltration route for moving North Vietnamese troops and supplies into South Vietnam. In fact, it was the only way to get from Hanoi to South Vietnam. And contrary to the name, it wasn't just one trail. It was actually a network of piss-poor roads dating back to World War II that by the end of the Vietnam War covered more than two thousand miles. But no matter how many times we bombed them, the routes would spring back seemingly overnight because the trails were maintained by about half a million soldiers and local farmers working under the cover of darkness. Intelligence reports say there were about three hundred tons of supplies moving along the trails at any given time. No wonder we had a rough time over there!

Range: one hundred yards.

COMBAT HAND SIGNALS

"What kind of hand signals do our warriors use when they have to zip it up?"
—Eric, Frederick, Maryland

"It all began with him!"

Combat can be a pretty noisy thing.

On the other hand, if you're close to the enemy, any sound you make may give away your position. So ground-pounders developed a bunch of hand and arm signals. They're used to communicate basic infantry maneuvers and important information about a situation.

There are some pretty standard signals for "halt," "take cover," "envelop right," "enemy spotted," "range one hundred yards," "range two hundred yards," and "cease fire."

There's one more hand signal you won't find in the manual, but it's probably the most popular among the troops. Now, I know that you know what I'm talking about, but I betcha don't know why we flip the bird. Well, according to one story, way back in 1415, the French threatened to cut off the middle fingers of the British during the battle of Agincourt. That way they couldn't operate their bows. In defiance, the Brits displayed their middle fingers to the French soldiers to show that their bow fingers were ready, willing, and able.

TEST YOUR MILITARY IQ

What does a fist pumped twice mean? No, numbskull, we're not asking for the check!

Answer on page 232.

SNIPER RIFLES

> **"What kind of rifle do our military snipers use these days?"**
> —Richard, El Paso, Illinois

"Sure fires smooth as silk."

Well, Richard, if you take a stroll through Scout Sniper School at the Marine Corps' Camp Pendleton, California, you'll see that the new weapon of choice for hard-charging Devil Dog sniper wannabes is the M40A3 sniper rifle.

From the minute the M40A3 hit the battlefield in Operation Iraqi Freedom, it lived up to the reputation that it first earned out here on the range—it is beyond the shadow of a doubt the best sniper rifle in the world. It shoots 7.62-caliber ammo, and at a little more than nineteen pounds, the M40A3 is heavy. But thanks to a rock-steady bipod, a free-floating barrel, and a sweet bolt action, this enemy-stopper fires smooth as silk, and it's unbelievably accurate up to a thousand yards.

Army soldiers use the sniper rifle too.

Now, I'm not bragging when I say I can hit just about anything with any rifle up to about four hundred yards. That's just the way it is, folks. But the targets at Pendleton were between 625 and 700 yards away. And they're only eighteen by twenty-four inches—or about the size of a human torso.

But being an expert sniper takes more than a trigger squeeze. That's why the number two man on the team is also important. The observer recommends windage settings to the sniper. In English, that means he's figuring out how wind is affecting the flight of the round as it travels downrange. His tool of choice is the M49 spotting scope. With this little honey, he can actually follow the vapor trail created by the round as it speeds to the target. And he's telling the shooter just what adjustments to make for his rifle fire.

Carlos Hatchcock, legendary Marine sniper.

With snipers, consistency is accuracy. They put their face on the gun, and it stays there until they're done shooting. The only hand that moves is the one that pulls the trigger.

I shot pretty damn well at Camp Pendleton, but nothing like the snipers in training who have already proven themselves as expert marksmen with the M16. And today, with the M40A3, these students can hit with better than 80 percent accuracy. So rest assured, America. With the lethal combination of rifle, scope, and well-trained eagle-eyed Marines, we've got nothing to worry about. And just in case we need a few more good men—well, I can always step into the breach.

THE MOST FAMOUS MARINE SNIPER EVER: SERGEANT CARLOS HATCHCOCK

Folks, all true Marines remove their covers at the mention of Carlos Hatchcock's name. I myself met him and have an autographed copy of a book about him. He's the legendary Marine sniper who plagued the Vietcong behind their own lines, making kills from up to an incredible twenty-five thousand yards. Every time he walked out of that jungle, he came out with another kill—ninety-three confirmed. His exploits are legendary. Alone, in daylight, at eight hundred yards, after three days of stalking, he killed an NVA general and escaped. He went face-to-face with a famous Vietcong sniper—and shot him right through the scope!
Hats off to Carlos Hatchcock, greatest of them all.

TEST YOUR MILITARY IQ

Where did the word *sniper* come from?

Answer on page 232.

Trailing two miles of wires, the TOW can't be stopped by enemy signal jammers.

TOW MISSILES: WIRED WONDERS

"What exactly is a TOW missile and how does it work?"
—Ryan, Detroit, Michigan

If you ever find yourself in a situation where you might want to engage and destroy an enemy tank, one of your best bets is a TOW missile.

TOW stands for "tube-launched, optically tracked, wire-guided." And let me tell ya, these fifty-pound missiles are real tank terminators. TOWs can be launched from helicopters and a variety of ground vehicles, including the Army's Bradley Fighting Vehicle, the Marines' light armored vehicle, Humvees—heck, there was a time you could fire these suckers from my beloved jeep!

The latest version is the TOW 2B. It has a range of 2.3 miles—which is about the time you run out of wire. You see, two thin wires actually unspool from the back of the missile and stay connected to the tube as the missile zips downrange at about 670 miles an hour.

Now, before you start thinking that having long wires trailing out the back of your missiles is kind of primitive, think about this, smarty-pants: The signal moving those wires can't be jammed by the enemy, the way radio or other wireless guidance systems can. The direct connection between you and the missile lets you adjust its flight to the target. So nothing is going to stop that puppy from delivering its world of hurt. Depending on how the TOW is mounted, gunners use a joystick or a helmet sight, or manually turn the traversing unit to keep the crosshairs focused on the tank. These adjustments move the small fins on the back of the missile, until—gotcha!

The Army got their hands on the original version of the TOW in 1970, and the weapons were used near the end of the Vietnam War. The few times NVA troops were dumb enough to bring out their tanks, we toasted them with the TOW. Those first TOWs didn't work at night and penetrated only a little more than half the armor thickness that today's TOWs take care of.

So what happens these days if you need to knock out some enemy armor at night or on a smoky, hazy battlefield? No problem. The sights are now infrared.

• **Lance Corporal Bill Sweeney, USMC TOW gunner:** At night it'll pick up heat signatures. When you see a vehicle, what you'll see is mainly the engine and the outline of the vehicle because it picks up the heat from so far away. Basically it's almost a guaranteed kill. •

The latest TOWs actually explode just above the turret of the tank, where the armor is usually a little thinner. Two projectiles shoot straight down from the missile and take care of business. Earlier versions, which are still in use, like the type used in Desert Storm, smack right into the side of the tank. A small shaped charge softens the outer layer of armor; a split second later the main warhead slams right in through any tank in the world. Kaboom!

We fired three thousand TOWs during the 1991 Gulf War, and boy, did they earn their keep. The TOW 2B takes twenty-one seconds to reach its maximum effective range. Which, coincidentally, is about the same amount of time it takes for the enemy to bend over and kiss his ass good-bye.

"Hey, Gomer, this ain't Mayberry, this is *Mail Call*. Wake up and turn the page!"

TOW: the best anti-tank weapon around.

AVENGER AIR DEFENSE

"Do you know anything about the Avenger air defense system?"
—Kevin, Austin, Texas

The Avenger is a lightweight, mobile, surface-to-air missile system that our armed forces use all over the world.

Well, Kevin, I know it's an all-fired big can of whup-ass!

Seriously, I went out to the Marine Corps base at 29 Palms, California, my favorite stompin' grounds, to visit with my fellow leathernecks from the 3rd LAAD Battalion; LAAD stands for "Low Altitude Air Defense." They showed me the Avenger, everybody's favorite big-boy toy these days, a lightweight, mobile surface-to-air missile system that's seeing service all over the world. We've even got a bunch stashed around Washington, DC, just in case anybody tries to mess with us again.

Now, the only purpose the Avenger has in life is to launch Stinger missiles and destroy enemy aircraft. Oohrah! The Avenger is a mobile missile launcher that can shoot on the move—taking down aircraft when it's going up to thirty-five miles an hour, and moving right along with convoys to protect them.

The Avenger has a 360-degree rotating turret with eight Stinger missile pods ready for action. The system uses FLIR—that's "forward-looking infrared" for you civilians out there—to lock on to the heat coming from the target and go in for the kill.

Add an MP3 .50-caliber electronically fired machine gun, which can shoot eleven hundred rounds per minute, and you've got one heapin' helpin' of high-explosive fun.

STINGER VS. REDEYE

"What's the difference between a Stinger and a Redeye?"
—Mike, Hartford City, Indiana

Well, first off, Mike, a Stinger's made with brandy . . .

No, wait a minute, I'm just kidding . . . Mike wants to know about shoulder-fired surface-to-air missiles, what the folks in research like to call man-portable whup-ass. The biggest difference between today's Stingers and the Redeye is that the Redeye came first, developed way back in 1958 for anti-aircraft self-defense. Redeyes are basically solid-fuel rocket launchers that shoot armed missiles. The missiles have an infrared seeker that locks on to the hot exhaust of an aircraft, and kaboom. We started replacing the Redeye with the Stinger back in the early 1980s, because

Stingers have better steering and are a lot less likely to get confused by flares or other anti-infrared counter-measures.

"Real men don't eat quiche-and they don't drink Stingers, neither!"

These days, when nothing but a Stinger will do, the Army has a dedicated Stinger section that goes into action. During Operation Iraqi Freedom, the section parachuted into northern Iraq with their missiles.

Now, that's what I call cojones.

WHAT MAKES SMART BOMBS SMART

"What makes smart bombs so
damn smart?"

—Price, Los Angeles, California

A smart bomb can vaporize enemy targets with unbelievable accuracy.

To find out just what it means when the military "educates" its bombs, the *Mail Call* team traveled to the Florida panhandle to visit the Precision Strike System Program at Eglin Air Force Base.

The good folks at Eglin put it in plain English—making a bomb smart means giving it a computer brain that will make it hit exactly where you want it to, no questions asked.

Technically a smart bomb is a guided bomb unit, or GBU for short. The most popular type of GBU is the LGB, or laser-guided bomb, known by its code name Paveway. A Paveway uses a special seeker head loaded with laser-detecting sensors. As the bomb is released from a plane, a crew member on board or somebody on the ground aims a laser beam at the target. A tracking device on the nose of the bomb follows that laser to the ground and boom! Mission accomplished!

• **First Lieutenant Bill Clements, Air Armament Center, Precision Strike System Program Office:** The pilot has a targeting pod on the aircraft to where he's reflecting a particular target. Let's say a truck. As the laser's pointing on the truck, this swivels and follows the target that's illuminated by the operator. •

Smart bombs were first put to the test in the early 1970s in Vietnam. These weapons were awesome, but they're downright Stone Age compared to what we've got going today. State-of-the-art LGBs are a wonder to behold. They're packed with high explosives and can weigh anywhere from two thousand pounds up to my very favorite, the five-thousand-pound bunker buster used during the 1991 Gulf War.

Another bomb that comes out of Eglin is the sensor fused weapon. It's the ultimate surprise package—delivering up to forty bombs for the price of one.

• **Second Lieutenant Tracie Martin, project manager:** Once the bomb has been released from the plane and it hits a certain altitude, linear-shaped charges strip through the outside of the shell and actually make the panels peel like a banana. Each submunition has a parachute that ejects, so you'll see ten parachutes in the air. A rocket motor will fire and help it climb and give the spin capability to the projectile. Once the rocket motor fires, the arms are extended with forty different projectiles. The copper plate becomes a molten slug, which actually penetrates armor. •

The enhanced smart bomb: the ultimate surprise package.

THE HIGH-IQ BOMB OF THE FUTURE

What's in store for the future? Something called the Low Cost Autonomous Attack System, or LOCAAS. This pint-sized version of a smart bomb graduated from high school a long time ago and is now at the top of its class working on a Ph.D.! Up to twenty-four LOCAAS can fit onto one fighter jet.

The LOCAAS carries a powerful warhead and guidance system. And it's about as smart as they come. It has the ability to think for itself. Before the LOCAAS takes off, you can program it with different types of targets. It knows not to go after a school bus, for instance, but after a SAM site or a tank instead.

TEST YOUR MILITARY IQ

Today one target point can be destroyed with one smart bomb. How many did it take during World War II?

Answer on page 232.

NEW KID ON THE BLOCK: THE XM29 RIFLE

The XM29 rifle: the bad boy of the future.

> "What's all the buzz I hear about the new XM29 rifle?"
> —Tony, 23rd Marines

The XM29 rifle: the bad boy of the future.

Now, Tony, my girlfriend has always been the trusty M16, nicely equipped with the M203 grenade launcher. She's sweet, but there's a new combat weapon on the test range right now that's gonna send this honey straight to the *Antiques Roadshow*. That's the XM29. Is it really the bad boy it looks like?

You bet!

The XM29 is expected to become the standard-issue rifle for the twenty-first-century soldier. It fires normal bullets and high-explosive rounds.

To find out all about this futuristic firearm, we went to a top-secret firing range in Minnesota, run by Alliant Techsystems.

• **Randy Strobush, weapons expert:** I take the magazine, and I put it into the weapon, and then I pull the charging handle back, and now the gun is loaded. For the remote firing, what we do is we have a remote-controlled trigger mechanism, and we basically line that up and put it so that it's in front of the trigger. •

The rounds are air-bursting 20mm high explosives—a new type of ammo the military is pretty psyched about. This thing can shoot targets no other weapons system in the world today can shoot. For instance, it can shoot soldiers in foxholes, behind walls, and inside rooms. This is the only gun around that can do that.

For our test, several enemy combatants, represented by the cardboard silhouettes, are hiding in a house a little more than a hundred yards downrange. The twenty-millimeter shell has been programmed to fly through the window and explode in midair about two yards inside the makeshift room.

But how do these rounds know when it's time to burst?

Well, the key is a high-tech brain that sits on top of the weapon. It's called the fire control system, and it's stuffed full of computer chips.

Looking through the eyepiece, the soldier sees a red dot called the aim point. This is simply placed on the target. Invisible to the naked eye, a laser beam shoots out to the target. It then bounces back to the XM29's fire control system. The computer automatically calculates the range, bearing, and angle to the target. It's then up to the soldier to decide exactly where the 20mm air burst should explode for maximum impact.

• **Lieutenant Colonel Matthew Clarke, Army product manager, individual weapons:** The gunner gets the range by pressing a plus or minus button right on the side of the weapon that'll increase or decrease the range of the round by increments of one meter [about three feet]. The operator then just pulls the trigger; the round will fly and it'll explode at the correct spot. •

When it's battle-ready in 2008, the XM29 will be modified to weigh fourteen pounds. That's four pounds lighter than today's prototype. And the electronics will be designed to link up with all kinds of other futuristic infantry gear. All in all, the XM29 promises to give the twenty-first-century American soldier the decisive edge on tomorrow's battlefield. So if you're the enemy, be warned—the XM29 is coming soon to a theater near you.

"If you're tired of reading, just look at the pictures, lard-ass! Now flip the page!"

Everything right at your fingertips.

PART TWO:
GEAR

"Hey, all you
gearheads-try
this stuff on
for size"

"Don't run into these dudes".

ERMEY IN SHINING ARMOR

"What about all the different pieces of armor that medieval knights wore?"
—Rob C., Little Rock, Arkansas

"The baddest dude around."

Heckuva question there, Rob. Did you think of that all by yourself? I'm only gonna go through this one time, so you better pay attention!

To answer this question I talked to Cliff Bassett, who sported gothic armor from about the 1380s. Cliff told me that all this stuff together can add up to between forty-five and seventy pounds . . . and that's really not much more than a combat Marine would be carrying into battle today.

• **Cliff Bassett:** Exactly. But what's different about medieval armor is that the weight is distributed through the whole body. Part of it's on our shoulders, part of it's on our hips. We're not as encumbered as we would be with all the weight on our back, like with a backpack. So we're able to move a lot better. This is actually tailor-fitted, so it's made just like a very fitted set of clothes. In combat, you really have to be able to fall off your horse and stand up before you get trampled. If you can't move, you're just not going to last very long in combat, no matter what the era. •

And the soldiers wore leather underneath everything, so they didn't get pinched by the hinges in places where the metal moved—I can hear you laughing! Button it!

"Button it, maggot! You think you can do any better?"

Now, if you were a knight getting dressed in medieval times, you'd have a squire assisting you. A knight in training. His family would have loaned him to you so that he could learn about chivalry, about how to serve. The idea was that only when you knew how to serve could you know how to command. I tell you, I woulda loved to have a squire when I was in the Marine Corps . . . boots needing shining . . . rifle needing cleaning . . . well, I can dream, can't I?

As armor styles changed and progressed over the years, different pieces were added or dropped. Here's what I got strapped into:

Protecting my coconut is the helmet or salet and the gorget.

Moving down, the breastplate and matching back piece together are called the cuirass. There's the pauldron on my shoulder, and the vambrace on my arm with the cowter covering my elbow. Strapped to the cuirass are the tassets to protect, well . . . you know what. The poleyn is on my knee; the greaves, kinda like a catcher's shin guard.

And I take my sabatons in a size 11D.

Much to my surprise, once I got into all this gear, my freedom of movement was pretty good. I felt like a warrior. Until I proceeded to have my little set-to with Cliff. Then the sun got in my eyes and my sword was probably twice as heavy as his was. Hell, I'd rather crank out twenty on a bed of sharp nails than fight in that thing again.

"Take that, you vile varlet!"

CAVALRY IN THE CIVIL WAR

"How were the cavalry outfitted for battle back in the Civil War?"
— Drew, Baltimore, Maryland

W ell, for starters, Drew, during the Civil War, the cavalry wasn't much appreciated at first, being used mainly for reconnaissance and message delivery. But generals on both sides soon realized that the cavalry could play a major role on the battlefield.

•Bob Zaricor, Civil War reenactor: As the war progressed, they found out how effective a cavalry charge could be. And I don't think there's anything that's more awesome than having an entire regiment of nine hundred to twelve hundred men riding down on horseback. That will turn an infantryman in a second. •

To be effective in combat, cavalrymen needed some specialized gear. The first thing you had to have on horseback was a good pistol. These were great for close-up fighting, and you could aim them really quickly. The guys from the North and the South typically used the same one: a Model 1860 Army six-shot .44-caliber rifle. It was a very effective weapon, good for probably about seventy-five yards.

A Confederate cavalryman and his nine-shot Le Mat pistol.

Now, when a cavalryman needed a slightly larger variety of kick-ass, a state-of-the-art Model 1859 Sharps carbine came in real handy. A carbine was shorter and lighter than a normal rifle. This made it easier to fire on the run, but still packed a big enough punch for the soldier to use once he had dismounted.

Then there was the signature weapon that a smart cavalryman kept close at hand—a nice, sharp saber. Back in the Civil War days, this wasn't just some fancy-shmancy ceremonial blade. The saber was an important weapon of last resort, used in the heat of battle when there was no time to reload a firearm. The saber's razor-sharp blade was curved so it wouldn't become stuck in an enemy soldier and yank the cavalryman off his horse.

The 1859 Sharps was the choice of cavalrymen on both sides.

And in case you're wondering how those cavalry guys walked around with these big-ass sabers, reenactor Dan McCluskey tells us.

• **Dan McCluskey, Civil War reenactor:** I attach the saber high when we walk. When I mount the horse, I drop it down into the lower position in order to ride. •

See? Don't you nimrods learn a lot in this book? And aren't you grateful to Gunny?

Now, Union forces usually outgunned Johnny Reb because the federal government was running a naval blockade in the South, which kept foreign weapons from reaching Confederate shores. But much to the Union's dismay, hundreds of Confederate cavalrymen did manage to get their hands on some highly effective handguns. They liked a French model called the Le Mat in particular.

The Model 1860 Army six-shot .44-caliber pistol—a quick shot from close in.

Most pistols at the time fired six shots. The Le Mat fired nine. And here's my favorite part: It had an additional chamber below the barrel that fired a shotgun shell. Talk about reaching out and touching someone. About twenty-five hundred of these beauties got through the blockade, and quite a few cavalrymen used them.

Finally, since a lot of missions lasted many days, cavalrymen needed to carry a bunch of other stuff besides weapons. Riders needed to have supplies and gear not only for themselves, but for their horses, too—say, a standard-issue 1859 McClellan saddle, blankets, and a bunch of bags for everything from food to extra horseshoes.

All this gear weighed up to sixty pounds, which meant the cavalrymen had to be slim and trim themselves— weighing no more than 140 pounds.

You'd probably need to recruit some jockeys to make that kind of weight limit these days!

The curved blade made it perfect for slashing from horseback.

TEST YOUR MILITARY IQ

When was the last mounted cavalry charge the U.S. Army made?

Answer on page 232.

THE M1910 WORLD WAR I PACK—AND WHY IT WAS SO AWFUL!

"What was in a World War I backpack?"
—Mark F., Emporia, Kansas

"Check out this pimplehead."

Well, Mark, here's your answer. Listen up!

When American doughboys marched into battle in World War I, they not only faced the brutality of trench warfare, machine guns, and gas attacks, but also had to contend with their own inferior equipment. None of which was worse than their clumsy backpack. To help answer Mark's question, I quizzed a group from the Great War Historical Society.

• **Mike Phillips, doughboy reenactor:** This is not a combat pack. This is almost impossible to move around in; this thing's so ungainly that just trying to run and turn, you've got an extra foot or so sticking off your back. And the sheer time involved in unloading it and loading it just does not make it feasible to use in a combat situation. •

It was no accident that what our boys carried had severe limitations. The pack was, if you can believe it,

SPIKIN' IT!

Ever wonder why they had a spike on top of the brain bucket that they were using back in Germany in World War I? Officially, it's called a helm, but mostly the guys called it a *pickelhaube*, which means "pimplehead" in German. Nice. The spike started in 1842, when the Prussian king Friedrich Wilhelm thought his infantrymen would look more aggressive with a spike on their heads. By the middle of World War I, though, the Germans started catching on that the spike was stupid when Allied snipers started shooting them off the heads of the guys in the trenches. At first, the helmet geniuses made the spike detachable, but by the end of the war the pimpleheads were popped off for good.

meant to be inflexible. In the early 1900s, the U.S. Army decided that a soldier should carry no more than one-third of his body weight in gear and equipment.

So they set out to design a pack and specific items to meet the doughboy's everyday needs. In 1910, they came up with what they called the M1910 pack. Nothing more than a bunch of straps and flaps. It's not a bag; it appears to be a bag, but it isn't, trust me. You pull the straps and flaps and this thing just explodes. And this is exactly what the World War I doughboy had to put up with.

• **Harlan Glenn, author-historian:** The idea of the design was like a squaw's papoose, all swaddled up on a packboard. They were forcing the soldier to take into battle what they thought he should take with him. But the problem is that they really didn't think about the soldier's mobility. It's like a huge lead weight on his back. •

Anyway, gearheads, here's what was inside one of these M1910s.

The bottom section of the pack, known as the diaper, was detachable and carried the soldier's blanket, shelter half, and shelter half stakes. On the belt you'd find ammunition, a first-aid kit, canteen cover, canteen, and cup. Inside the flaps were a bacon tin and condiment can for salt, sugar, and coffee. There were boxes of bread rations, sometimes packed in metal to protect them from gas attack. Also a towel, soap dish, shaving kit, handkerchief, foot powder, and extra socks. Attached to the outside were the bayonet, shovel, and mess kit.

And guess what? Due to the placement of the bayonet, most soldiers could not withdraw it from its sheath or put it back themselves. They had to have a buddy do it for them.

Incredibly, this terrible design remained in service until early in World War II. It's a wonder we didn't lose that war. We could all be speaking German right now. In fact, I'd be telling you: *Sprung auf marsch, marsch, hinlegen!* Ding-dong!

Inside the M1910 pack.

SAVING LIVES: AIR FORCE SURVIVAL GEAR

"What's inside an Air Force survival vest?"

—Paul and Bennett, Daytona Beach, Florida

Everything the flier on the run needs, from GPS to strobe.

It took two guys to write this e-mail?!

Unlike the old days, rescues today are fairly easy with long-range helicopters. But not every rescue mission is a success, so our airmen always wear a survival vest.

What's inside? Let's check it out.

When an airman takes to the skies, the enemy isn't the only danger he faces. There's always a chance that a problem with the flight, even in a training exercise, could force him to eject. Whether in hostile territory or wilderness, the flier will need more than just his sidearm. He'll also need a darn good survival kit. Pilots in the 8th Fighter Squadron at Holloman Air Force Base in New Mexico take along one of the best.

In fact, Master Sergeant Buddy Gurnari of the squadron's life support section helped design it.

• **Master Sergeant Buddy Gurnari:** As far as the pilot's survival equipment goes, he would have the survival vest, along with his parachute harness. And attached to the parachute harness would be his survival kit. During flight, the survival kit fits in a slot under the pilot's ejection seat. Crammed into this small container are all kinds of goodies. If a pilot has to eject, about a split second afterward, the container will open up and the rest of the survival kit will deploy out of that. •

Once a pilot hits the deck, he ditches his parachute harness and determines which gear he has time to take with him. If the enemy's already on him and he has to get the hell out of Dodge, it might end up being just the vest he's wearing. The survival vest has lots of high-tech gadgets that can help the unlucky flier tell his buddies where he's at. There's a high-powered, waterproof radio . . . a handheld global positioning system . . . even a strobe light that can be seen at night from great distances. It's waterproof, and it's also directional.

The vest also has a signal flare and a compass, along with a couple of packets of always-critical drinking water. But that's just the beginning of this first-rate survival system. If the pilot has only a few extra seconds, he can scoop up what they call the "hit-and-run" kit and the rucksack—two pieces of gear that will make his life a lot easier.

• **Master Sergeant Gurnari:** The hit-and-run kit is packed in a waterproof container—so even the bag itself can be used as a water storage device. But inside here you'll find additional items for communications and for signaling. Backup survival radio, along with the one that's in the survival vest. A fixed-blade knife, another flare, compact pen gun flares that'll shoot up about a thousand feet. Some sort of fire-starting device, a flint bar, a camouflage stick. A signal mirror . . . a multitool for improvising and as a backup to the knife. And more of that all-important emergency drinking water. •

LET'S SEE—IS THAT MAE OR PAMELA?

A lot of people wonder why life jackets used to be called Mae Wests.

Back in the old days, there were a lot of bombshells in the movies. But nobody put it out there like Mae West. When she asked you to come up and see her sometime, trust me, she wasn't inviting you to a tea party. Ol' Mae had it in all the right places—fore and aft. Especially when it came to her top deck. So a life jacket as Mae West is a no-brainer.

Nowadays they'd probably call it a Pamela Anderson!

Radios, GPS units, first-aid kits . . . lots of handy stuff. But when it comes down to it, a pilot's most important survival equipment is what he has right up in his head. It takes some equipment, but it really takes knowledge and also, most importantly, the will to survive.

Hell, throw in some high-caffeine coffee and a bag of doughnuts, and I'd be more than happy to hang out in the woods for months!

WHAT DID OUR WORLD WAR II GIs PUT IN THEIR PACKS?

"What personal items did fighting men of World War II carry?"

—Kirk, Amarillo, Texas

Whether they were clearing dragon's teeth or storming beaches in the Pacific, our guys in World War II were loaded down with weapons, ammo, grenades, all sorts of combat gear. There wasn't a lot of room left over for personal stuff. So those little luxuries had to be chosen carefully . . .

• **Harlan Glenn, author-historian:** Some of the personal items that were carried by GIs and Marines in World War II were issued by the government; some you could buy in the PX or were donated by volunteer groups like the American Red Cross. Others, of course, were sent from home. They had a special, scaled-down shaving kit, very compact. Everything in this shaving kit is small and lightweight. Even the toothbrush has been hacked off so it can fit inside here. Folded up and put in your pack, it hardly takes up any room. •

Once the men came off the line, one of the very first things they wanted to do was shower and shave. And after a

Keeping clean helped maintain morale and combat readiness.

few days of boonie stompin', a Marine can get pretty ripe! Shaving off weeks' worth of beard growth helped to make a guy feel less like an animal and more like a human being again.

Now, although there was a lot of leeway for what the men could bring into battle, a few items were completely banned.

• **Harlan Glenn:** Two personal items that were strictly forbidden to be carried in the field were cameras and diaries. If a soldier were killed or taken prisoner, the enemy might be able to get valuable intelligence from the photographs or from the notes made in the diaries. •

"If you're gonna play, you're gonna pay!"

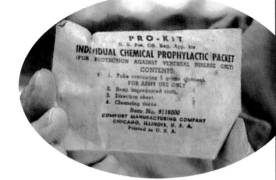

"This is my rifle, this is my gun, one is for fighting, one is for . . . need I say more?"

Besides fighting the enemy, our guys also had to do battle with wildlife and body vermin. Mosquitoes, sand fleas, ticks, lice that could eat a guy alive. And all the soldiers had to combat them was bug repellent and delousing powders. Water purification was also an issue, especially in the Pacific, where there was no fresh water, so tablets were provided for that.

Finally, reminders from home were considered to be the most treasured personal items of all. A simple letter from a loved one, or a novel, or a magazine could do wonders for morale.

The American fighting man of World War II had quite an array of personal items. Some kept him fit and ready for battle. Others served to make the hell of war just a little more tolerable.

WHAT DID OUR PARATROOPERS CARRY ON D-DAY?

"What kind of special equipment did paratroopers use on D-Day?"
—Tristan, Fresno, California

When the hard-charging paratroopers of the 82nd and 101st Airborne Divisions jumped into France on June 6, 1944, they weren't sure what they'd face when they hit the ground . . . so they had to be ready for anything. You bet they carried all the weapons and ammo and chow that they could stuff into the pockets of those M1942 jumpsuits, but they also carried a bunch of unusual gear, special gadgets for specific situations.

• **Mike Phillips, reenactor:** The troopers were issued a variety of knives, one of which was a switchblade to cut themselves out of their chutes should they become entangled in a tree when they landed. Give a quick cut to your risers and you're out. Or if a guy got stuck in a tree too high to jump down, he could slide to safety with his thirty-three-foot "let down" rope. •

The infamous "leg bag."

A gas mask pouch. The mask was soon tossed away, and the pouch became a valuable waterproof carryall.

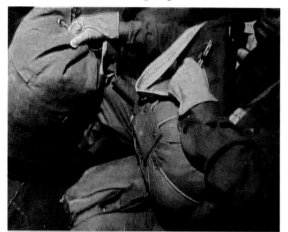

Maybe the handiest creations used in the invasion of France were the custom-made ammunition pouches sewn by a unit's riggers, which could hold nearly twice the number of bullets and grenades carried by the standard-issue equipment. These modified Thompson machine-gun magazine pouches are a shining example of GI ingenuity—by rigging two pouches together across the chest, a guy had plenty of ammo close at hand.

The men carried gas masks in special watertight assault bags. These bags kept the gas masks dry even if the troopers landed in a bog. Also, every paratrooper wore a gas detection brassard over his shoulder. It was treated with chemicals that changed colors in the presence of poison gas to give the wearer a warning to grab that gas mask now!

It became pretty apparent after the second or third day at Normandy that there was no gas going on, so most paratroopers either ditched the brassard or ditched the gas mask and used the bag as a watertight container for cartons of cigarettes and rations.

Being out there on your own, behind enemy lines, without a medic, what would you do if you got wounded? Well, you'd find help in your personal first-aid kit, that's what.

• **Josh Henneger, reenactor:** A paratrooper is issued a different first-aid kit than the regular army and infantry. They actually had morphine and a tourniquet in there as well as a bandage. If these guys hurt themselves on the drop or misdropped away from the rest of their guys, they had no medical attention. •

Now, some of our men tried the British-made leg bag. It was designed to carry all the heavy stuff tied around one leg with a rope. Sounded good, but it was a dog! When the heavy bags hit the wind, they snapped the rope and scattered the gear to hell and gone. The unlucky paratrooper landed without his weapon, or his ammo, or his chow. Not a good way to start the largest operation of the whole war.

POKER, ANYBODY?

What the heck did those markings on World War II paratrooper helmets mean, anyway? The brass was concerned that the green paratroopers on D-Day wouldn't be able to tell who was in which unit. So they decided to paint marks on the sides of their helmets. To make it easy, they used the four suits from a deck of cards, one for each of the division's four regiments. The diamond signified the 501st Parachute Infantry Regiment. The heart was the 502nd. The spade was the 506th. And the club was the 327th Glider Infantry Regiment.

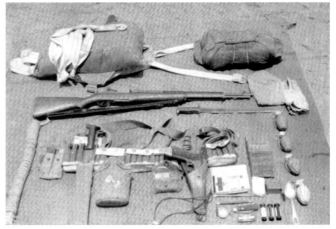

A paratrooper's gear. Note the .45 automatic.

THE FIRST SPECIAL SERVICE FORCE

"What kind of gear and equipment did U.S. Special Forces use during World War II?"
—Michael, Seattle, Washington

Michael says his granddad was a member of the First Special Service Force during World War II, and that's quite an honor. Of all the Allied units that fought the Nazis, this one in particular scared the Germans right out their lederhosen!

The First Special Service Force was an all-volunteer outfit. The unit was one-half Canadian and the other half American. They were rugged guys. For them, there was no terrain too extreme, and no mission that they couldn't handle!

• **Harlan Glenn, author-historian:** The First Special Service Force first saw combat in Italy. Italy was very mountainous terrain, and the Germans, being masters of defense, had the Allies in a stalemate. What better job for this force of highly trained mountain fighters? They were able to knock the Germans off mountaintop after mountaintop. •

The Germans called them Black Devils because they came out of the night, with painted faces.

To get the job done, the First Special Service Force had some cool weapons and gear, like the V42 dagger for stealthy, close-quarters work. The V42 was made only for the First Special Service Force, by the Case knife company. Each dagger was actually handmade; no two were the same. But all the V42s were designed to be used in a very specific fashion.

• **Harlan Glenn:** There's a thumbprint at the base of the blade, and the idea is that it forces the GI to hold the knife in a particular fashion: You can insert it in your enemy's chest and it goes between the ribs. If you were to insert it vertically, it could get stuck between the bones. •

The V42 is the most highly collectible fighting knife used by our boys in World War II! And speaking of collectibles, how'd ya like an M41 Johnson light machine gun, the other very unique weapon of the First Special Service Force, designed by Melvin Johnson? The beautiful thing about the Johnson is that it was ten pounds lighter than other machine guns, making it an ideal weapon for airborne troops and mountain troops. It had a twenty-round magazine. It could be fired fully automatic or single shot. It was a lot more effective than the BAR in these kinds of situations.

And the First Special Service Force had some pretty slick garb and gear to wear into combat—all tailor-made for their kind of war! Most of it was designed for mountain warfare, such as reversible snow parkas, white on one side for snow camouflage, olive drab on the other for use in forests. And mountain rucksacks ideal for tossing in anything and everything.

With their combination of toughness, training, special weapons, and custom gear, it was no wonder the Germans feared 'em so much. In fact, the German troops called them the Black Devils, since they'd usually blacken their faces before kicking some butt on midnight raids.

Author-historian Harlan Glenn demonstrates the V42 knife, made only for the First Special Service Force.

The M41 Johnson light machine gun: a superb assault weapon.

WORLD WAR II RADIOS

"What kind of radios did they use in World War II?"
—Jerry, Lubbock, Texas

Hey, all you radioheads, tune in! The key to winning a battle is being able to maintain good communications between you and your men. Three types of radios did the most to make this happen for the lowly ol' ground-pounders. They had handheld models, man-pack sets, and team-operated component sets that would make ol' Ma Bell's head spin!

• **Andy Miller, military radio collector:** The BC-611 Handie-Talkie is probably one of the most widely recognizable pieces of World War II radio equipment. In its day, it was an amazing accomplishment in microtechnology, and although by today's standards it's no lightweight, it certainly was a miracle to the soldiers who had to operate it back then. Designed to be used by somebody with little or no experience in electronics, it has only a few basic controls. Simply hold it up to your head like it's a telephone, listen without pressing the button, and when you're ready to send a message you push that button and you're on the air. •

It was a great little radio, well designed and able to stand up to the punishment of combat usage. The BC-611 had a range of about two miles

Top: The BC-611 Handie-Talkie—don't confuse this with the walkie-talkie.

Middle: The *real* walkie-talkie.

Bottom: Cranking it sent out a message, while batteries were saved for reception.

under ideal conditions—good for communicating at the platoon level. Now, some of you have probably committed the heinous crime of calling a Handie-Talkie a walkie-talkie. I'm not surprised because it was all you civilians out there who screwed that up when you were playing with your little army men.

The real walkie-talkie was the SCR-300. It was called that because you wore it like a backpack and walked around—duh! It had a little wider range than the Handie-Talkie—up to about three miles—so one company commander could figure out what the other one was doing. This was a great little radio that came out late in the war. It was designed to be an FM set, which is a big departure, technologically speaking, from the earlier sets. FM had less static and less interference, which allowed soldiers to get the message through when they really needed to.

Before going out into the field, all the operator had to do to get this set ready to use was turn on the on/off switch, set the frequency, and lock it so it couldn't be moved while he was walking around. Then he'd turn on the squelch—which was new to the FM sets and eliminated all the static in the set when nobody was talking—and close the top.

Now, you couldn't just pick up any old radio set and call in air support or reinforcements! The one-man Handie-Talkies and walkie-talkies couldn't handle that. For those bigger jobs, you needed the TBX-8 radio, operated by a team of skilled and highly motivated Marines.

• **Andy Miller:** The TBX-8 radio set used by the Marines and Navy during World War II was a higher-power set and able to transmit its messages farther than the small field-pack radios. It was able to transmit both voice signals and Morse code. To operate the TBX-8, you needed at least one other team member to supply the electricity that the radio would need to get the message out. •

The hand crank was used to provide power for the short bursts of outgoing messages from the transmitter. Batteries took care of the lower-power job of listening to incoming messages.

Hope that answers your question, Jerry. Next time, try to be a little more specific 'cause I can't spend all day on our answer! But I think we covered the most common and most faithful sets that kept our boys "in the know."

Oohrah!

"Hey, puke!
Keep your butt
down and your
ears up. And
turn the page!"

FABULOUS FLOPS: THE JETPACK

An idea whose time never came.

"Did the military ever experiment with jetpacks?"
—Martin, Cleveland, Ohio

"Ready to kiss the sky, Mini-Lee?"

One of the things that makes my beloved military so outstanding is that we've got an awful lot of brilliant minds coming up with new and better ways to do things.

But not every invention has been a success story. So when I got Martin's e-mail, it was time to go into my fabulous flop file.

It's a bird, it's a plane . . . it's a guy taking his life in his hands to fly fifty feet. The idea for using rocket belts—or jetpacks—got started in science fiction. Inspired by dreams of becoming a real-life Buck Rogers, early experimenters in this kind of travel date back to the 1920s.

The first workable jetpack wasn't invented until 1958, when Wendell Moore, an engineer with Bell Aerosystems, took some tethered flights in the lab. The flights were short and rough, and when Wendell fractured his knee on one flight, his jetpack-flying days were over. But almost immediately the U.S. military took an interest in the device. In the 1960s, they were able to get a peroxide-powered jetpack to carry a man over a thirty-foot hill, across a river, and over and around a variety of obstacles. The only problem was that the packs were dangerous and unreli-

able. Today a private company is still working with the jetpacks, but it's probably going to be a cold day in hell before we see a platoon of Buck Rogerses whizzing around the battlefield. Trust me on this.

I wanted to go for a ride myself, but at ten thousand bucks a pop a flight is way over my budget—and nobody around here wanted to pick up the pieces if the old Gunny went splat. So I got my little buddy here a jetpack of his very own.

Oohrah! Semper fi. Carry on!

TEST YOUR MILITARY IQ

What was the jetpack's maximum flight time?

Answer on page 232.

A GREAT PLACE TO FLOP: THE FART SACK

"Hey, Gunny, what's a fart sack?"
—Mike, Plano, Texas

"Is that a Gunny or a Mummy?"

Well, Mike, you crude piece of civilian puke, here's a quiz.

A fart sack is (a) you after a mess of chili cheese fries, or (b) one of these mummy-type sleeping bags.

The mummy sack is a lot better than most American soldiers ever had it. It wasn't until the Civil War that any type of sleep equipment, besides tents, became standard issue. Civil War soldiers were lucky to receive one scratchy piece of fabric known as a horse blanket. During World War I, soldiers still got just one wool blanket. And even in World War II, sleeping bags were few and far between. Plus, they were pretty darn heavy.

During the bitterly cold winters of the Korean War, troops were provided with nice cozy "mummy sacks." But they came up so high and were so snug that guys often couldn't get out of them quickly enough during surprise night attacks. Their solution was to cut arm- and legholes in the sacks so they could make a run for it instead of getting skewered by North Korean and Chinese bayonets.

Sleeping bags weren't in too high a demand in hot, muggy Vietnam. And these days, lighter-weight synthetic materials have made sleeping bags a lot easier to bring along.

FROM SALT PORK TO C-RATIONS— MEALS BEFORE MRES

"What kind of rations did our soldiers eat before MREs?"
—Richard, New York City, New York

Top: Softened up "sheet iron."

Bottom: A K-ration, opened sixty years after it was packaged. Verdict: "Dog food!"

Good question, Richard. Now I know, living in New York and all, you're probably used to some pretty fancy eatin', but your average combat Joe ain't had it that way, believe me, buster!

Civil War historian Paul Schoeman prepared a dish for us using salt pork, the meat most commonly available to Civil War troops, along with an ingredient that many consider to be the first official combat ration: hardtack.

• **Paul Schoeman, historian:** Hardtack is a simple wheat and water biscuit. It was manufactured in large quantities by both sides in the war. It was issued to all the troops, usually nine or ten biscuits a day. But these biscuits, usually baked months earlier, were often so hard and stale, troops nicknamed them "tooth-dullers" or "sheet iron crackers." To soften them up a little, soldiers mixed them with salt and pork grease to add flavor, then fried them up. •

But since there isn't always time to build a fire on the battlefield, and most young soldiers aren't Cordon Bleu–trained chefs, the Army needed a more standardized, ready-to-eat ration. Food-canning technology, developed after the Civil War, helped make that happen. The soldiers who fought World War I ate a variety of canned foods.

• **Gerald Peterson, historian:** They had crackers packaged in a tin can. And they also had a product called bully beef, which was also packaged in a tin can with a key opening. There were two varieties. There was one that came from the United States or Canada. And there was one that came

Eating out of a can gets monotonous after a while.

from Madagascar that the troops hated. It was called monkey meat because it had a very unpleasant, greasy taste to it. •

Most combat troops in the early days of World War II lived off so-called C-rations, which consisted of three parts—a B-unit, an M-unit, and an accessory packet. The accessory packet provided some "nice to have" items like toilet paper, along with luxuries like gum and cigarettes. It also contained the famous P-38, a clever device for opening the tin cans. The first can, the B-unit, contained candy, crackers, sugar, and coffee. The second can, the M-unit, held the main course, which was often meat and vegetable hash or meat and vegetable stew or meat and

beans. And sometimes only one ration would get through.

This ain't "have-it-your-way," like Burger King, ding-dong! Things got pretty monotonous. And those early C-rations in metal cans were heavy to carry.

To lighten the load—especially for paratroopers—the Army introduced the Type K ration, their first attempt at getting everything jammed into a single, lightweight container. As a special treat, historian Gerald Peterson opened a surviving World War II K-ration, just for us. Gaawwd! Sixty years ago, the crumbling hockey-puck-like mass we saw would have looked like the potted meat sold in stores today. Basically, like food for Fido!

After World War II, the K-ration was replaced by a new and improved C-ration; this time, the different cans were packed together in one box. Designated "Meal, Combat Individual," the new C-ration would become the staple for troops in Vietnam and would continue its service into the 1980s. But all that's been replaced these days by the MRE.

Don't remember what that is, Gomer? Tough luck. You're just gonna have to wait.

TEST YOUR MILITARY IQ

Okay, Dr. Atkins—how many calories in each C-ration?

Answer on page 232.

The combat cupcake: dee-licious baked goods, right under your hood.

MREs: THE GOURMET FOOD OF GI RATIONS

"What do our guys eat in the field?"
—Brad, Sacramento, California

The "MRE," or "Meal, Ready-To-Eat," has filled the bellies of U.S. fighting troops for almost twenty years now. Since its introduction in 1983, this self-contained dinner-in-a-pouch has served as the U.S. military's standard individual combat ration.

To find out more about what's inside an MRE pouch—and why a pouch in the first place—we visited an MRE factory: Ameriqual Foods in Evansville, Indiana. We met up with Gerry Darsch, director of the Department of Defense Combat Feeding Program.

• Gerry Darsch, director, Combat Feeding Program: The intent behind the MRE was to reduce the weight of the individual combat ration that the soldier in the field would carry. And in doing so, we had to come up with a new packaging concept that did not rely on conventional cylindrical cans. •

The new package had to be not only lightweight, but also flexible and as tough as a Marine. The answer: a bag with layers of nylon, plastic, and aluminum foil. But it takes a heckuva lot more than just a sturdy package to make a good combat ration. Designers of the MRE had to make sure the new meal met a long list of other requirements.

• Gerry Darsch: The MRE has to provide approximately thirty-six hundred calories per war fighter per day. And we provide that with three meals, so each meal provides around twelve hundred. They have to meet the surgeon general's military recommended dietary allowances in terms of micronutrients—vitamins, minerals, fats, carbohydrates, and protein. We have to be able to throw these bad boys out of an airplane with a parachute. And toss 'em out of a chopper at a hundred feet with no parachute. And if you don't think that's enough, after all that's done, the meals have to look good, taste good, and be consumed by the soldier in the field. •

At the heart of each MRE is one of twenty-four main menu items—dishes like beefsteak with mushrooms and gravy, or chicken tetrazzini. They've even got a couple of vegetarian meals. While I was at the factory, they were making buttered noodles, yum, yum, yum!

Huge pressure cookers heat the pouches to kill any microbes sealed inside. After cooling, the pouches are slipped into chipboard cartons and loaded into the outer MRE bag, along with a bunch of other goodies. There's an accessory packet in there containing items like matches, toilet paper, utensils, condiments, and hot sauce. There's also, usually, a bakery item in each of the pouches. And there are snack items like M&M's, pretzels, peanuts.

Why, there's even a handy-dandy flameless heater to rewarm the entree and side dish. The heater contains a mixture of chemicals that get hot when you add water.

Ain't no escapin' it—the MRE contains just about all the comforts of home a combat soldier could hope for in the field. And it's pretty good chow, too. Maybe we should offer extra MREs as enlistment bonuses.

THE COMBAT CUPCAKE

Some guys in the field shared one of their special dessert recipes with me, which I know you maggotheads would just love to try out at home. What you're gonna do is you're gonna take about a third of a canteen full of water and put it in your canteen cup. You're gonna sprinkle in some cocoa beverage powder. Stir it up just a wee bit. Then to kick it up a notch, toss in some Chiclets, and it's all ready to go in the oven. And by "oven," I mean the engine of my jeep. It may look like a jeep to you civilians, but to us old military dogs it's an in-the-field microwave. You give it about two minutes and—voilá, ding-dong!—a combat cupcake.

A lightweight pouch, easy to carry, easy to open.

Chowing down in the field—one of the great delights known to man (and woman!).

A lot tastier than your old C-ration.

The Gibson Girl—1890s sex siren.

GEARHEADS IN LOVE

"What was so attractive about the Gibson Girl?"
—Elwood, Grand Prairie, Texas

"What makes ALICE such a sweetheart?"
—Chris, Golden Valley, North Dakota

Elwood, something tells me you're not really interested in hearing about the Gibson Girl who was the creation of fashion illustrator Charles Gibson, back in the 1890s—the real hottie with the hourglass figure who was all the rage. My guess is that you're sitting there in Grand Prairie pondering the SCR-578 rescue radio, also known as the Gibson Girl radio because of its hourglass shape.

Starting in World War II, the Gibson Girl is what downed pilots used when they had to ditch in the ocean. The radio is completely self-contained and practically waterproof; it floats, and it has a hand-cranked generator for power. It would automatically send out SOS signals alternating with long dashes and could also sometimes be used to transmit messages. The rescue radio kit also came with a box kite or a balloon so you could get it up—the antenna, that is—where the signal was better.

The Gibson Girls hung around until the 1970s 'cause they were pretty ingenious—and not bad looking, either. Especially if you'd been at sea (or in Grand Prairie) for a while.

I swear, you gearheads and your love affairs. First a Gibson Girl, now ALICE! Hey, whatever floats your boat—or in this case, rides your back!

No matter how you get into combat, you can't go empty-handed. You gotta be prepared for just about anything. Back when I was in Vietnam, we wore a special rig to hump our ammo and gear. What the Army called the M1956 Load Carrying Equipment, the Marine Corps always referred to as 782 gear. It had a butt pack, ammo pouches— pretty good gear. But after the war, the Army came up with a new system called the All-Purpose Lightweight Individual Carrying Equipment . . . ALICE for short.

In Vietnam, our web gear was made from cotton canvas fabric. And that little butt pack couldn't really carry much. Late in the 1960s, the Army started testing new gear made from nylon. It was lighter to start with, and when it got wet it didn't grow much heavier. It even dried off quicker. In 1974, the Army officially adopted the new ALICE system. It snapped together easily and let guys customize their gear in a lot of different ways. Plus, that ALICE pack could hold everything but the kitchen sink.

In the past few years, ALICE has been sent packing in favor of new gear like the tactical load-bearing vest. And there's a brand-new system called MOLLE, which stands for "Modular Lightweight Load-Bearing Equipment." The MOLLE gear is being tested on the front lines right now as we speak, but reviews are mixed.

So don't start falling in love with MOLLE yet, dirtballs!

This "Gibson Girl" was the muse of many a man lost at sea.

COIN OF THE MILITARY REALM

What is a Military Challenge coin? Well, most are about the size of a silver dollar. They're carried by unit commanders, senior staff NCOs, and officers—and then they're handed out to their troops as a way of saying thanks for a job well done. Their most popular unofficial use is to see who buys the next round when you're off duty. If someone pulls out a coin and taps it on the table, everyone else is supposed to follow suit. If you're empty-handed, then you're buying. But if everyone has a coin, then the person who issued the challenge in the first place has to pick up the tab.

And so it's only right that *Mail Call* should have its own Challenge coin. It's pretty handsome, if I do say so myself. We've got **The History Channel** logo on one side and the Marine Corps eagle, globe, and anchor on the other. Now, you can't buy these. I give 'em out to folks we feature on the show and to troops I meet out in the field as a way of saying thank you for their service to our country! Semper fi.

Carry on!

Gunny's very special Challenge Coin.

The ALICE backpack holds everything a lonely soldier needs.

MILITARY SPIDERMEN

"What's the difference between fast-roping and rappelling?"
—Ed, East Windsor, New Jersey

Rangers have rappelled down cliffs from Normandy to the present day.

Well, Ed, if you want me to explain how our troops get outta high-flying helicopters or descend a rocky cliff, then I want you to meet some guys who put Spider-Man to shame.

Welcome to Ranger School in Fort Benning, Georgia. This is where the Army trains its elite commando force. When these bad boys come callin', the war's on! Their job is simple: Attack with lightning speed across land, sea, and air and kill the enemy before he knows what hit him. Fast-roping and rappelling are two of the coolest ways they hit the battlefield.

"Don't make me knock your ass off that couch, pal. Keep on reading!"

Students learn firsthand the fundamental differences between fast-roping and rappelling. So listen up, Ed! At its most basic, Rangers fast-rope from helicopters and rappel over natural terrain. Rappelling has played a vital role in their training for decades. Rangers have roped their way into history from the cliffs of Normandy in World War II to Mogadishu in Somalia, and in more recent conflicts as well. The basic techniques haven't changed much, but the gear is a helluva lot better.

• **Staff Sergeant Michael Black, Ranger instructor:** The difference between fast-roping and rappelling is that in fast-roping—or what we call FRIES, Fast Rope Insertion Extraction System—they utilize a rope that is three inches in diameter, one hundred feet in length, and made of hemp. It attaches to the aircraft or helicopter. The Rangers slide down this like we would a fire pole. In rappelling, we utilize a rope eleven millimeters in diameter, 150 feet in length, that has a tension strength of approximately forty-eight hundred pounds. •

These hardy Rangers also use what's called SOFME, or Special Operations Forces Mountaineering Equipment. They wear a nylon harness. Heavy leather work gloves prevent burning of the hands. There's a locking snap link with a tension strength of two thousand pounds, and a figure-eight descender that acts as a friction break. This allows you to support your weight and control the rate of descent.

Now that we've got the gear down, let's check out the proper technique for rappelling and fast-roping . . .

• **Staff Sergeant Black:** The proper technique for fast-roping is quite simple, but it's actually very dangerous because the Ranger is not hooked up to anything. He grasps the rope and slides down, utilizing his hands and his boots. Once he's approximately three feet off the ground, he releases his feet and prepares to land. Once he lands, he moves away from the rope, allowing the next roper to hit the ground. •

The proper technique for rappelling is that the Ranger utilizes one hand for a break and the other hand as a guide. He gets into a good L-shaped position and either walks backward down the cliff or uses successive bounds. When utilizing successive bounds, he'll flex his knees and loosen the grip of his break hand and continue sliding down the rope. When he wants to stop or slow down, he tightens the grip with his break hand and places it into the small of his back. Once at the bottom of the cliff, he clears his ropes and walks backward off the rope.

No matter which one you do, rappelling or fast-roping, remember one thing, genius: Hang on!

Speed and safety lie in top-notch modern gear.

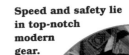

Fast-roping from helicopters—a means of quick insertion.

Mike's e-mail got me thinking about the very first guy who tried parachuting. It seems that back around the time of the Revolutionary War, some English guy tested the theory by jumping out a two-story window with an open umbrella! I'll bet the jackass damn near broke every bone in his body. Ouch!

Actually, the invention of the parachute back in 1797 is credited to James Blanchard, who never used one himself—but legend has it that he proved a chute would work by pushing his dog out of a hot-air balloon. Apparently, what had not been invented yet was the Humane Society.

Well, things have changed a lot since then, as a little trip to the Army Airborne School at Fort Benning, Georgia, showed us. No matter what branch of the service you're in, if you want to learn how to jump out of an airplane and survive, you go to Fort Benning, at least for initial training. The airborne school pumps through some seventeen thousand students a year. That takes a lot of parachutes. And every one has to be carefully

"No, I ain't Mary Poppins, smart-ass! Drop and give me fifty!"

packed by a platoon of specialists called riggers.

Sergeant First Class Michi White oversees the rigger platoon. A former exhibition parachutist, Sergeant White has more than three thousand jumps to her credit. She knows the standard-issue parachute about as well as anybody else in the Army.

• **Sergeant First Class Michi White, parachute rigging supervisor:** We refer to it as a T-10 Delta. It weighs approximately twenty-six pounds when it's fully packed. We have thirty tables here where we do pack the parachutes. And it takes our average rigger about ten or twelve minutes to pack one up. •

"Okay, maggot, get your sandwich and then come right back. Your dear old Gunny'll be here waiting for you. Not!"

The T-10 canopy has thirty individual sections and thirty suspension lines and is made of a special ripstop nylon, so it's tough. Tears are few and far between. That's one of this model's few improvements over the T-7—the World War II parachute. The T-7's canopy was made of silk. The nylon version came along by the end of World War II. Another, more recent improvement is the anti-inversion net at the bottom of the canopy. This net keeps the canopy from flipping upside down during deployment.

Speaking of which, how does this puppy deploy?

• **Staff Sergeant Jeffrey Mader, parachute rigging inspector:** When they're actually in the aircraft, a soldier's attached to a cable, secured to the body of the aircraft via a static-line and snap hook. And this'll always stay connected to the aircraft. As the soldier jumps out of the plane, the aircraft's going to keep going forward, deploying the static-line in a neat, orderly manner. •

The soldier's weight then pulls the canopy suspension lines from their stow loops, and the canopy deployment bag starts to open—and baby, you're flying! The jumper can move right or left a little by pulling on the straps that connect the harness to the parachute itself, but it's kind of tough to steer the round canopy. That's on purpose. Mainly what you want is the entire force to exit that aircraft while drifting in approximately the same direction until they hit the ground, so there is less possibility of entangling in the air.

So there you go, Mike. The parachute for an airborne soldier hasn't changed much since World War II for a reason—if it ain't broke, don't fix it.

A parachute rigger at Fort Benning, Georgia, carefully prepares a chute.

With a few modifications, the T-7 chute of World War II . . .

. . . became the T-10 our airborne troopers use today.

A vintage U.S. Army combat desk.

FROM GUNNY'S TENT TO THE TOC

"Can you give us a tour of your tent?"
—Earl, Coos Bay, Oregon

Well, a man's home is his castle, Earl, but I guess I could take you around. For a guy who spends a lot of his time out in the woods, I've got a pretty sweet setup here!

My humble little abode is 100 percent cotton and specially treated to be water-resistant and fire-retardant. Technically, it's an M1945 command post tent. But I just like to call it my little canvas mansion. It's got my cot, where I rest my weary head after a hard day in the woods. I have an office complex, of course, where I handle all the e-mail that you people send me. There's a vintage combat field desk. Field stove, Handie-Talkie, all the latest electronics.

And my ammo boxes out front make great modular furniture. I can make a nice easy chair with a matching ottoman, or even elegant patio furniture.

Hope you like my crib, but of course it's got nothin' on what happens in the Army's battlefield TOC tents these days. For the uninformed out there—and that seems to be most of you meatheads—*TOC* stands for "Tactical Operations Center." The TOC is designed to give modern commanders real-time intelligence so they can better take control of the battle.

• **Colonel Robert Brown, TOC:** Imagine you have thousands of separate elements maneuvering all over a battlefield. They're all doing good stuff—fighting, agile, adaptive leaders making decisions. But someone's gotta take all that and piece it together and figure out the bigger picture. And that's what the Tactical Operations Center does. •

Using the TOC is kinda like standing over a big war-gaming table with all your soldiers at your fingertips. In place of the sand table, though, you've got a wall of computer screens that instantly transmit every detail from the battlefield into one command center.

Once the enemy has been pinpointed, you can begin deploying your troops. And that's the beauty of this system: All your men are online, from ground-pounding infantry to hell-on-wheels mechanized units. All ya gotta do is type out a message on the keyboard and bingo—you've got mail!

This ain't your daddy's battle, bub! Back then, you had to hardwire phone lines, or wrangle carrier pigeons, or wait on messengers. Bigwigs like Eisenhower and Bradley had to twiddle their thumbs, waiting in the rear with the gear for word from their junior commanders on the front line. Heck, by the time they got the info, it could be yesterday's news!

• **Colonel Brown:** Before we had this technology, it would take you twenty to thirty minutes—and this is the best-case scenario—once you saw the enemy to report it on up over a radio. And it was all done verbally. •

TOCs can be set up and run in any type of weather and on any kind of terrain. If you're on the move, you'll only need a few Humvees. But if you've got some time, you can set up the whole kit and caboodle! All you have to do is back up, unload, plug in, and turn on!

WHERE DID THE NAME *PUP TENT* COME FROM?

The term *pup tent* is said to have originated with the Sixth Iowa Infantry in 1862. It seems to go along with *dogtags, dogface,* and *dog biscuits,* which were already popular nicknames with the Sixth Iowa. But another version of the story says the name comes from the Fifteenth Infantry at Chattanooga, which called their tents "doghouses" starting around 1864. Either way, the name *pup tent* goes all the way back to the Civil War. And since then, the doghouses have gotten a whole lot cushier!

Targeting the enemy.

Patio furniture, Gunny style!

NIGHTTIME ON THE BATTLEFIELD

"How do troops get any shut-eye when they're on the battlefield?"
—Kyle, St. Francisville, Louisiana

Setting up your perimeter: the key to good night defense.

Hey, good question, Kyle. I mean, let's face it, it is really important not to get your ass shot off in the middle of the night—so how do troops get any sleep at all on the battlefield?

And the flip side of this is, how does an exhausted soldier stay awake?

To get a closer look at how our hard-fighting soldiers bed down for the night, we visited the Army's Stryker Brigade Combat Team at Fort Polk, Louisiana.

• Captain William R. Jacobsen Jr., Stryker Brigade Combat Team: There is not a specified number of sleep hours, because the enemy's always out there and you have to be aware of that. •

During the stalemate of World War I, both sides hunkered down in their miles of trenches. World War II was a more mobile war, so units set up temporary defensive lines or circles with enough firepower to keep the enemy from getting through. The same kind of formations still work, although these days our grunts prefer triangles over circles, with a vehicle at each point.

• Captain Jacobsen: At each of the apexes of the triangle, you place your most casualty-producing weapon—possibly a .50-caliber machine gun, or something like that. And then in between each of those apexes you place your soldiers, and they pull security in that local area. •

Usually there will be one guy pulling security for every three soldiers in the unit. Sometimes they're in groups of three: one guy manning the gun, one keeping a lookout for the enemy, and the third catching some z's.

But when it's their turn to keep watch, many guys invent their own remedies for drowsiness. Some soldiers will take the coffee packet out of their MRE and actually put it in their mouth and suck on it. Others put Tabasco sauce from the MREs in their eyes to stay awake. Yeooww! Don't try that at home, maggothead!

Another technique is to drink an entire canteen of water right before you go to sleep; then the normal bodily functions will force you awake basically in a couple of hours. Hope you can find the latrine!

SEEING BETTER THAN A CAT!

No matter how their eyes stay open, the boys pulling security need to see what the heck is going on. The same Stryker Combat Team we spoke to was the first to try out the latest high-tech night-vision gizmo—the AN/PAS-13. It's a thermal device that can be handheld or mounted on a weapon.

With regular night-vision goggles—also known as NVGs—you can only see what the available light allows. But this baby has a range of eighteen hundred yards even in complete darkness. You can't hide from a thermal. Your heat will give off a signal, and the guy holding the thermal will orient everybody else's fire on that target. Which is you! Not to mention, these new thermals have one more trick nobody can beat. They can be used in an urban environment, where our guys can see the heat signatures in the rooms inside cinder-block walls. This gives U.S. soldiers an advantage they've never had before over anybody else in the world.

Here's hot sauce in your eye— using Tabasco to stay awake.

Turning night into day.

GEAR FOR THE SOLDIER OF TOMORROW

"What kind of gear will our soldiers be equipped with on the battlefield of tomorrow?"
—John, Augusta, Maine

The face of future warfare.

The soldier of tomorrow will have incredible advantages over today's fighters using the latest groundbreaking technology. Land Warrior is the system that will revolutionize the way our soldiers fight.

So what is Land Warrior? I met up with Sergeant First Class Chris Augustine, an expert on the system, and Sergeant First Class Alton Stewart, our very own Land Warrior, to check out this futuristic gear.

• **Sergeant First Class Chris Augustine:** Land Warrior is a digital soldier system that allows soldiers to communicate and share information among themselves on the battlefield, as well as providing enhanced lethality and protection for the individual soldier. •

So basically it's a better weapon combined with a better way to communicate and navigate. At the heart of this system is a small but powerful computer—kinda like what you might be using at work or at home. You probably use a mouse with your computer—well, so does Land Warrior. And just like you, the Land Warrior needs a monitor. But this monitor is the "head-mounted display."

• **Sergeant First Class Alton Stewart:** The head-mounted display is equivalent to a seventeen-inch monitor. If you were sitting in front of a computer desk, you'd get the same type of view. •

Maps are created using this navigational unit. It's more accurate than using a protractor and compass. And thanks to precise tracking info from a GPS, each soldier knows not only exactly where he is, but also the locations of all his buddies. The soldier communicates via radio through this microphone. Or he can send still images or text messages—just like your e-mail.

• **Sergeant Augustine:** If I tell three soldiers to move around the side of a hill, I can actually follow them on my map as they move. I can draw the plan and send it to them digitally so that there's no doubt in my mind that they know exactly what it is I want them to do. I can also snap a picture from my daylight video sight and send that up the chain of command to have it verified that it is the correct piece of equipment or individual that I'm looking for. •

That's the technology side. Now let's get to the firepower of this baby! It's an M4 carbine assault weapon. It's very accurate, with a maximum effective range of three hundred yards. It can hold a thirty-round magazine.

On top is a lightweight thermal weapon sight. The enemy target can be behind a tree or even in a foxhole. The Land Warrior can now shoot accurately in the dark and even around a corner without exposing you to return fire.

But all this high-tech gear wouldn't be much good if it couldn't protect the guy using it. So Land Warrior will improve the survivability of the soldier through protective eyewear and body armor. The eyewear not only stops dust and grit but also keeps the soldier's retinas from getting fried by enemy lasers.

Land Warrior won't be seeing any real action for a few more years. Still, one of its beauties is that it's fully integrated and modular. When technology changes, we won't have to scrap the whole system; we can simply upgrade the software.

Think of it as GI Joe meets Robocop!

Inside the eyepiece of the Land Warrior, a computer world with the clarity of a seventeen-inch monitor.

M4 carbine assault weapon: the Land Warrior's weapon of choice!

NEW CAMOUFLAGE FOR TOMORROW'S MARINE!

The Gunny looking like a new man.

"How did the Marines design their new camo pattern?"
—Jason, Cedar Rapids, Iowa

Jason, how nice of you to notice! When you consider that Marines in combat often depend on stealth and concealment for their very survival, any changes to their camouflage are gonna be taken pretty seriously. The man with all the answers on the new uniform is its project director, Lieutenant Colonel Gabe Patricio of the Marine Corps Systems Command.

• **Lieutenant Colonel Gabe Patricio:** To improve the uniform's effectiveness, the commandant of the Marine Corps personally handed down three main goals for the new design. One was to improve durability over the old uniform. Two was to make the uniform go back to its roots, really, and have more combat utility. And three was that the uniform should be uniquely Marine. •

Patricio's team talked to hundreds of Marines to hear any complaints they had about the current uniform and then started making changes, like smarter placement of the pockets.

On the old uniform, you see two symmetrically aligned pockets—neither of which has much utility in a combat environment once you have your flak jacket or backpack on. So what Patricio and his team did was convert the old pockets into shoulder pockets. Now a Marine can get to them, even with load-bearing straps coming down.

The design team also worked in several other improvements, like adding pouches on the inside of the uniform to hold knee and elbow pads. But the most noticeable change is the new camouflage pattern, called MARPAT—for "Marine pattern."

Camouflage is all about breaking up the outline of the body and helping it blend into the background . . . which, for a combat Marine, is usually trees and grass, so Marine camouflage uniforms have tried to mimic natural vegetation since World War II. But this new pattern doesn't.

• Lieutenant Colonel Patricio: The camouflage does two things. Number one, it disrupts. So whatever body is in the pattern, it gives it a sense of disruption. And the second thing that it does is blend with the background. It's designed by a research lab in Natick, Massachusetts, and made up of clusters of little squares called pixels. Before we actually printed our very first version of the material, we actually did this on paper, by optimizing and shifting around the pixels to different sizes, different locations, and different color percentages to the point where we felt comfortable taking it through the manufacturing process. •

Of course with new outfits, you need new footwear. Out with the shiny black boots, and in with the brown suede boots. They blend in better with most environments.

But not everything about the old uniform was thrown out.

Lieutenant Colonel Patricio: One of the features that they absolutely wanted to keep was the cover that I'm wearing. And this cover is the exact current cover, with two exceptions. Number one is the obvious one, the pattern. And number two is, we actually embroidered the eagle, globe, and anchor on the cover, whereas the current one has an iron-on decal.

The new camouflage uniform has just become standard issue for new recruits. And it's giving the Marines of tomorrow a whole new look!

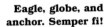

Eagle, globe, and anchor. Semper fi!

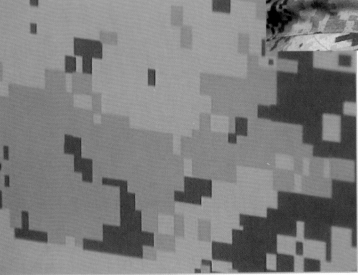

The MARPAT pattern.

PART THREE: GRUNTS

"Whether you're a crazed Viking, a Leatherneck, or a tank driver in Baghdad—you're still a grunt!"

GOING NUTS! THE HISTORY OF VIKING BERSERKERS

> **"What's the origin of the word berserk?"**
> —A. J., Grand Ledge, Michigan

A.J., *berserk* means "crazy, wild, and ferocious," terms your old Gunny is intimately familiar with, especially when I'm dealing with you grabasstic maggots out there.

The word comes from a bunch of old Norse warriors who were all that—and more. *Berserker* is a combination of two Norse words—*bjorn*, meaning "bear" or "bare" (naked), and *serkr*, meaning "shirt." You see, berserkers went into battle wearing bearskin shirts or just plain naked. They thought that by wearing the skin of a bear, they would become possessed by the animal's ferocious spirit.

Before battle, berserkers prepared themselves by painting their faces, banging helmets, howling like animals, drinking large quantities of alcohol, or eating hallucinogenic mushrooms— sort of like your average frat party these days!

Interestingly enough, their act was meant to terrify an enemy so much he wouldn't fight. But if he chose to— look out. The berserkers formed groups of twelve and charged. They always fought to the death, and their courage was so outstanding that even non-Viking kings of the period used them as bodyguards. Problem is, they got too dangerous to their own side, sometimes killing friends in their frenzied state, and eventually they were outlawed.

Frenzied warriors who could not be stopped.

GRUNTS AND DOUGH BOYS WHAT'S IN A NAME?

Stars and Stripes called them "doughboys"—and it stuck.

"Why were World War I soldiers called doughboys?"
—Tom, Romeo, Michigan

"Why are soldiers called GIs?"
—Kevin, Ashland, Oregon

Well, there's a bunch of theories here, Tom, so try to keep up. Some people say the name comes from the buttons the soldiers had on their uniforms during the Mexican-American War. The buttons looked like the dumplings—or dough balls—that the soldiers ate . . . so they were called "doughboys." Then there's the theory that those same soldiers built their quarters out of adobe mud and got a lot of it on their boots tramping around the Southwest. People started calling them mud crushers or adobe crushers and eventually just plain "dobees"— which sounds a lot like "doughboys."

Or maybe the term comes from the fact that infantrymen back in those days used pipe clay to whiten their belts and trimmings. When it rained, though, the clay got sticky and dough-y.

Nobody can quite agree on which explanation is the right one, but somehow by the time the First World War was under way, *Stars and Stripes* was calling all the Yanks "doughboys," and it stuck.

Kevin, frankly I thought your question was pretty damn stupid! But as it turns out, the answer is real interesting.

According to military historians, the term *GI* may go all the way back to the turn of the twentieth century when cavalry buckets—we're talking the cans that hung under the wagon axles—were stamped GI, which meant "galvanized iron." By World War I, *GI* had gained another meaning—"garrison issue," referring to certain accessories to the standard-issue uniform. Somehow, by the 1930s *GI* started being used at West Point to refer not only to the uniforms but also to the soldiers in them. And by World War II, it had come to mean "general issue," or more commonly "government issue."

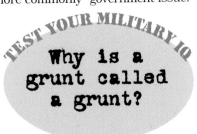

TEST YOUR MILITARY IQ

Why is a grunt called a grunt?

Answer on page 233.

GUNNY SEZ: SEMPER FI, ALL YOU GUNG-HO LEATHERNECKS!

I've gotten a lot of e-mail asking me all kinds of questions about why I say "Semper fi" all the time, and what does "Gunny" mean, and, hey, how about this "oohrah" thing and what's a "leatherneck" and by the way, "Can you explain gung-ho?" and, guess what, numb nuts—I'm sick of it!

Once and for all I'm gonna tell you the story of what these famous Marine terms mean . . .

The term *gung-ho* may have started with Marine Raider Colonel Carlson.

Semper Fi

It's right on the U.S. Marine Corps flag flying from the beak of the bald eagle: SEMPER FIDELIS. That's Latin for "always faithful"—which we are. Marines shorten the motto to "Semper fi" and use it to mean hello, good-bye, I got your back, and so on.

Now, "Semper Fidelis" wasn't always the Marine Corps motto. Back around the War of 1812, we were greeting each other with "Fortitudine," which meant "with fortitude." But that didn't last long—too hard to say. Then in 1883, Commandant Charles G. McCawley came up with "Semper Fidelis" and that's the one that stuck. And here's something else you need to know. If a Marine comes up to you and you're not a Marine and he says, "Semper fi, Mac"—well, that's the equivalent of the middle finger salute, if you know what I mean.

Leathernecks

Starting in 1798, the standard-issue neckwear for every American Marine was a leather collar. It was designed to protect the jugular vein and to keep the Marine's chin up. And it worked. Maybe too well. It was such a distinctive look that people started calling Marines leathernecks. Even when they

"Now, listen up! Gunny ain't got all day!"

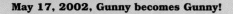

May 17, 2002, Gunny becomes Gunny!

stopped using the darn things in 1872, the nickname stuck. And there's another name for Marines we can blame on the uniform. People thought it made us look like our heads were screwed on our bodies. So some deck apes started calling us jarheads. But I better not catch you calling me that, buddy-boy!

Gung-Ho

The strongest theory pins the origin of gung-ho on Lieutenant Colonel Evans Fordyce Carlson. In 1937, Carlson was a USMC observer in China studying the movements of the Chinese Eighth Route Army. He was really impressed by how the troops worked together using a system of cooperation called the gung-yeh-ho-dzo. The short version of that was gung-ho, meaning "work together." When Lieutenant Colonel Carlson got back stateside, he became commander of the Second Marine Raider Battalion and introduced the term with his own troops.

Gunny

Okay, this is the most important question you can answer, puke! What's a "Gunny"? Listen carefully, 'cause I'm only going to go through this once.

We're talking enlisted rank structure of the U.S. Marine Corps here. It starts with private, which is your lowest rank, and goes to pay grade E7, which is gunnery sergeant—or Gunny for short.

The name goes back to the 1890s, when the corps was looking for a way of promoting sergeants who displayed exceptional skill with naval ordnance. I was a staff sergeant E6 when I was medically discharged from the Marines in 1971. But as we all know, once a Marine, always a Marine.

So on May 17, 2002, the commandant of the Marine Corps signed an order to promote me to gunnery sergeant at the Marine Corps Recruit Depot in San Diego, California. And that's why you can call me "Gunny." Right now, smart-ass!

"Don't hang it like this."

POMP AND CEREMONY: FROM HOW TO HANG THE FLAG TO THE MILITARY SALUTE

"Hang it like this."

"What's the deal behind the twenty-one-gun salute?"
—Len, Appelton City, Missouri

"What's the proper way to hang the flag?"
—Sid, New Haven, Connecticut

Sid, I want to say how proud I am that many of you are flying the American flag, but let's get it right, people! If you've got a flag in front of your house, the union—that's the part with the stars—should be uppermost at the top and to the flag's own right (that means to your left).

This rule is part of the U.S. Flag Code, and if you want to know all the rules, check it out on the Web.

Great question, Len. And here's the 411 on the twenty-one-gun.

Sometime around the fourteenth century, when ships started carrying cannons, gun salutes were instituted to let folks on shore know that your navy was friend, not foe. Since early cannons carried only one shot, discharging them meant you were unarmed. Originally, ships fired seven of their guns.

Why seven? This is where it gets mystical. Some people say it was because God rested on the seventh day, or because the phases of the moon changed every seven days, or because people thought seven was just a lucky number. But nobody really knows why. Anyway, the guys on shore would respond with three shots from their land batteries for every one fired from sea. That adds up to a twenty-one-gun salute.

In the nineteenth century, the U.S. military laid out some rules and regulations on cannon salutes. Today, you get a twenty-one-gun salute in this country only if you're the head of a foreign government, you're a member of a reigning royal family, or you're the president, or president-elect, or ex-president of the United States.

Now, lots of other bigwigs can be honored with gun salutes, just not the big twenty-one. If you're the vice president, speaker of the house, or a member of the cabinet, for example, you're entitled to a nineteen-gun salute. Four-star generals, admirals, and chairpersons of house committees get seventeen, and so on down to five-gun salutes for certain embassy consuls.

What do you think gunnery sergeants ought to get? Think hard before you answer, puke!

"Where did the military salute come from?"
—Kevin, Worcester, Massachusetts

Well, thank the old knights in shining armor for this one. History eggheads tell me the salute originated when knights raised their visors so they could be recognized and also to show that their right hand—their "weapon hand"—was unarmed.

Now, the Army's Quartermaster Center and School has a different explanation. It says the salute started when junior officers were required to take off their hats in the presence of superiors. Eventually the hat stayed on but the gesture remained.

All right, I'm going to show you how to do a hand salute real quickly here. Fingers extended and joined, thumb along the forefingers, wrist straight. Your arm should be parallel to the deck. Your right forearm should be at a forty-five-degree angle. And your index finger and your social finger should be touching the brim of your hat just forward of your right eye. Carry on!

HOW MANY SOLDIERS . . .

. . . are in an Army squad, platoon, and company?

Time for some math education, military style! The smallest element in the Army is the squad. That's eight to ten soldiers, depending on their function.

Combine two to four squads and you've got a platoon. Three to five platoons form a company. Four to six companies and you've got a battalion. Three to five battalions and we're talking brigade, baby. We're up to three to five thousand soldiers by now.

Three brigades is a division. Two to five divisions is a corps. And two or more corps is an army. That's a whole lotta whup-ass!

THE STORY OF THE HEROIC PJS

"What exactly is a PJ, and are they truly the elite of the U.S. Air Force?"
—John, Hamilton, Montana

You're asking what a PJ is, John? It sure as hell ain't your Winnie-the-Pooh pajamas! PJ stands for "pararescue jumper" and hell, yes, they're the elite of the Air Force.

PJs are a combination medical technician and supercommando, the baddest of the bad. They go deep behind enemy lines in places like Kosovo, Somalia, Afghanistan, and Iraq. Their dangerous missions require two years of intense training—and 90 percent of PJ wannabes wash out. Why? Because these guys are like Army Rangers, Navy SEALs, Green Berets, Delta Force, and top-notch

SSgt Chris Mercendetti
38th Rescue Squadron

Staff Sergeant Chris Mercendetti, PJ: "That others may live!"

superparamedics all wrapped into one. That's why.

• **Staff Sergeant Chris Young, PJ:** Being a PJ is literally one of the best jobs in the military. It's one of those high-profile jobs where you get a lot of training. You get a lot of good equipment. But it's also very rewarding. Our job is one of the few jobs that has no politics involved in it. If we are launched on a mission, it's not because of somebody's political agenda. It's because people are in danger and they need our help. •

• **Staff Sergeant Chris Mercendetti, PJ:** Our motto is "That Others May Live." And it's more than a motto to us. It really is a way of life. We'll do

PJs are equipped to fight their way through any obstacle.

whatever it takes to bring our people back. •

These guys work in all kinds of conditions—from dealing with heavy seas to confronting enemy gunfire. Anywhere a pilot can fly a plane—and potentially crash and need help—is where PJs are trained to go. They've been around since 1943. And besides saving downed pilots, they've also pulled astronauts out of the ocean after successful splashdowns in the Pacific. Part of their rescue equipment is the Stokes litter—a fancy term for a big wire basket used to hoist whomever they're rescuing up to a helicopter. The litters can move a person weighing up to 225 pounds.

• **Staff Sergeant Young:** The main reason why the maximum weight is important is that we never seem to rescue really skinny, small people. The guys that always seem to get in trouble are, you know, really big. If we have to jump in the ocean, we have a dry suit right here. It's actually a wet suit that keeps you dry. •

I'm personally scared of being lost at sea forever. So you notice my helmet has a whole bunch of white reflective tape on it, because if you jump into the North Atlantic at night, you really want people to be able to see you.

• **Staff Sergeant Mercendetti:** There's a reason why we take these risks and are trained to such high standards. We're there to save lives. And the fact that we've recovered someone alive and brought them back to fight another day, or back to their family, is just an incredible feeling. •

No doubt about it, those boys have guts. Back in 1989, you might remember when a section of double-deck freeway collapsed during the San Francisco earthquake. PJs from the 129th Rescue Wing volunteered to squeeze in between the layers of concrete to recover and treat injured motorists. Nicely done, boys. Oohrah!

"Stay where you are or there will be consequences!"

PJs make an astronaut pickup.

PJs' favorite: The PRC-117-F satcom radio can be submerged in sixty feet of salt water for two hours.

THE MEDAL OF HONOR AMERICA'S BRAVEST

"Exactly what does it take to receive a Medal of Honor?"
—Jeff, Peoria, Illinois

The highest award our country bestows.

"In a word: It's all about bravery."

Jeff, the Medal of Honor is the highest military award our country bestows.

It took a couple of acts of Congress to set the present-day parameters for who can receive the Medal of Honor, sometimes called the Congressional Medal of Honor.

And in a word, it's about bravery.

All personnel, enlisted or officer, in all branches of the service are eligible as long as their actions meet the following criteria. First, the act of bravery must occur while engaged in an action against foreign opposition or an enemy of the United States. Second, the act must be so outstanding that it can be distinguished as above and beyond the call of duty. It must involve the risk of life, and it must be confirmed by at least two eyewitnesses.

All told, 3,459 Medals of Honor have been awarded since the award was

Fighting men from all walks of life fought to save their fellows.

first presented in 1863. Nineteen men are double recipients.

There are three different designs of the medal, one for the Air Force, another for the Army, and one shared by the Navy and Marines. Today there are only 142 living recipients of the Medal of Honor. The last action for which these medals were awarded was during the operation in Somalia in 1993. The medals were presented posthumously to U.S. Army sergeants Gary Gordon and Randall Shughart, whose exploits were chronicled in the famous book and movie *Black Hawk Down*.

A FEW MARINE RECIPIENTS OF THE MEDAL OF HONOR

Lieutenant Colonel Harold W. Bauer, Marine pilot, who received the medal for an action near Guadalcanal in 1942 in which he shot down four enemy planes . . .

Private First Class James D. LaBelle (posthumously), who threw himself on a Japanese grenade on Iwo Jima in 1944, thus saving the lives of his comrades . . .

Corporal Charles Abrell, who died while single-handedly storming a North Korean bunker in 1951 . . .

And Sergeant Richard Pittman, who fought off a charge of some thirty to forty Vietcong in 1966 to save wounded comrades.

VIETNAM FIREBASES

"What were Vietnam firebases and how were they built?"
—Jeff, Arroyo Grande, California

American firebases dotted the Vietnamese hilltops (note the artillery emplacements at right in this photo).

The 155mm howitzer could be brought in by chopper.

Jeff, ol' boy, this is a topic I can talk about with some authority.

Before Vietnam, it was common practice to keep the artillery securely behind the front lines. In the rear with the gear, these long-range, accurate weapons could deliver a world of hurt to the bad guys without taking any flak themselves. But Vietnam was a different kind of war with a different game plan. Because there were no front lines, and enemy attacks could come from any direction, it was tough for our forces to use the old playbook. The VC had a tendency to sneak up on us and strike hard and fast, often retreating well before the artillery could be called in.

Solution? Well, mix a bunch of combat engineers with heavy artillery pieces and an infantry battalion, and bam, you've got yourself a fire support base! Fire support bases, or FSBs, or just firebases, were islands of artillery smack dab in the middle of the jungle, totally surrounded by the enemy. They varied in size, but they all had the same three objectives: to support infantry operations, to defend Vietnamese villages threatened by the enemy, and to defend other fire support bases. If one base did get knocked out, the others close by could pick up the slack thanks to something called interlocking fire.

• **Eric Hammel, historian and author of *Khe Sanh: Siege in the Clouds*:** Interlocking fire is based on the concept that if one gun goes down or one position goes down, the band of fire, the arc of fire from other positions, could help cover what would otherwise be a dead zone. •

An ideal location for an FSB was on the high ground, but you can build them just about anywhere. Once a site is selected, the engineers arrive and clear a suitable helicopter landing zone. Cue the demolitions experts.

Once the initial LZ was established, heavy engineering equipment was brought in to create the gun pits, bunkers and berms, and fighting positions.

At this point, it was time to bring in the guns and their crew. It was standard practice to move the troops in by helicopter. But thanks to the new, lighter alloys that the big guns were made from, they could use the friendly skies, too. The 105mm and 155mm howitzers could hitch a ride on the CH-54 Sky Cranes and CH-47 Chinooks.

A typical firebase might have a battery of six 105mm howitzers and a bunch of 81mm mortars as well as an infantry battalion for protection.

• **Eric Hammel:** The advantage to mortars and howitzers is they can do what's called indirect fire or high-angle fire. *High angle* means that they can actually fire pretty close to themselves by lobbing a shell high and it will come down in an enfiladed position— which is something the artillerymen can't see but could be the back of a hill within sight of them that can't be reached by firing straight at it. •

Now, if terrain permitted, the firebases also made room for the M109 self-propelled gun. The M109 carried a standard 155mm howitzer tube in an armored chassis that weighed twenty-three tons. It also had a .50-caliber machine gun, just in case the enemy got too close. And if you got really desperate you could lower the

The NVA
fiercely
attacked
American
firebases.

A GI digs
a fighting
position as a
firebase is set up.

The howitzer was an effective firebase weapon because of its high angle of fire.

The 155mm howitzer was the firebase's mainstay support.

big gun and blast away at anybody trying to get inside the perimeter. All that firepower out in the middle of nowhere made the firebase a pretty dangerous place to be. They were prime targets for the North Vietnamese and Vietcong. The enemy kept the FSB gun crews on alert at all times with unrelenting attacks.

• **Eric Hammel:** The objective wasn't to overrun a base and take a position, because they were't going to hold it anyway—they were going to melt back into the countryside. Their objective was to kill people, make headlines, and demoralize our troops, and they did a great job over the course of time. •

The gunners had some deadly new shells to counter these attacks. The improved conventional munitions, or ICM, contained many smaller submunitions within a single shell; these would break apart in midair, raining down grenade-like explosives on the enemy. Another innovation was the M546 "beehive" round. This little nasty had a two-part aluminum body loaded with eight thousand dart-like flechettes; as the shell came apart in flight, the darts would spiral outward, creating something that looked and sounded like a swarm of angry insects. Now, that's what I call killer bees!

But a lot of people still felt fire support bases weren't such a great idea, because they were kinda like mini Alamos spread all over the place. They were supposed to be temporary, in and out—a place to put artillery pieces where they could support a unit moving around in the field. However, because you were covering the same field all the time, it made sense to keep the fire support bases in one place, so what started out as a position for an artillery battery would soon have a permanent assignment of a platoon of tanks, at least one infantry company, service and support units, supply clerks, kitchen, and so on—which resulted in fixed targets for the enemy.

It would be easy enough for our forces today to set up firebases, if needed. But in this day and age, our modern military is moving too fast to make them worthwhile. Back in Vietnam, the firebases never stopped bailing out the grunts in the field. Whether laying fire support for the troops, halting a VC attack, or even covering each other's asses, the firebase gun crews knew they were number one in the protection racket. Although far from

perfect, the firebases played a major role in a difficult war, and those who served on 'em fought hard to get the job done.

HEY, CHARLIE!

There were two major forces we were fighting in Vietnam. There was the conventional North Vietnamese Army—the guys who were usually in uniform. They were the ones we called NVA.

Then there were the harder-to-spot Vietcong, made up of guerrilla fighters wearing civilian clothes. They lived right in among the South Vietnamese population. And you know how us military types love to come up with short ways of saying stuff, so there was no way "the Vietcong" was going to stick. We started calling 'em VC for short, or sometimes we used the call signs for VC—that's Victor Charlie. But Victor sounded like some waiter in New York City, so we just started calling 'em Charlie. Not too politically correct, but if you want that kind of stuff, you're asking the wrong guy.

TEST YOUR MILITARY IQ

How far could an M109 self-propelled gun blast its projectiles?

Answer on page 233.

WAR GAMES THE MODERN INFANTRY WAY—OOHRAH!

"What's OPFOR training?"
—Steve, Cleveland, Ohio

Lasers register "hits," which simulate wounds.

Since 1981, U.S. soldiers from all over the country have come to Fort Irwin, California, to face off against a ferocious, well-trained enemy. Fort Irwin is situated in a piece of desert—more than a thousand square miles—which you could call the world's largest sandbox. But nobody's playing nice.

The day we were there, the historic First Cavalry Division from Fort Hood, Texas, stepped into this hostile territory. The moment the First Cav rolls in, they become the Blue Force—or "BLUEFOR"—bringing all the high-tech gadgets they need to blow away the enemy. The bad guys are the opposing force, otherwise known as the "OPFOR." In the real world, they're known as the Eleventh Armored Cavalry Regiment. It's their job to make the visiting team

sweat it out. The OPFOR's arsenal consists of U.S.-made vehicles converted to look like Russian-style war machines, like the T-80 tank. For thirty days, the First Cavalry must fight the OPFOR on the OPFOR's home turf. And it's not just Ruskie-looking tanks they need to worry about, either.

• **Joe Moore, commander, Eleventh ACR, OPFOR:** We provide guerrillas who work in the rear and civilians who walk around in blue jeans. These mock civilians will protest out your gate, they'll blow up a truck bomb, they'll come and ask for food or medical aid. We also provide air so the

A thousand square miles of some of the toughest desert around.

soldiers don't have to deal with just our ground forces, but the threat of helicopters, too. •

To simulate casualties on this battlefield, the BLUEFOR and the OPFOR use special equipment called MILES gear. *MILES* stands for "Multiple Integrated Laser Engagement System"— basically a super-high-tech plugged-in kind of paint ball.

All the soldiers and all the weapons on both sides of the conflict are equipped with MILES gear. The weapons shoot lasers instead of lead, and sensors register the hits. There are sensors all along the belt. And they receive data from any kind of laser that's transmitted from any caliber weapon. It's processed through the MILES box in the back, which has a nine-volt battery. This sends a signal through, and if a large-enough-caliber weapon hits a soldier in a certain area or enough times, it'll set off the alarm.

Even the vehicles have MILES equipment, and fire off simulated rounds. A yellow whoopee light comes on when a tank gets blasted. And when that MILES alarm goes off, a soldier boy better start crying for Mama— or the nearest medic— 'cause medics are here to train, too.

• **Sergeant Tiwanda Brown, medic, First Cavalry Division:** Everyone throughout the whole battalion is given what we call a "casualty card." Say that person is determined to be a casualty—they come to us at our aid station and we look at the cards and decide what kind of treatment we're gonna give that patient. And with a lot of them, we don't know what's coming, so we have to immediately be on our toes and figure out what to do with that patient. •

What happens to every soldier and vehicle out in the desert is tracked with a GPS system in what is known as the Star Wars building. Here the top dogs can evaluate what went right— and what went wrong. No matter what form the OPFOR may take, their mission is to fight it out till the last fighter gets knocked out of the battle.

Each soldier carries a casualty card.

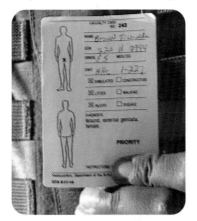

TEST YOUR MILITARY IQ

What's the range of a MILES laser?

Answer on page 233.

GOLDEN KNIGHTS OF THE SKY

> **"Hey, Gunny, what about the U.S. Army's parachute team?"**
> —John, Oak Creek, Wisconsin

The world-famous Golden Knights Diamond Formation.

Okay, pipe down, whiner! Do you really think I'd to forget to tell you about the Golden Knights?

Everyone always asks, "Why would you ever want to jump out of a perfectly good airplane?" Well, first of all, there's no such thing as a perfect airplane. Second, if you're asking, you obviously haven't seen the U.S. Army's Golden Knights. The men and women who wear the black-and-gold uniform represent the best precision freefall parachute team in the world.

With their eye-popping aerial maneuvers and on-the-mark accuracy, they take the high-octane art of skydiving to a whole new level.

Parachutes were originally invented to save a pilot's life when he jumped from a disabled aircraft. We've relied on this little deceleration device ever since. And in 1959, a general got the notion to put together a parachute team to show the world the airborne capabilities and superiority of the U.S. Army.

• **Sergeant First Class Billy Vansolen, Golden Knights:** We have performed in all fifty states and in thirty-four different countries. We jump four hundred times a year. We hold the current world record in freefall formation skydiving. We haven't relinquished that crown in the last fifteen years. It's a very, very, very prestigious unit. •

Approximately a hundred men and women throughout the Army apply each year. Being selected to join this elite team takes more than being a hotshot in the air. Once they weed out all but the best, the "appies," or applicants, are invited to tryouts on the team's home turf at Fort Bragg, North Carolina. Tryouts are make-it-or-break-it time, sometimes making white-knuckle jumps up to seven times a day—hope these rookies packed plenty of changes of underwear!

In addition to serving as goodwill ambassadors, the team represents the

Army's elite airborne divisions, demonstrating the highly mobile, quick-strike capabilities that paratroop units have executed in combat over the years. And with each show, they give the public an up-close and personal look at the teamwork, discipline, and excellence of the U.S. Army.

The Golden Knights' various jumps highlight the maneuverability of the human body while falling at speeds in excess of 120 mph. One dramatic maneuver is called the Cutaway . . . which shows what happens if your parachute doesn't work. The parachutist is wearing three chutes. He'll open one a lot higher than normal and then make it malfunction. He'll release that one, go back into freefall, and then deploy his main parachute—and land on target!

Then there's the world famous Golden Knight Diamond Formation. Four jumpers exit the plane and fly to within inches of each other . . . then perform a little bomb-burst maneuver, open their parachutes, and land on target. The team counts on the high-performance nine-cell elliptical canopy called the Stiletto to get them safely back to earth.

For more than four decades, over forty million people's jaws have hung open in awe as the Golden Knights continue to hit the bull's-eye every time. I've got an open invitation from the Knights to jump with them . . . and I think I just might take them up on that.

A Golden Knight checks his gear.

Living large at 12,000 feet.

The Golden Knights' unique twin-doored F-27 Friendship Fokker.

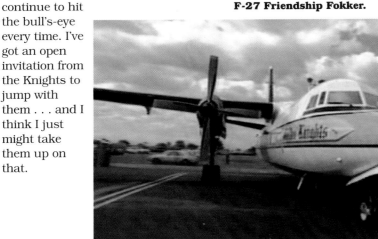

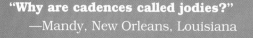

GI JARGON

"I don't know but I've been told / Mail Call is mighty bold!"

Mandy says she's a junior Air Force ROTC drill commander—Oohrah!—so she's probably bounced a few jodies around in her time.

As far as we know, the name goes back about fifty years. It's hard to imagine there was ever a time when raw recruits didn't march or do double-time without chanting jodies, but the cadences we all know and love only started in 1944. Back then—the story goes—a private named Willie Duckworth started chanting, "Sound-off; 1-2; sound-off; 3-4; cadence count; 1-2-3-4; 1-2—3-4." That motivated his exhausted squad members as they returned to their barracks at Fort Slocum, New York.

Fort Slocum's commander liked the cadences, too. The "Duckworth chants" spread like wildfire from base to base, and somewhere along the line somebody started chanting about a guy named Jody. So who was Jody? Well, he's the mythical guy back home most likely sitting in your kitchen having a good time with your sweetheart.

I've barked a helluva lot of jodies in my day, and here's one of my favorites . . .

Ain't no use in going back
Jody's got your Cadillac
Ain't no use in calling home
Jody's got your girl and gone
Ain't no use in feeling blue
Jody's got your sister too!

William, I like a man who knows his place!

The military alphabet was developed so that we'd all be on the same page, 100 percent intelligible, in the heat of battle.

In World War II the alphabet was a little different than it is today—a was *able* and r was *roger*, for starters. But the alphabet was standardized in 1956, and it's been that way ever since. So listen up, because here's the alphabet: alpha, bravo, charlie, delta, echo, foxtrot, golf, hotel, india, juliet, kilo, lima, mike, november, oscar, papa, quebec, romeo, sierra, tango, uniform, victor, whiskey, x-ray, yankee, zulu.

Whew!

Well, Ron, *G2* is GI jargon for "information," "the skinny," "the 411." It comes from the military designation G2, which is the general staff section in charge of military intelligence. Since G2 officers are supposed to know what's what, asking for the G2 is asking, "What's going on?"

THE MIRACLE OF V-MAIL

Kilroy WAS HERE

"Can you explain what V-mail was and how it worked?"
—Don, Biloxi, Mississippi

Okay, Don, first thing you've gotta know is that we're headed back to World War II here, and back then they didn't have cell phones or e-mail or any of that—hard for some of you numbskulls to understand, but it's true! So folks wrote letters—tons and tons and tons of letters—and moving all that mail got to be almost as big an operation as D-Day. Yet letters were the soldier's lifeline to home and family. The troops needed their mail, but the military needed to figure out a way to get it overseas more economically.

So in 1942 the U.S. Post Office started using a British system called V-mail.

Here's how it worked. You'd write your letter on a special V-mail form. Then you'd fold it up, put a stamp on it, and mail it to your local post office, where your letter was photographed and put on microfilm. Overseas, they took the film and printed out the letters at one-quarter size. With V-mail, twenty-five hundred pounds of regular mail ended up weighing a mere forty-five pounds. Between 1942 and 1945, more than a billion letters were sent as V-mail. That's a billion, bozo!

KILROY WAS HERE

The most famous name of World War II wasn't on a letter, but in a graffito—see, I betcha ya didn't know I knew how to say that! The name is Kilroy, folks. But who the hell was he?

During World War II, Kilroy was everywhere. And it all started at the naval shipyard in Quincy, Massachusetts, with an inspector named James J. Kilroy. It was his job to count how many holes a riveter filled on his shift. To make sure the rivets weren't double-counted, ol' Kilroy came up with his legendary cartoon to show that he'd done his job. Now, when those ships went out to sea, sailors who didn't know about Mr. Kilroy and his rivet counting were baffled. All they knew was whoever Kilroy was, he always got there first, so they started drawing Kilroy's signature all over the place—and a legend was born. Almost as good as the legend of Gunny, huh? Oohrah!

UNSUNG HEROES: MILITARY FIREFIGHTERS

"Can you tell me anything about military firefighters?"
—John, Tucker, Georgia

GI firefighters putting out a fire on a simulator airplane.

As far as I'm concerned, John, military firefighters come under the heading of "unsung heroes." They don't get a lot of press, but when it comes to the hot spots, those guys are right in the middle of it.

To find out all about them, we hotfooted it on down to San Angelo, Texas. Goodfellow Air Force Base is the home of the Louis F. Garland Fire Academy, which is where firefighters from all branches of the military learn and practice their trade.

The curriculum here covers everything a modern firefighter might be expected to face, including structural and aircraft firefighting, containment and disposal of hazardous material, and disaster rescue.

We asked Course Director Scott Hebert about the difference between military firefighter training and civilian firefighter training.

• **Scott Hebert, course director, apprentice fire training:** For the most part, we do the same exact training as the civilian community. We go a little bit further when we teach airport firefighting, and we go into a lot more extensive training as far as hazardous materials, munitions, and so forth. •

Simulators such as generic burning airplanes give students hands-on experience in knocking down jet fires. For training purposes—and to keep the environment clean—this fire is fueled by propane, and these guys are putting it out with water. In an actual crash situation where jet fuel is burning, they'd be using aqueous filmforming foam. Thank God they decided to just call it AFFF.

Foam is the agent of choice for flammable fuel fires because it blankets the fuel, keeping out oxygen and halting the burning process. At the same time, foam lowers the temperature of the fuel and adjacent surfaces. The training structure at this academy is literally a flaming classroom. It's three stories high—forty-five hundred square feet of measured inferno. The temperature inside can reach nearly five hundred degrees Fahrenheit. If it gets hotter than that, special sensors kick in and shut down the heat to protect the student firefighters.

The attacks on September 11 and beyond demonstrated that our firefighters must be ready to deal with new and more sophisticated threats. In the event a chemical or biological agent is spilled or released, these hazardous material or hazmat, guys are gonna get the call.

• **Technical Sergeant Brian Kyser:** We're teaching a weapons of mass destruction course here. What we're doing right now is training individuals on different kinds of containers and the leaks that they might come across in a normal, average hazmat or WMD incident. •

When buildings go down, trapping people inside, that's when the GI smoke eaters switch into "urban rescue" mode. They've got a number of highly effective tools, such as a petrogen torch that cuts through metal to make a rescue.

That torch actually has the capability of cutting through heavy-gauge metal almost like it was butter. A petrogen torch can cut through eight layers of half-inch steel in twelve seconds. It's a lot quicker than a standard oxygen acetylene torch, and a lot safer, too. It's also cheaper. Two and a half gallons of it will cut as much steel as 250 cubic feet of acetylene.

There are so many classes going through the Garland Academy that they hold a graduation ceremony every other day. In a single year, forty-five hundred military firefighters will be certified right here. They'll be deployed all over the world.

And believe me, when the smoke fills the room, you want these unsung heroes on your side!

This GI firefighter receives training he can take with him anywhere in the world.

Dealing with hazmat and WMD emergencies: just part of the GI smoke eater's job.

TEST YOUR MILITARY IQ

Who were the first military smoke jumpers?

Answer on page 233.

SPECIAL SECURITY THE MARINE WAY!

"Have the Marines set up a special unit to fight terrorism?"
—Gary, Broken Arrow, Oklahoma

No matter what the provocation, these Marine special forces must keep their cool.

Terrorist threats have become a colossal pain in the butt for U.S. embassies around the globe. And Marines from the Fourth MEB, the Fourth Marine Expeditionary Brigade, are learning how to handle 'em.

We stopped off at the Marine Corps Security Force Training Company, near Norfolk, Virginia, to learn the latest techniques for dealing with likely terrorist shenanigans. In a few days, the Marines we saw were headed for Afghanistan to take over security of the U.S. embassy in Kabul. But before they went, Gunnery Sergeant Henry Aguero and his team put these future guardians through an intensive week-long training course.

For instance, what if the trainees have to deal with a flag burning?

They set up security around a mock embassy, and their mission was to defend the building against approaching demonstrators—really just a group of fellow Marines in disguise. This was a "no shoot" scenario, so the trainees didn't have permission to fire simulated rounds unless fired upon. They had to exercise restraint—not usually the strong suit of hard-charging Devil Dogs.

• **Gunnery Sergeant Henry Aguero, instructor:** We're trying to antagonize these Marines. We're trying to push their buttons to see if they're actually going to react to a situation that they maybe shouldn't react to. The trainees also receive classes on high-level threat security procedures. We actually show them physically how to inspect a vehicle, how to inspect a person, how to set up security. •

The training company here at Norfolk also schools an elite, specialized Marine unit called FAST, which stands for "Fleet Anti-Terrorism Security Team." You might think of FAST as kind of a 911 force. After the USS *Cole* was bombed in October 2000, for instance, FAST responded to the scene to put a stop to any potential follow-up attack. But in most cases, they're used to ward off trouble ahead of time.

• **Sergeant Kelly Crawford, former FAST company member:** FAST company has been designed as sort of a preventive medicine for potential aggression in any region. They go in, set up security, and provide stability for U.S. personnel and interests in the area. •

Besides operating in foreign hot spots, another typical mission for a FAST company might be to safeguard nuclear material on a submarine while the boat is docked. Since they have to be prepared for anything, FAST Marines also receive specialized training on how to storm enemy strongholds, including close-quarters fighting in buildings.

And when they're handling perimeter defense, they get to play with some very cool toys.

• **Sergeant Chris Harris, weapons and equipment instructor:** FAST Marines use the Saber 2000 as an explosive detection device. They'll swab suspected areas of either a vehicle or any type of baggage that some personnel may have. They'll swab the areas, then run a test on it using the Saber 2000.•

I sure wouldn't try to slip anything past the Marines of the Fourth MEB or FAST. But it would be kinda nice to

have one of those thermo imagers with the remote monitor to keep an eye on my kids at night. That should help you get a good night's sleep, America.

Oohrah!

The Saber 2000 detects even trace amounts of explosives.

The FAST strike team must prepare itself for any eventuality.

MORE GI JARGON

Time to play that GI Jargon game again. Right now we'll start with Gene, up there. Gene, what do I look like, a friggin' dictionary? I'll tell you, but I'm only going to do it once.

Click has two meanings. The most common is shorthand for the word "kilometer," as in "the nearest head is three clicks up the road"—that would be three kilometers, or about two miles. The other meaning refers to the adjustment on the sight of a weapon for elevation and windage. The "dope" on a rifle is the number of clicks left or right for windage and the number of clicks up or down for elevation required to get a round to hit where the sight is pointed.

Typically, a foxhole is dug for one man. It can be anywhere from four to seven feet deep and two to three feet square. A sump is dug into the floor of the foxhole to allow a soldier to step up and fire a rifle or to sit down and avoid gunfire and enemy tanks. Another variety of hole in the ground is known as a fighting hole. It's a horseshoe-shaped trench four feet deep and two feet wide. An elevated piece of ground in the middle serves as a platform for a machine gun.

The time it takes to dig a hole depends on the condition of the soil. But it doesn't matter if it's soft, hard, rocky, or frozen . . . when you're pinned down by enemy fire, you don't get a choice. Dirt is molded into one-foot-high berms along the outer perimeter of the holes to give better protection.

Well, Rebecca, I have a feeling you're asking that question because you think you're going to see a little U.S. prime beefcake. But the Gunny ain't going there. No sir. Instead, I'm going to direct your attention to my weapon. *Field strip* means breaking your rifle down into its component parts so you can check it and clean it. To help new recruits, they use something called the field strip cloth, which lays it out for you piece by piece.

I have a feeling that wasn't the answer you were looking for, Rebecca, but it's the only one you're going to get!

Before I can tell you that, Ryan, you gotta know what I mean when I say "stack arms." Which you probably don't, cause you're a civilian puke! Anyway, that means stow your rifle in a kind of tripod, with three or more weapons placed barrel-up and butt-down. What keeps the rifles from falling over is the proper use of a small metal bracket that hooks the rifles together. It's called the stacking swivel, and it's located right here on the throat of your typical M1 rifle. Throughout our nation's history, American fighting men have been using the stacking swivel so they don't have to lay their rifles in the dirt. It's also where the Marines get the slang phrase *Grab him by the stacking swivel*, which means "grab him by the throat."

The stacking swivel is held on to the weapon by the stacking swivel screw, and that's slang for . . . well, Ryan, I don't want to offend your tender ears! Semper fi! Dismissed!

The digging implement of choice.

Digging was hard work, but saved plenty of lives.

PART FOUR: AIRPLANES

"Butts down and ears up, maggots— we're headed for the wild blue yonder!"

DOGFIGHTING WORLD WAR I PILOTS

"How did World War I pilots shoot through their propellers?"
—Rich, Baltimore, Maryland

The short answer, Rich? Not very well . . . at first.

Up until 1914, using an airplane for anything other than reconnaissance was literally considered a war crime. But all that changed in World War I, as aviation historian Craig Schmitman explains . . .

• **Craig Schmitman:** The first weapons used were things like pistols, and shotguns, and rifles; then the machine gun found its way onto combat aircraft. These machine guns were not very easily mounted and would often fire from rearward positions. Finally, someone had the idea to mount them on the upper wing to fire above the arc of a propeller. It got to the point where people realized that the best way to use the airplane as a military weapon was as a gun platform, with the machine gun firing straight ahead. •

The first flying gun platform.

One French pilot, Roland Garros, devised a method whereby he would just shoot through the propeller and let the hits fall where they may. Studies showed that 25 percent of the time, he would hit his own propeller—which, believe me, folks, represents a problem!

So he invented a shield that was situated at a forty-five-degree angle. And he put it on both sides of the propeller, exactly where the bullets would hit.

Unfortunately, the Garros Wedge, as it was sometimes called, deflected some of the bullets back into the cockpit. The French equipped a small number of their planes with deflector gear, but in 1915, while attacking a train station, a bullet fired by a rifleman on the ground pierced Garros's fuel line. He managed to put the aircraft down safely, but failed in his attempt to destroy it before he was captured. The Germans passed on the captured plane to a young Dutch aircraft designer named Anthony Fokker and ordered him to produce something similar. Within forty-eight hours, he returned with a plane equipped with his soon-to-be-famous interrupter gear. Fokker first demonstrated it from the ground, but the Germans demanded that he actually shoot down an aircraft.

He took the plane up himself, but when he finally flew near an unarmed observation plane, he found that he could not bring himself to pull the trigger. He was a lover, not a fighter! On August 1, 1915, German lieutenant Oswald Boelcke became the first to shoot down a plane with the Fokker-designed interrupter gear.

How did the interrupter work?

• **Craig Schmitman:** The propeller and the engine revolve, and there is a plate with a cam on it; this cam hits a rod. The force goes up, and then it's transferred horizontally to the trigger of the machine gun. And when the propeller is in front of the machine gun, the gun cannot fire. This technology revolutionized combat and created a whole new type of plane—the fighter. •

Thanks for clearing that up.

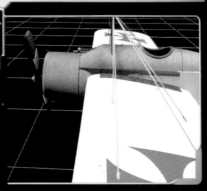

The Garros Wedge sometimes deflected bullets right back into the cockpit.

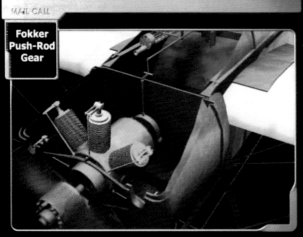

Fokker's revolutionary "interrupter gear" kept the machine gun from firing when the propeller was in front of it.

TEST YOUR MILITARY IQ

Oswald Boelcke's second in command was Max Immelman. What did he become famous for?

Answer on page 233.

WORLD WAR I ACES

American ace Eddie Rickenbacker survived the war to become head of Eastern Airlines.

Back in World War I, Manfred von Richthofen, better known as the Red Baron, racked up eighty aerial kills—more than anyone else. The plane he scored most of those victories in was the Fokker DR 1, or Fokker triplane.

Those three wings looked pretty wild. But they helped make the Red Baron's aircraft more maneuverable than your typical biplanes of the era.

• **Dr. Peter Fedders, San Diego Aerospace Museum:** The strength of the Fokker triplane was that it could make much tighter turns than other airplanes, and it had a very, very fast rate of climb. That's because it had a large wing area, having three wings. So in an actual dogfight, it was effective because it could turn very fast. •

The main disadvantage to having three wings was that it created more drag than one or two wings, cutting down on straight-ahead speed. Von Richthofen made full use of the innovative German fighter planes. But more importantly, the Red Baron brought new strategies to the skies.

Essentially, he developed tactics for pilots flying not as individuals but as part of a group. He set down a bunch of rules, which was probably his greatest significance to the German air force.

But the odds finally caught up with the Red Baron just months before the end of the war. It's still unclear if it was ground fire or Canadian ace Roy Brown that did him in on April 21, 1918. While the Germans were using the Fokker, the Allies developed a few deadly fighter planes of their own. The French made the Spad and Newport series, while the British focused on the Sopwith Camel.

Sopwith Camel

The Spad was built for speed. Early versions, like the Spad 7, had 170-horsepower engines, making this one of the fastest aircraft in the first part of the war. The later Spad 13 had a 235-horsepower engine and could reach a top speed of 138 miles per hour. French ace Ren Fonck flew

Fokker DR1 Triplane

without experience. In fact, it's said that the Sopwith Camel killed more British pilots than German. Still, British ace Albert Ball and Canadian ace Billy Bishop, who was flying for the Brits, knew how to get the most out of their Camels. They downed a lot of enemy fighters, although coming up with exact numbers back then was always a little fuzzy.

But considering the flimsy aircraft and the short life spans of the pilots, World War I produced some of the toughest and bravest SOBs around. In just four years, they changed fighter aircraft from novelties to an essential part of warfare.

the Spad series. Fonck was the Allies' highest-scoring survivor of the war. He missed the Red Baron's record of eighty kills by just five planes.

American ace Eddie Rickenbacker flew in the Newport series, which still had machine guns mounted on top of the wings.

• **Dr. Fedders:** The Newport 28 was a standard biplane, a very elegant-looking airplane, but it had a lot of defects in it and the French pilots wouldn't fly it. So it was actually the Americans who bought them from the French. •

Rickenbacker scored twenty-six kills and survived the war to become head of Eastern Airlines.

The British Sopwith Camel, so called because it had a hump between the pilot and the propeller, was armed with two .303-caliber Vickers machine guns. It was considered an excellent fighter in the hands of a good pilot, but it wasn't a good fighter for somebody

Von Richthofen, the Red Baron (inset), racked up eighty victories before being shot down in 1918.

Newport II or Bebe

Spad 13

Fokker DR1

HOW THE MIGHTY ZEPPELIN ALMOST BOMBED NEW YORK CITY

"Where did the name zeppelin come from?"
—Peter, Oscoda, Michigan

Well, Pete, unless you're harking back to your no-doubt decadent days as a stone maggot rock-and-roller listening to that English band Led Zeppelin, zeppelins are airships built by Count Ferdinand von Zeppelin in Germany starting in 1900. There is an incredible story surrounding these German Zeppelins, which came this close to carrying World War I right into downtown Manhattan!

At the start of the World War I, mass bombing of cities from the air had never been done. But the Germans had a fully operational zeppelin with a top speed of forty-seven miles per hour and a maximum ceiling of six thousand feet. So they decided to use it to put a world of hurt on the Brits.

On the night of January 19, 1915, two German zeppelins carried out the first successful bombing raid on British soil. The British got wise to this pretty quick and started sending up fighters to meet these babies. Now, putting tracer rounds into bags full of hydrogen can sure blow up your world pretty quick, and the Sopwith Camel got to be so good at this that it was known as the Zeppelin Killer.

To beat these fighter aircraft and the increased British anti-aircraft ground defenses, the Zeppelin Company built a special series of zeps called Height Climbers, which routinely operated at altitudes above twenty thousand feet. Cruising at seventy miles per hour, beyond top range of British fighters, crew members fought oxygen deprivation, dizziness, bitter cold, snapped oil lines, frozen radiators, and cracked windows.

On the night of October 19, 1917, they launched a massive eleven-ship raid against England using nothing but Height Climbers. The ships were so far above the earth that their engines couldn't be heard by observers on the ground. Following the raid, Allied fighters destroyed nearly half of the eleven climbers as they dropped altitude to come in over Germany. But one

airship, the L-55, flew unscathed over the Western Front by maintaining altitude. Dawn found the ship in France at over twenty thousand feet. The rising sun increased the temperature of the hydrogen, and immediately the ship began to rise farther. She reached 24,606 feet before the captain and a few men were able to force her into a downward angle. L-55 crashed in Germany, but not before setting the all-time airship altitude record, including the number of hours surviving crew members spent above twenty thousand feet.

On August 8, 1918, the Germans launched their last zeppelin raid against England. A British fighter scrambled and caught three of the giants cruising in the dark at 17,500 feet. The aircraft's pilot attacked the lead ship, lacing her three-hundred-foot bow with two drums of tracers. The sucker blew up, and immediately the other ships increased their altitude, then turned tail.

Count Ferdinand von Zeppelin

The zeppelin blown out of the sky that night was the L-70. Not only a Height Climber, the L-70 was the most advanced of a special breed of extremely long-range zeppelins. Her commander's next mission had been to cross the Atlantic and bomb the city of New York, then return without stopping. The British pilot changed the course of history that night, and the raid on New York City never occurred.

How's that for history, meatheads!?

COMBAT GLIDERS

The CG-4A—better known as "the flying coffin."

Now, I know this sounds nuts, but back in World War II we did in fact send guys into combat inside flimsy wood-and-canvas aircraft. These things didn't have any defensive weapons—they didn't even have an engine.

But we had good reason to use these gliders: When paratroopers get chucked out of a plane, they can end up spread out all over the place and lose valuable time regrouping for an attack. If you pack a squad of men in a glider, however, they land together and are ready to hit the enemy right away.

There were thousands of infantrymen specially trained to take these risky rides into combat . . . they called themselves "glider riders"!

• Bob Bridge, 325th Glider Infantry Regiment: I hadn't even seen a glider until a couple of days later and then they took us out and started to load us. Showed us how to lash and load gliders and how to get in and out of them under fire and whatnot. •

The combat glider used most often by the Army was the CG-4A, designed by the Waco Aircraft Company. Some fourteen thousand of these gliders were built during the war by twenty-three different manufacturers—from automakers like Ford to companies that made caskets. That may be how the glider got its nickname, "flying coffin"!

The CG-4A had a welded tubular steel fuselage and plywood floor; the rest was canvas—crude and cheap, but it got the job done! The model was used in airborne operations all over Europe and in the Pacific. The glider was a real workhorse. It could haul a squad of thirteen infantrymen, a Jeep, an anti-tank gun, or even a 75mm pack howitzer. The whole cockpit of the glider flipped up, and you could then

An arrestor chute helped slow down the plane on the ground.

drive your Jeep or roll your gun into the belly. You had to really tie the load down, otherwise the gear might shift and tear right through the canvas . . . and ruin your whole day.

To get airborne, the glider was hooked to a tow plane like a C-47 by means of a nylon towrope. Once the tug took off, the glider followed behind as far as the transporters could take it.

A glider pilot had to be careful to keep the aircraft out of the prop wash created by the big transport plane. Otherwise the turbulence could get so

Mother Earth. Since the glider doesn't have an engine, the pilot's only got one shot at a landing. No second chance to come around for a better approach. And when you've come to a complete stop, it's time to get the hell out.

• **Bob Bridge:** You're gonna be a target, 'cause the Germans were not settin' around watching this with a picnic in mind. They were ready to come at you with a lot of artillery or mortars or small arms. •

Once on the ground, troops had to move fast.

bad that you'd end up eating your lunch twice. Once they got near their landing zone, the glider pilot cast off the towrope and steered the glider in for a landing.

• **Bob Bridge:** Smacking into another glider was the pilot's biggest fear. And of course he was up front. He was gonna bear the brunt of the damage in the collision, so he did his best not to get into that situation. But we had gliders that hit each other and, of course, wingtips. A lot of wingtips hit. •

An arrestor chute helped slow you down once you started to slide across

Those gliders that landed in one piece could be retrieved and used again. High-wire pickup rigs were set up so a transport could fly by, snatch a glider, and tow it back to base. The Army Air Force's version of recycling, I guess!

After World War II, helicopters took on the job of hauling troops into combat, and the rickety combat glider went the way of the dodo bird.

Glider pilots had special wings with a G in the center. Officially, that G stood for "glider," but among themselves, the pilots said it stood for "guts."

EJECTION SEATS: GETTING OUT FAST!

EJECTION SEATS
GETTING OUT FAST!

"How were ejection seats invented and how do they work?"
—Mike, Chicago, Illinois

"It feels like you've been hit by a charging hippo—but you're alive!"

Sometimes the only thing between you and certain death—if you're a fighter pilot, that is—is an ejection seat.

To answer Mike's question, hats off to First Sergeant Lawrence Lambert, who in 1946 had the guts to be the first pilot to test an automatic ejection seat fitted in a AP-61. Ejection seats have come a long way since those early models, but the how-they-work part is pretty much the same.

It begins when the pilot activates the ejection system. Explosive charges jettison the canopy, shatter the canopy, or blow the escape hatch, depending on what kind of plane you're in. A catapult shoots the seat off its rails, and a rocket fires to propel the seat farther away from the aircraft. Then the parachute opens, the seat tumbles away, and our flyboy floats to safety.

And it all happens in less than four seconds.

A pilot bailing out at mach 2 is gonna be hit with about 20 G's—which is basically the kind of force you'd get if you were body-slammed by a hippo. So we're not talking joyride here. You're gonna get hurt, but you will be alive.

Here's a bit of trivia you can lay on your friends. Did you know there are actually ejection seats in helicopters? The Russians developed these to eject pilots from attack copters. These work about the same as with fixed-wing aircraft systems, but they've added explosive bolts to jettison the chopper's rotors. That way, the ejecting pilot doesn't end up as somebody's sausage. The United States tested the system with Cobras but said no thanks.

Semper fi. Carry on!

TEST YOUR MILITARY IQ

Has anyone ever ejected at supersonic speed?

Answer on page 233.

NOSE ART: ARTISTS OF THE SKY

"Why did pilots paint nose art on their planes in World War II?"
—Brian, Boise, Idaho

Well, I'm no shrink, Brian, but I know it never hurt morale to have a half-dressed babe waiting for you out on the flight line.

Although it was strictly against military regs to decorate equipment with anything but officially sanctioned insignia, the brass turned a blind eye to the nose art the guys were painting during World War II. And the farther from home and command headquarters, the racier the art got. But pinups weren't the only subject matter our planes were sporting. Fierce-looking animals made it onto a lot of aircraft. Cartoon characters also took to the skies. And symbols like swastikas or bombs counted a plane's successes.

The artists weren't generally professionals and usually got paid for their efforts with booze and cigarettes. But famous artists, most notably the animators who worked for Walt Disney, were pressed into nose art service during the war.

By 1944, the Army Air Force passed a regulation officially allowing nose art on aircraft, but with the end of the war, the golden age of aircraft art was over. And although decorated planes saw service in Korea, Vietnam, and even Desert Storm, the nose art of World War II has never been equaled. So when did this idea of painting the noses of airplanes get started? Well, it goes back to the early days of World War I, when a painted sea monster showed up on the nose of an Italian flying boat. The Germans also started painting a lot of open shark mouths under the propeller spinner on their airplanes. Things just took off from there.

The artists were amateurs, but their work was larger than life!

THE FABLED BALL TURRET GUNNER

"I've read that the life expectancy of a ball turret gunner in World War II combat was seventeen seconds. Is that true?"
—John, San Diego, California

Well, the official line from the brass is that flying the ball was no more dangerous than any other crew position, but it was one helluva place to be when the flak started flying. Precision bombing was the name of the game for the American Army Air Force in World War II. And that meant that our bomber crews in B-24 Liberators and B-17 Flying Fortresses had to fly their raids against Nazi Germany in broad daylight. Our flyboys in the big, slow bombers were sitting ducks for the German fighter planes.

Before the days of friendly fighter plane escorts, it was up to the gunners of the Eighth Air Force to protect their planes.

A bomber typically had a crew of ten men. Five of them manned machine guns. There was a tail gunner way in the back. Left and right waist gunners shooting from the sides. A top turret gunner. And down below, the ball turret gunner. In a B-24, the ball turret

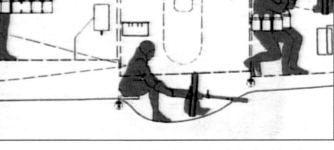

An original schematic of the inside of the Boeing B-17 combat aircraft.

could be retracted into the aircraft, but in a B-17, the turret was permanently fixed to the bomber's belly. The ball turret gunner was exposed, alone, and had nowhere to hide.

• **Wilbur Richardson, ball turret gunner, Ninety-fourth Bomb Group:** Some guys had said that if they were going to force me in there, I would refuse to fly. •

• **John Hurd, ball turret gunner, 401st Bomb Group:** It's kind of spooky down there. And it can make you nervous. Just cooped up. You can't move around or anything hardly in there. •

The glass bubble of the ball turret was considered state-of-the-art in World War II. In fact, it was the end of a long line of improvements that Boeing had made since they introduced the B-17 back in 1936. The original small turret evolved into a bathtub shape. But the gunner had to kneel, and that made it awkward and difficult to shoot accurately. An improved belly gun was operated by remote control, but the aiming periscope gave the gunner severe vertigo and nausea . . . and that's not good. So Boeing tried stuffing the gunner inside an exposed ball turret. It worked.

When enemy fighters attacked, or when flak started exploding all over the place, the ball turret gunner just had to ride it out. And if hanging out there during an attack wasn't tough enough, consider this: The hatch on the ball turret could be opened only when the bubble was in just the right position. If the hydraulics were shot up, the gunner was trapped. And if the landing gear was out, too, the plane would have to make a belly landing, crushing the ball turret gunner to death.

But was the average life expectancy of a ball turret gunner really just seventeen seconds? Well, not quite. It appears that all the airmen—no matter what position they flew—had about the same odds of survival. The tour of duty for an airman in the Eighth Air Force was twenty-five combat missions. After your twenty-fifth mission, you could go home, which sounds pretty good—until you realize that the life expectancy of a bomber crewman was only fifteen missions. So, you do the math. They all had it pretty tough.

For sure, when the airmen were on the ground, they had it better than the guys in the trenches. But comfortable beds and good chow didn't make up for the dangers they faced in the air.

"Hunched in the belly . . ."

The B-17's ball turret did not retract, leaving the gunner exposed to serious danger during crash landings.

THE GREAT DOOLITTLE RAID

"How did the United States pull off the Doolittle Raid against the Japanese?"
    —Jeff, Des Plaines, Illinois

Top: Doolittle's B-25s get ready to launch from the deck of the USS *Hornet*, April 18, 1942.

Inset: Jimmy Doolittle receives our nation's highest military honor.

Now, that's a hefty hunk of history, Jeff, but it does give me the chance to tell you a little something about one of the greatest American war heroes of all time.

Jimmy Doolittle was a World War I vet, a daredevil pilot and the first to fly across the country in less than twenty-four hours, setting a world speed record in the process. These exploits made him famous, but the Doolittle Raid during World War II made him a legend.

Doolittle's first challenge was to see if it was even possible to launch B-25 Mitchell medium bombers off an aircraft carrier—that's something that had never been tried before. But after modifying the B-25s to lighten the load and make more room for fuel, Doolittle made several test runs at Eglin airfield in Florida. He found that with a decent headwind, the B-25s could take off using about 450 feet of runway—just enough to make carrier-based takeoffs possible. He then handpicked his crew from members of the Seventeenth Bomb Group.

Sixteen bombers would take off from the western Pacific and fly about 450

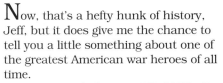

One of Doolittle's Raiders, captured by the Japanese.

miles to major Japanese cities, including Tokyo. Then the planes were supposed to continue on and land safely at friendly airfields in China, another twelve hundred miles away.

The planes were loaded on board the USS *Hornet*, a Yorktown-class aircraft carrier. In April 1942 she began an eleven-day journey across the Pacific. On April 18, 1942, a Japanese trawler sighted the *Hornet*, kicking the secret operation into high gear. The trawler was quickly destroyed, and the decision was made to launch the attack then and there in case any more Japanese ships were heading their way. Doolittle's Raiders would have to fly 650 miles to get to Tokyo—200 more than they'd planned. They would be pushing their maximum fuel range to get to China safely. The weather was also deteriorating, but at least a thirty-knot headwind would help make their takeoff easier.

Each of the sixteen B-25s carried five crew members and four five-hundred-pound bombs. With just 467 feet of runway for the first aircraft, it was tense on the flight deck as Colonel Doolittle took off in the lead plane. He made it—and once he was airborne, the other planes followed.

As the bombers headed for Japan, a strange stroke of luck was playing out in the streets of Tokyo. The Japanese were simulating an air raid just as the real air raid began, and by the time the Japanese anti-aircraft gunners figured out that this was the real thing, it was too late. Low on fuel and unable to pick up a homing beacon to an airfield at Suchow, China, Doolittle and the seventy-nine other airmen on his team were forced to sacrifice their aircraft to save their

own lives. Four planes crash-landed. Another ditched offshore. The remaining eleven crews, including Doolittle's, bailed out.

Five crewmen died while ditching their aircraft. Eight airmen were captured, three of them executed. One more died from malnutrition. For the remaining fliers, there were immediate awards and honors. Doolittle was promoted to brigadier general on the spot in Chungking. Later he received the Medal of Honor. And all the airmen of the Doolittle Raid received the thanks of a grateful nation.

You know, folks, another way they took weight off the B-25s was to take the rear guns out. Well, Jimmy Doolittle was concerned that this might be sending the wrong message to the Japanese, so he put black broomsticks sticking out the rear to make the Japanese think they were real guns and discourage any attacks from that direction.

That's the kind of guy Jimmy Doolittle was!

"Don't go anywhere, maggots—or you'll be history!"

The men who launched the first American strike against the Japanese homeland.

The Flying Tigers were the first to challenge the Japanese in the air.

THE FLYING TIGERS

> "Can you go into detail about the Curtiss P-40?"
> —Zack, Ledyard, Connecticut

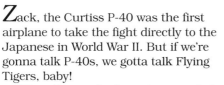

Retired U.S. Air Corps officer Claire Chennault, at right, founded the Tigers in China.

Zack, the Curtiss P-40 was the first airplane to take the fight directly to the Japanese in World War II. But if we're gonna talk P-40s, we gotta talk Flying Tigers, baby!

When the war broke out, we needed to really crank up our aircraft production lines. At the time, the best fighter plane we had was the P-40, built by the Curtiss-Wright Corporation. A sturdy, low-wing monoplane, the P-40 was powered by a twelve-hundred-horsepower Allison engine. It packed three .50-caliber machine guns in each wing and could carry a five-hundred-pound bomb. It could fly at speeds over 350 miles an hour and as high as thirty-two thousand feet.

During the war, we sold or gave the P-40 to a lot of our allies, and this war-

bird saw action all over the world. Depending on which air force was flying it, the P-40 was nicknamed the Tomahawk, the Kittyhawk, or the Warhawk.

Probably the most famous outfit to use the P-40 was the American Volunteer Group, but you know 'em as the Flying Tigers. These were American pilots who had volunteered to fight for China before the United States had even entered the war.

Early in 1941, Madame Chiang Kaishek, wife of the Chinese leader, asked a retired U.S. Air Corps officer named Claire Chennault to help organize a group of fighter pilots. And since China was a key American ally, and already at war with Japan, President Roosevelt signed an unpublished executive order on April 15, 1941. It authorized reserve officers and enlisted men to resign from the Army Air Corps, and naval and Marine air services, in order to form the volunteer unit.

One hundred pilots and two hundred ground crew members arrived in the summer of 1941 to begin their training. But there was one big problem—Chennault didn't have enough P-40s for his guys to fly. Luckily the airplane builders had a solution. Because they were already building P-40s for the British, the folks at Curtiss-Wright decided that they'd give the Brits updated P-40s a little later, so they could give the Tigers the older P-40Bs right away.

By late December, just two weeks after Pearl Harbor, they were facing the Japanese air force in combat over Asia. These were the older P-40Bs that the Tigers were flying—not the best of the bunch. They weren't equipped with a gun sight, bomb rack, or extra fuel, and they weren't very fast at high altitudes. But the Flying Tiger pilots made do. Using the planes' low-altitude

speed and stability, Chennault trained the pilots to exploit the enemy's weaknesses and make the best of their equipment.

During their first combat, on December 20, they shot down nine out of ten Japanese bombers they were targeting and lost only one P-40. During another key mission, on Christmas Day 1941, the Tigers knocked out twenty-three Japanese bombers and fighters without losing a single P-40. The Tigers also supplied critical air cover for forces moving along the Burma Road, the most vital supply line for the Allies through Asia. When it was all over, the total numbers for the Tigers were impressive—286 Japanese planes shot down and only twelve Flying Tiger pilots listed as killed or missing in action.

Finally the U.S. Army Air Force absorbed the Flying Tigers in 1942. Most of the men of the squadron stayed on to fight in the Pacific; Claire Chennault remained their leader. He rejoined the Army and earned the rank of major general. By the end of the war, these brave and skillful P-40 pilots had shot down 650 Japanese planes. Not bad for a team flying a fighter that a lot of people felt was second-class.

The Flying Tigers head for their planes.

TEST YOUR MILITARY IQ

What was a "blood chit"?

Answer on page 233.

SUPPLIES FROM THE SKY: MILITARY CARGO AIRLIFTS

"What kind of cargo can our military air-drop, and how do they do it?"
—Jerry, Scottsboro, Alabama

Cargo, ready to go!

Wow, Jerry,—a two-part question—you must be exhausted, maggot. So take a load off and watch how the big boys do it!

Fliers have been dropping supplies to troops on the ground for about as long as planes have been in the air. But one of the earliest large-scale air-drops by the American military was in 1932. Crews loaded the bomb bays of B-2 Condors with food and other supplies wrapped in heavy blankets and dropped them to starving Navajo Indians in Arizona who had been cut off by severe winter storms. By World War II aircrews were dropping equipment and paratroopers all over the world from aircraft like the C-46 and C-47. And in Vietnam, C-130 crews provided a vital lifeline from the sky when American troops were cut off from all other ground units at Khe Sanh. Between the end of January and the beginning of April 1968, more than twelve thousand tons of air-dropped supplies allowed the vastly outnumbered

American ground units to withstand repeated North Vietnamese attacks.

How does the U.S. military do it these days? Here's how: the Air Force C-17. And let me tell ya, you can shove a lot of cargo into the belly of this beast! Problem is, there's not always a runway to land on at the other end. So in order to get supersized equipment to the troops on the ground in one piece and on the money, you need some riggers and aircrew who know a thing or two about airdrops.

Today's air-drop process is pretty much the same as it's ever been. And it all begins with the airlift riggers. It's their task to pack the gear right in the first place, with all the proper ropes, knots, and parachutes, because when it lands in the combat zone it's gotta be in one piece. When training, riggers use dummy loads, filled with concrete and wood, to simulate the weight of real equipment. And you'll notice that all the loads are cushioned by a small amount of cardboard, called honeycomb. It's only a few inches thick, but on impact it crunches down just enough to help keep stuff from breaking. These boys use three types of pallets, which can take anything from a hundred pounds of MREs to two Humvees side by side.

Once the platforms are aboard the C-17, the flight crew takes charge. The cargo is now in the safe hands of the loadmaster and it's up to the pilots to get it to the drop zone on time and on target.

There are two main kinds of cargo airdrop: extraction and gravity. The extraction method is used for bigger loads and is done with some high-tech help. The aircrew puts the drop zone coordinates into the onboard com-puter. An orange tarp, placed by the ground crew, marks the spot.

When the cargo door opens, a computer sensor factors in wind and altitude, then triggers a special mini extraction chute. At the right moment, the computer releases the locks and the load is pulled out. Because the second heavy is tied to the first, it quickly follows, and geronimo!

The gravity drop is used for lighter loads, which don't need the help of a parachute to pull them out. The plane tilts up at an angle. Then, at the drop zone, the computer releases blocks holding the platforms. They roll right out and the chute deploys.

Simple, ain't it? Till you try it.

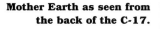

Mother Earth as seen from the back of the C-17.

Special honeycombed cardboard cushions the shock of landing.

TEST YOUR MILITARY IQ

What's the heaviest vehicle that can currently be air-dropped?

Answer on page 233.

BEAUTIFUL BABY HUEY: FROM SLICK TO GUNSHIP

"What was the first helicopter used in combat?"
—Rusty, Laurel Hill, Florida

"What's the difference between a slick, a dustoff, and a gunship?"
—Don, Gresham, Oregon

Not a bad question at all, Rusty. It all started with Russian immigrant Igor Sikorsky, the inventor who took the helicopter from a pipe dream to a combat flying machine. Sikorsky had been fooling around with rotor blades since the 1900s, but 1943 was the year when his R-4 became the world's first helicopter to go into mass production. It was also the first helicopter in U.S. military service and the first to operate from a ship's deck.

A couple of modifications later, the R-4 became the YR-4B, and on April 25, 1944, the YR-4B was the first helicopter in combat. Lieutenant Carter Harman of the First Air Commando Group flew his eggbeater deep behind enemy lines in Burma to rescue four men who had crash-landed in extremely rough terrain. Three of the men were severely injured, but they all got out safely thanks to the YR-4B.

You know that chopper had pretty severe weight restrictions, so Lieutenant Harman had to take the men out one at a time. The mission took three days. We sure have come a long way since then.

Well, Don, you're talking about one of my favorite helicopters—the Huey.

Helicopters have really changed the way armies fight. And in this Marine's humble opinion, none was greater than the Bell series of helicopters known as Hueys. The Huey is essentially the basis from which all of today's helicopters have evolved.

"Stop playing Nintendo and listen up, you grabasstic snotballs, or I'll Skyhook your ass!"

These babies aren't going to win any beauty contests, but believe me, when you heard the Hueys coming in over the jungles of Vietnam it was music to your ears. To give you a comparison, an infantryman in World War II with four years' involvement had perhaps forty days of actual combat. In Vietnam, an infantryman with a one-year tour experienced 240 days of combat, which really says that the helicopter took the fighting man to where he was needed.

Huey helicopters came of age during the Vietnam War, but you gotta rewind at least a decade to have a look at where they were born. In 1955 Bell Helicopter came up with a sweet little air ambulance called the Model 204. It was the first production helicopter to fly with a gas turbine engine. The Army liked what it saw and ordered a bunch in 1959, giving them the military designation HU-1: H for "helicopter," U for "utility," and 1 because it was the very first. Well, with that designation it was a no-brainer that the first pilots nicknamed the choppers Hueys. The name was such a hit that even when the U.S. military went to a new aircraft designation system in 1962 and HU became UH, the guys still called them Hueys. I guess it was better than calling 'em "uhhhhs"!

The first Hueys were used now and then for medevac. But Vietnam was where they proved themselves every day. In order to be successful with an air mobility strategy, we needed to find a helicopter platform that was reliable, had a lot of payload capacity, and could meet a variety of missions. Well, the Huey was perfect for that.

Bob Asbell flew Hueys when he was a warrant officer in the 116th Assault Helicopter Company, Vietnam. He knows firsthand how tough they were.

• **Bob Asbell, Huey pilot, Vietnam:** I had an engine failure where it quit over the jungle and we exercised what we called an autorotation. And we were able to fly that helicopter into a very small landing area and safely land without damage to any people or the helicopter itself. •

Although they began life as medevac helicopters, at the height of the war Hueys had three different functions: They were either slicks, dustoffs, or gunships.

Slick was the name for the transport version of the Huey, given because it was smooth. It didn't have any external armaments on it. Dustoff

was the official call sign for medevac choppers. During the war, dustoff Hueys completed more than half a million medevac missions. And gunships—well, I guess that one is self-explanatory, ain't it?

Gunships had a whole bunch of different armament packages they could carry, depending on what kind of action they expected to see. Hueys could be equipped with a grenade launcher or 20mm cannon in the nose, 2.75-inch rockets or machine guns attached to the skids, and flexible M60 door guns. I think it could be said that the Huey was a symbol for the Vietnam War. I challenge almost anyone to come up with a story about Vietnam that doesn't show a picture or talk about a Huey. I mean, think about it. The Hueys flew more than seven and a half million hours. For those of us who saw these babies in action, they'll always be our helicopter of choice!

THE SKYHOOK RECOVERY SYSTEM

Between 1966 and 1982 if you wanted to get somebody out of the water or off a mountain where a helicopter couldn't go, this is how you did it . . . with a Fulton recovery system called the Skyhook. Here's how it worked: You dropped your stranded Devil Dog a bag containing a harness, a cable, and a helium balloon. He put on the harness and attached one end of the cable to himself, the other end to the balloon. The balloon sent the cable aloft, where it could be snagged by a Y-shaped yoke rigged on the end of the aircraft. The ride was actually pretty gentle, and once your guy was aloft, the crew clipped on a cable and reeled him in!

FIGHTER FACTS

The Mikoyan MiG-25 fighter. Code name: Foxbat.

Air Force Captain Steve Ritchie, Vietnam era, America's most recent combat ace.

Well, pull back on your throttle, Jake, and listen to this.

It pains me to admit it, but the fastest combat jet in the world isn't one of ours. It's a Russian Mikoyan MiG-25 fighter, code name Foxbat.

The Foxbat's been clocked at mach 3.2, just over twenty-one hundred miles per hour. And not only is it fast, but this jet also likes it up in the stratosphere. The Foxbat can take off and reach an altitude of 114,000 feet in under four minutes. Wow! But don't expect this baby to turn on a dime. Apparently it's not very maneuverable—you might even say it drives like a tank.

Ever since fighter pilots have been flying, they've been keeping track of their aerial victories on the sides of their airplanes. To tally a kill, you have to knock an enemy plane out of the air. Ground kills don't count. And here's the catch: Somebody on your team has to witness the kill. Five of these confirmed aerial kills and you're an ace. In World War I, there were 110 American aces; probably the most famous was Eddie Rickenbacker, with twenty-six confirmed kills. The American ace of aces was a World War II pilot named Richard Bong, whose record still stands—a whopping forty kills. Atta boy, Richard. Our most recent pilot ace was Air Force captain Steve Ritchie. He scored his fifth victory in Vietnam on August 28, 1972. And by the way, this isn't just a men's club. There have been two female aces, both of 'em Russian. Ouch!

BOGEYS

Nobody knows for sure, but the word bogey seems to come from an old Scottish word for an evil phantom that is believed to haunt the countryside. Scottish kids still get threatened with a visit from the bogey if they don't do their chores—it's where we get the term bogey man.

Now, how bogey ended up being American military slang I can't say, but there must have been some Scottish pilot involved somewhere. And remember this . . . a bogey is a suspicious aircraft that may or may not be hostile. If the aircraft is known to be hostile, then it's called a bandit.

AIR FORCE ONE

"What was the first aircraft to be called Air Force One?"
—Todd, Scottsdale, Arizona

The first presidential aircraft was a tricked-out C-54 Skymaster that had all the comforts of the White House—well, sort of. Nicknamed Sacred Cow, this plane had a retractable elevator to accommodate its first passenger, the wheelchair-bound Franklin Delano Roosevelt. The C-54's first flight carried FDR to and from the Yalta summit in February 1945. It was also the president's last flight on the Sacred Cow; he died just two months later. President Truman inherited the C-54 and used it to fly all over the place, until it was replaced by a bigger and better C-118 in 1947.

But neither of these planes was actually called Air Force One. That distinction goes to President Eisenhower's C-121. Up until then, presidential flights were identified only by the tail number on the aircraft. But in 1953, a near-hit between Ike's plane and an Eastern Airlines plane with a similar tail number convinced the Secret Service to give all future presidential planes the special designation Air Force One.

Nowadays, of course, it's a whole new ball game. There are actually two Air Force Ones—two specially configured Boeing 747-200Bs, tail numbers 28000 and 29000—with the Air Force

designation VC-25A. When the president is aboard either aircraft, or any Air Force aircraft, the radio call sign is Air Force One.

Accommodations for the president include an executive suite consisting of a stateroom (with dressing room, lavatory, and shower) and the president's office. A conference/dining room is also available for the president, along with family and staff. Other, separate accommodations are provided for guests, senior staff, Secret Service, security personnel, and the news media. Two galleys provide up to a hundred meals at one sitting. Six passenger lavatories, including disabled-access facilities, are provided, as well as a rest area and mini galley for the aircrew. The VC-25A also has a compartment outfitted with medical equipment and supplies for minor medical emergencies.

They really know how to do it, don't they!

FDR made this his flying home.

WHO WERE THE RAVENS AND WILD WEASELS?

> **"Who were the Ravens?"**
> —Leroy, Gold Canyon, Arizona

> **"What can you tell us about the Wild Weasels?"**
> —Ken, Coopersburg, Pennsylvania

The Ravens were a supersecret bunch of forward air controllers who flew in Laos and had the highest casualty rate of any aviation outfit during the Vietnam War.

They wore blue jeans and cowboy hats to hide their military affiliation and were a breed apart. To find enemy targets, order up fighter-bombers, and mark their targets with smoke rockets, the Ravens flew in unarmed single-engine Cessnas, and the danger was real every time they went out. They would skim the treetops, looking for targets and drawing a lot of fire. After they marked a target and the sky jocks came screaming in with their bombs and napalm, the Ravens had to stick around until it was all over to do bomb damage assessment.

One hundred thirty Air Force pilots volunteered to be Ravens, and when it was all over more than 30 percent of the unit had died from combat injuries. Thank goodness years later some of their secret files were declassified, and we can now acknowledge the incredible job they did. Hats off to you, Ravens! Oohrah!

Ken, during the Vietnam War, we were flying a lot of missions. But the juiciest targets were heavily defended. The North Vietnamese were kicking the snot out of our flyboys by using SAMs, or surface-to-air missiles, to hit our aircraft. The military brass needed a fearless unit to take out those SAM sites, even if it meant the odds were completely stacked against them. The unit the Air Force created was code-named the Wild Weasels.

These guys flew into North Vietnam airspace at the head of a strike force, allowing themselves to be tracked by Vietnamese radar and even fired at by enemy missiles. Then they headed straight for those enemy missile sites and tried to blow them up.

Each crew was made up of a pilot with at least two thousand flight hours, along with a backseater called an EWO or electronic warfare officer. EWOs used radar-tracking technology to reveal the location of the SAM sites so they could be taken out. At first the Weasels flew in converted F-100Fs, but they were getting blown out of the

skies way too often. So they moved to the faster, more nimble F-105F Thunderchiefs. The Weasels' more maneuverable aircraft allowed them to learn the fine art of dodging or "dancing" with the missiles. They'd let the missiles, traveling at mach 3.5, get dangerously close to their planes. Then they'd nose down until, just in the nick of time, they'd power up at full throttle. Usually the SAM couldn't match this quick maneuver.

Dodging SAMs.

It took talent, guts, and luck to complete the hundred-mission tour of duty. Thirty-five-year-old pilot Leo Thorsness was one of the toughest. He could be counted on in any situation—once even shooting down a MiG that was threatening his wingmen. His wingmen survived, and Thorsness kept

flying straight into danger. Then in April 1967, he was shot down on his ninety-third mission, just seven shy of completing his tour. He and his EWO spent the next six years as POWs in the Hanoi Hilton. On March 4, 1973, Leo Thorsness and hundreds of other servicemen were finally released and brought back to America. He was later awarded the Congressional Medal of Honor from President Richard Nixon.

Congressional Medal of Honor winner "Weasel" Leo Thorsness.

Based in Laos, the top-secret Ravens hid their military affiliation.

SAY HELLO TO SPOOKY!

> **"Gunny, have you ever checked out a real war machine—the AC-130U gunship?"**
>
> —Lee, Fort Walton Beach, Florida

Known as Spooky, the AC-130U flies close air support for grunts in danger.

Well, no, I hadn't, Lee, but once I found out that this baby has the biggest gun in the sky, it was an offer that I just couldn't refuse.

We hauled ass down to the Florida panhandle to visit Hurlburt Field, home to the Air Force's Sixteenth Special Operations Wing and Fourth Special Operations Squadron. The men and women of the Fourth SOS are known as "ghostriders," and the AC-130U gunship they fly is dubbed "Spooky."

Spooky's job is to help the grunts on the ground with close air support firepower and armed reconnaissance. With a 25mm Gatling gun, a 40mm rapid-fire cannon, and a 105mm howitzer mounted under the left wing, Spooky circles the target like a big dark cloud hurling a hailstorm of lead.

Spooky is a converted Lockheed C-130 Hercules assault transport. The airframe hasn't changed much since the first C-130s of the 1950s. But on the inside, the AC-130U hauls one of the most complex aircraft weapons systems in the world.

• **Captain Jason Buss, pilot, 4th SOS**: We're able to literally put our rounds within meters or feet of the target, and we can engage at a relatively safe distance to friendly forces without risk of endangering them. We're big and we're slow, which can actually be an advantage. Whereas a fighter might come in and be able to make a quick pass and look at something, we can literally stay on station for hours. •

On the early gunships, dating back to the Vietnam War, the guns were fixed to the side of the plane; the pilot aimed them by maneuvering the entire aircraft. Today, Spooky's guns are on

The 25mm Gatling puts out eighteen hundred rounds per minute.

A 40mm Bofors cannon pours down hell on the enemy.

This plane even has its own artillery—the 105mm howitzer.

hydraulic mounts, guided by some sophisticated sensors and sights. And their three-gun system sure kicks butt! The 25mm Gatling gun fires eighteen hundred shots per minute, plus or minus a hundred rounds. With its massive numbers of rounds firing at a high rate, this is a good psychological weapon, basically saturating the area where the enemy is at.

The 40mm Bofors cannon nails larger targets with rounds weighing five pounds apiece pouring in at a hundred per minute. Oohrah! This gives us a little bit more capability on larger targets.

If that's not enough firepower for you, how about the number three gun—a 105mm howitzer? Yep, that's what I said. It's basically the same gun that the Army uses, just adapted for the aircraft. That's about ten rounds a minute of sheer hellacious whup-ass!

Beginning with their rapid-fire introduction in Vietnam, these gunships have seen action in just about every U.S. engagement since—including operations in Afghanistan and Iraq. And there is no doubt that enemies all over the world know the AC-130's reputation as a ghostly gunslinger.

Captain Buss: A lot of times just the noise of a AC-130 is enough that the enemy will not do anything. It stays pretty quiet when we're overhead. So a lot of times the ground users will like to have us just overhead just to make some noise.

You might just say that ol' Spooky can scare away the bad guys by just showing up and saying "Boo!" I like the squadron's unofficial motto . . . "You Can Run, But You'll Only Die Tired."
Oohrah!

DUSTOFF!

"What kind of advances have we made in getting our wounded out of harm's way?"
—Robert, Baltimore, Maryland

Top: The Bell Model 47 "Goldfish bowl": safe, fast, reliable.

Bottom: The modern military's way of saving lives, fast.

Bob was a medic in Vietnam and he knows how damn important this question is. To field it, I took a little off-road trip out to the Army's National Training Center at Fort Irwin, California. Every year, tens of thousands of soldiers come out here to hone their war-fighting skills. And with that many soldiers training in the field, the folks at Fort Irwin gotta be ready for anything. So meet the troops of the U.S. Army Air Ambulance Detachment, call sign Dustoff. They fly a special configuration, the Sikorsky UH-60 Blackhawk helicopter.

These guys need to be ready at a moment's notice, so the crew chief doesn't just keep the engines crankin' but is also responsible for the special gear that makes this bird a high-flyin' ambulance.

• Sergeant MacNaughten, crew chief, 247th Medical Detachment: We can take three to six wounded personnel, depending on whether we have a hoist in. There is also a kit we can install in the craft, which gives us a greater capability to carry more wounded. •

One lifesaving addition is the electric hoist that the sarge mentioned. It's used to fetch a casualty when the bird can't land—over water, say, or among dense trees, or on a mountain. The hoist is fitted with a jungle penetrater. It's basically a pointed weight that can clear tree branches on the way down to the ground. When these small legs are folded out, a medic can be strapped on and lowered to the injured. Once the casualty is properly secured, both medic and patient can be hoisted up to safety.

But getting to the casualty is only half the battle. The real hard part is up to the medic. Once aboard, he or she can begin immediate in-flight treatment of the wounded. That's because each flight medic has undergone rigorous medical training and has a lot of top-notch, lifesavin' gear aboard the

Top: Medics equipped with their own EKG equipment can diagnose almost instantly.

Bottom: The wounded were strapped to the skids and transported through the sky.

Probably the most famous dust off helicopter in the world is the Bell Model 47, one of the most popular light utility helicopters ever built. What makes this particular model of the H-13 Sioux so damn popular nowadays is her appearance at the beginning of every episode of *M*A*S*H*.

Back in the Korean War, the Model 47 was the belle of the ball because she saved lives every day. In fact, this whirlybird was nicknamed the "angel of mercy" for evacuating more than twenty thousand casualties during the three-year Korean conflict alone. The Model 47 also had some pretty nifty features, including a Plexiglas canopy for better visibility, nicknamed the "goldfish bowl"; the signature exposed aluminum tubing running aft to the tail rotor; and the skids, which were fitted with special stretcher pods to hold more casualties. The pilots loved the old goldfish bowls. They were so reliable that the guys said there wasn't any emergency they couldn't get themselves out of. The only thing that could bring these babies down was if the rotor came off. So they called the gizmo that held it on the "Jesus nut."

Let me tell ya, if that nut fell off, you found religion real fast.

Blackhawk. One item is called the Life Pack 10. It's able to interpret three-lead EKGs of the heart and see what the old thumper is doing. If an injured person's heart has stopped, this pack is also equipped with a defibrillator that can emit an electrical shock to jolt the patient back to life.

Now, these medical Blackhawks never carry weapons since they're on mercy missions. For these guys, speed is their best defense. With twin turboshaft engines, they can cruise along at 160 miles an hour, which also helps them land back at a division-level aid station and save lives.

GUNNY TAKES A WILD RIDE ON AN F-15

> "What's makes the F-15 the best air fighter in the world?"
> —Jim, Holyoke, Massachusetts

The F-15: unmatched anywhere in the world.

Well, I figured the best way to answer this question was to find out firsthand, but before the sky jocks would let me hitch a ride on an F-15, I had to take some special training and learn some real important things, like where to puke when the bird starts to dive.

To get my hands on the throttle of one of these birds, I headed on out to the 173rd Fighter Wing, 114th Fighter Squadron, at Kingsley Field in beautiful Klamath Falls, Oregon, where the boys of the Oregon Air National Guard invited me to take a test drive. First I had to undergo an intense day of training just to backseat it in an F-15D model.

Then I got my flight suit and had to get properly fitted with the gear that's gonna keep me from passing out—like a G-suit. It has a hose that pumps air into bladders within the suit during high-speed turns. That extra pressure squeezes blood out of your legs and torso and up toward your heart. Next stop was what the boys call the egress trainer: a cozy mock-up of an F-15, where they taught me how to be a safe passenger.

Oh man. Then I got a crash course—if you know what I mean—in parachute jumping.

"What was he lookin' for? Osama bin Laden?"

"Without a G-suit, I wouldn't get enough blood to the old noggin and I'd pass out."

I flew with Lieutenant Colonel Greg Imrich—call sign Eddie. He's an instructor and ops director at Kingsley. After a preflight check, it was time to head up into the ol' wild blue yonder.

Strapping in, I felt like a kid in a candy store. I thought I'd let you pukes listen in on a little of our cockpit conversation.

Eddie: All right, we're gonna do a final check here as we taxi a little bit. Double-check all your connections for your shoulder harnesses and your lap belt—if you can confirm that's all good to go . . .
Lee: I seem to be all intact.
Eddie: Okay, good.
Tower: Code one Kingsley Tower, runway three two, wind three five zero one two, cleared for takeoff.
Eddie: Let's get this show on the road.
Lee: Gimme a good ride, Eddie.
Eddie: No doubt about that.
Lee: Ha-ha, never a doubt in my mind, I know you'll take care of business. Semper fi. Off we go! How many civilian pukes get to come out and fly in an F-15?! This is fantastic!

At first we flew at eleven thousand feet. It didn't feel like much of anything.

Eddie: We're doing 0.8 mach right now, four hundred knots.
Lee: We are?
Eddie: It doesn't feel like much, does it?

Lee: No, it sure doesn't. It feels like we're just floating along.
But then Eddie really kicked it in!
Eddie: Okay, Gunny, we're gonna put some G's on you and let you feel what this jet really can do.
Lee: Just try not to kill us.
Eddie: That's not part of the plan. This is the airspace we normally fly in. We do a training out here over the eastern desert . . . That was about five G's.
Lee: How cool it is!
Eddie: Okay, go ahead and put your hands on the controls.
Lee: I got them.
Eddie: You fly the jet.
Lee: Okay.
Eddie: And like you told me, don't kill us.
Lee: I'll try not to.
Eddie: Do whatever you want to get a good feel for the jet. And I'll have to help you out here.
Lee: Arrgh!
Eddie: You got the jet.
Lee: No, you hold on to it.
Eddie: Okay.

By the time we landed, I knew I wasn't ready to go solo, but my trip sure gave me a lot of respect for these incredible machines. I now understand why the F-15 is the superior air fighter —because it is humongously bad! Oohrah! Semper fi!

Gunny at the controls of an F-15: "Arrgh!"

"The flight was physically demanding, but before I could hit the sack, the boys at the 114th Fighter Squadron have a little tradition for first-timers like me."

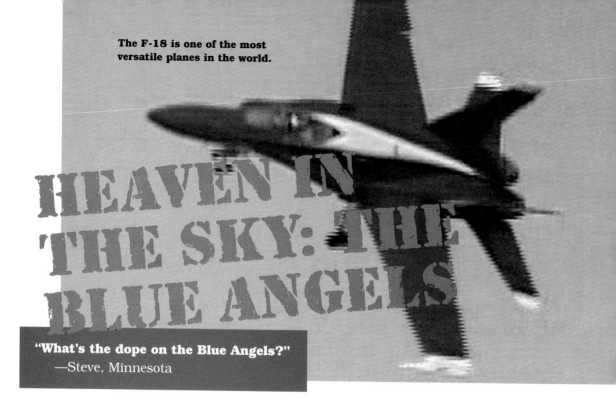

The F-18 is one of the most versatile planes in the world.

HEAVEN IN THE SKY: THE BLUE ANGELS

"What's the dope on the Blue Angels?"
—Steve, Minnesota

Okay, no problem, Steve, but you'd better buckle up!

With their unbelievable precision and heart-stopping aerial maneuvers, the Navy's Blue Angels have been dropping jaws and craning necks since 1946. Sometimes flying just thirty-six inches apart, the team demonstrates the very best in naval aviation. Four guys fly in the diamond; the other two fly as solos. When all six of them get together, it's called the Delta. Are you with me, Gomer?

The versatile Boeing F-18 Hornet is the team's aircraft of choice, with a design that lets pilots keep their eyes on the skies . . .

• **Captain Greg Wooldridge, Blue Angel:** The F-18 is such a beautiful airplane. It has a heads-up display looking through the front windscreen that gives me all the parameters I need: the air speed, the altitude, the G loading, the attitude of the airplane. •

The F-18 can fly nearly twice the speed of sound, but the Blues slow it

down to let the folks on the ground see what's happening . . .

• **Lieutenant Larry Packer, Blue Angel:** We usually fly about four hundred to five hundred miles per hour during the show. Anything faster than that and you really don't get a chance to see what's going on all that well. Now, there are times in the show when the solos will come by just under the speed of sound, but the maximum speed of the airplane is right around 1.8 mach. •

When the Blues perform their hair-raising maneuvers, they sometimes pull up to eight G's—that's eight times their own body weight. And listen up, all you iron men out there . . . they don't even wear G-suits!

• **Major Scott Wedemeyer, Blue Angel:** The way we fly in the airplane . . . your arm rests right on your leg, and so with a G-suit, in an airplane all it does is inflate. You can't have your arm moving up and down because you have a spring on the stick, which is

The Blue Angels are masters of instrument flying, even with powerful G forces.

about thirty-five pounds of pressure. So you don't want your arm moving. You have to brace yourself. •

Being a Blue Angel pilot is usually a two-year rotation, and it's one of the most coveted jobs in the Navy. More than five hundred people apply to the team every year. Once the pilots are selected, the fun really begins: You learn how to fly wingtip-to-canopy. This kind of precision takes a lot of practice. The Blues brief before each and every flight. I was allowed inside and I thought I'd stumbled into some sort of séance. These boys literally fly the mission sitting there at a conference table.

• **Major Wedemeyer:** The first time I went to a Blue Angel brief, I didn't know whether to get down on my knees and start praying or just start dying laughing. You'll see all the guys sitting around the table with their eyes closed and their heads nodding—and you look down and see their hands moving, left and right, and their little thumbs twitching. And that's all just to get your mind ready for the air show. •

So there you have it. Over the years, more than thirty-eight million people have seen the Blue Angels. After watching the Blues in action, I'll bet all of them left with big smiles on their faces.

And don't you forget, folks, the right wing in any Blue Angels formation is always flown by a Marine. Oohrah!

"Turn the page for the skinny on the violent world of attack helicopters. You have a problem with that, worm? I didn't think so!"

MODERN ATTACK HELICOPTERS PART 1: THE SUPER COBRA

"What's the story on the Super Cobra attack helicopter?"
—J. J., Colonial Heights, Virginia

Hey, pal, when I get an e-mail about anything that flies and fights, it's time to head on down to my friendly neighborhood Marine Corps base and check it out for myself.

To find out what makes the AH-1W Super Cobra such a bad-ass bird, I went to Camp Pendleton, California, and hooked up with Marine Light Attack Helicopter Squadron 369, better known as "the Gunfighters." Major Tony Gallardo, call sign Walleye, gave me the rundown on what they call the Whiskey Cobra.

• **Major Tony "Walleye" Gallardo, assistant operations officer:** The specific job of this helicopter is to provide close air support for the grunts on the ground. That's what we do, that's our bread and butter. What we live for is the guys on the ground, making sure that they're safe and that we can clear an access of advance for them anytime they're coming up against any opposition. •

And that's exactly why the Cobra was first put into combat in 1967. It was originally developed for the Army as a heavily armed chopper to support our ground troops in Vietnam. It relied on the same engine and transmission as the Huey but was a lot skinnier because of the tandem seating.

When the Marines saw how effective the Cobra was in combat, they immediately wanted one of their own. By 1970, the first Marine Corps Cobras were delivered, and to this day the Cobra remains a staple of Marine Corps aviation. For hunting its prey, this Cobra has got some serious fang, including a three-barreled 20mm Gatling gun cannon, which shoots at a rate of 650 rounds per minute.

Now, that's a lot of lead, but that's not the only way this so-called flying tank can bite the bad guys.

• **Major Gallardo:** We have a TOW missile launcher. We call it a TML for short. We can load either two or four. We hang another underneath it so we can carry as many as four TOW missiles on this side of the aircraft. •

The Cobra can also launch the laser-guided Hellfire, a fire-and-forget tank buster. And for air-to-air, the heat-seeking Stinger packs a knockout punch. That's what's so great about this attack helicopter . . . it can be loaded up with a variety of lethal goodies, including 150—you heard me, 150—2.75-inch rocket pods for lighter enemy targets.

But all that firepower isn't worth a damn if you can't spot the bad guys. So this bird comes with a telescopic sight unit and forward-looking infrared. It doesn't matter if the enemy's a long way away or sneaking around at night—the Super Cobra's still gonna put a world of hurt on him. Well, it's obvious that this chopper can pack a wallop, but what's underneath is just as impressive. The Super Cobra has twin T700 engines that can get this baby moving at about 170 knots with weapons fully loaded. That's 195 miles an hour.

With that kind of speed and firepower, it's no wonder the Cobra has such an outstanding battlefield record. Want proof? Check this out. During Operation Desert Storm, Super Cobras chalked up ninety-seven enemy tank kills, 104 armored personnel carriers and vehicles, sixteen bunkers, and two anti-aircraft artillery sites, without the loss of one aircraft. The official count from Operation Iraqi Freedom is still being tallied—I'll have to get back to you on that one.

Oohrah!

"Gunfighter" emblem of the Marine Light Attack Helicopter Squadron 369.

"Meet my good friend, the Cobra!"

The Cobra: close air support for grunts in trouble.

MODERN ATTACK HELICOPTERS, PART 2: THE KIOWA WARRIOR

> **"What's the real story on the Kiowa Warrior helicopter being used in Iraq?"**
> —Marc, Mobile, Alabama

The Kiowa: stealthy reconnaissance.

Well, Marc ol' buddy, you have come to the right place my because I've got all the dope on the Kiowa.

The OH-58D Kiowa Warrior is a two-seat, single-engine armed reconnaissance helicopter. It's the smallest, quietest, and—the pilots who fly them will tell you—best recon rotary airframe in the world.

The Kiowa Warriors and the Army pilots who fly them are throwbacks to the cavalry scouts of the old days because the Kiowa's mission is to sneak ahead of the main course looking for trouble. When she finds it, she can either call in the big guns or take care of business all by herself.

It's easy to spot the Warriors because they've got that ball that looks like an alien

The distinctive ball on top of the Kiowa houses two cameras, the heart of the chopper's electronic recon.

mounted over the blades. That little gremlin is called the Mast Mounted Sight, or MMS, and it's the heart of the operation.

• **Instructor-pilot Randy Morris:** The MMS allows the pilot and copilot to extend their eyes on the battlefield and find the enemy at a great distance. It houses two cameras, a TV and a thermal imaging system. The two windows house the two different cameras. The darker-tinted window has the thermal imaging system camera mounted behind it. The clear window has the TV camera. •

The TV camera is for daylight; the thermal imaging system works at night. The Mast Mounted Sight can spot a target up to

12.4 miles away and can be used like the periscope on a submarine to give the Kiowa stealth capability. Built by Bell Techstrong, the Kiowa Warrior is a Native American, armed to the teeth, with up to four different weapons systems.

• **Instructor-pilot Ed King:** The Hellfire missile system is a laser-guided missile using the MMS and the laser within the MMS or a remote designator. The seeker head in the front of the missile will acquire the laser-hit spot. It's a point weapon system. Depending on the delivery mode, the range for the Hellfire is eight hundred to eight thousand meters [875 to 8,750 yards].•

The Hellfire is primarily a tank buster. It can penetrate any armor out there today. The next weapons system is a 2.75-inch folding thin aerial rocket. This system's been around for a long time, upgraded over the years. The rockets can be equipped with high-explosive warheads, bomblets, or thousands of pieces of sharp metal called flechettes.

If you're expecting to come up against personnel or light-skinned vehicles, rockets are the way to go. Now, if you want to dish out some close-range bursts of lead, meet my old buddy: the .50-caliber machine gun, which is based on the same M2 or Ma Deuce machine gun that's been around since World War II. A laser sight can be mounted on it that can be controlled from inside the aircraft. And if you find the bad guys are crowding your airspace . . .

• **Ed King:** The air-to-air Stinger is an infrared or IR guided missile. It has a seeker head in the front of the missile similar to the Hellfire, but instead of tracking laser energy, it tracks IR energy off enemy aircraft, whether fixed or rotary wing. Then it tracks on the enemy target and destroys the aircraft. •

There you have it: the best recon helicopter on the planet. And it belongs to the Marines. Oohrah!

Loading Hellfire missiles, good up to 8,750 yards.

The Science & Technology International blimp contains the future of aerial surveillance.

MODERN BLIMPS

"What is state-of-the-art in aerial recon?"
—Chad, Greeley, Colorado

The war on terrorism means that we need a constant stream of new hardware to keep giving us the winning edge. But it might just surprise you to see that one of the newest things we're using these days is based on some pretty old technology. Like the blimp!

You're right in thinking that the blimp ain't exactly cutting-edge, but combine it with some new hardware developed by Science & Technology International and you may have the next weapon in the war on terrorism.

Now, basically a blimp is just a big gas bag attached to a gondola. You won't find any of the structure inside the bag that some of the old rigid airships used to have. The Navy started playing with airships back in the 1920s and '30s. During World War II, blimps flew along with our convoys across the Atlantic to protect them from German U-boats. They were more effective as scouts than fixed-wing aircraft since the blimps could move at the same speed as the ships. But because they were so slow, they weren't much good at taking out subs— although the blimps did usually carry a few depth charges just in case.

The new LASH spy system maps and photographs wide landscapes.

Finally, in 1961, the Navy gave blimps and rigid airships the boot. The brass decided to put their funding into faster fixed-wing surveillance planes instead, like the P-3 Orion. So why is the Navy considering getting back in the blimp business? Well, it's simple: Blimps can supply something that fixed-wing aircraft can't—a stationary eye in the sky. And that's important for homeland security these days.

Another advantage of the blimp over other aircraft is the fact that it requires less maintenance. It's a very basic craft, with very basic engines. A blimp doesn't have that many moving parts, so for every one flight hour you've got maybe three or four man-hours of maintenance. Most aircraft can tie up ground crews for up to fifteen hours per hour of flight time.

Some people assume that blimps are easy targets. Wrong! A blimp is virtually invisible to radar, since radar waves mostly pass right on through it. But suppose some hothead on the ground does start shooting at it. Well, even if he hits it, it would take hundreds of punctures to cause a leak big enough to bring the ship down. That's because the helium in the blimp is at such a low pressure that it barely leaks out when punctured. So it'll float down rather than pop like a balloon.

Now let's check out the hardware that's given the blimp a new lease on life. The LASH (Littoral Airborne

Sensor Hyperspectral) system uses cameras and sensors to capture light patterns that can't be seen by the naked eye and creates a very colorful map. It can read 256 shades of color to identify objects by their color signature. So if you know the specific color signature of an object—for instance, a certain shade of camouflage paint on a tank—you can program the image-processing computer to zero in on it.

But if you don't have a specific target in mind, this system is also handy in pointing out objects that just don't belong. When the LASH system maps a particular terrain, it remembers what it sees. So when it passes over the same area again, anything that wasn't there before is gonna get noticed.

What happens if the LASH system finds something suspicious? Well, the blimp is also equipped with telescopic and infrared cameras, so you can take a closer look. And when we do catch the bad guys lurking about, we can unleash the hounds immediately by sending our intel to friendlies in real time.

By combining the LASH technology with the right platform, this blimp just might make the perfect watchdog. Not only does it have an amazing set of eyes, but it also knows how to move. I'll bet you this supersnooper makes it to the front lines in the war on terrorism.

Information at the touch of a computer key.

MANNED. UNMANNED: WHICH AIRCRAFT WINS?

"Are unmanned aircraft getting so good they're going to replace pilots?"
—,Anthony, Las Vegas, Nevada

On the left, the manned X-35. Right, the unmanned X-45 UCAV.

W ell, I don't think our fighter pilots are going anywhere just yet, Anthony, but the latest X-plane is gonna give them a run for their money. X-planes are experimental aircraft, and you can find a flock of 'em at Edwards Air Force Base in California. Fasten your seat belts as we strap on the gloves for a battle royale between the latest manned and unmanned aircraft.

In this corner, an aircraft that's lethal, agile, and flown by a pilot—the X-35 joint strike fighter! Over here is a plane that's shaped more like a UFO than a UAV; it's the X-45 UCAV or Unmanned Combat Air Vehicle.

First, the X-35 . . .

The coolest thing about the X-35 is that it comes in three different versions—one for the Navy, one for the Air Force, and another for the Marines. So instead of laying out a ton of cash to develop three different planes, it's cheaper to build one that can make everybody happy.

Each of the three versions of the joint strike fighter has a unique way to take off and land. Need it to take off from a short field, like an aircraft carrier? No problem. Need a vertical takeoff? Piece of cake. Even if you want a regular runway takeoff, the X-35 can handle it.

Let's get the lowdown from the X-35's corner man, Lieutenant Colonel Edward "Fast Eddie" Cabrera.

• **Lieutenant Colonel Edward Cabrera, X-35 operations commander:** The joint strike fighter is the replacement for many different aircraft, including the Air Force's F-16, the Navy's A6, and the Marine Corps' F-18 and Harrier. It's an airplane that's easy for the pilot to fly and employ in combat. •

Like a rookie boxer getting into the ring, the X-35 joint strike fighter is scheduled to hit the production line by 2008.

Okay, what about the unmanned planes?

The feisty challenger in this bout is the X-45 UCAV. As an unmanned aircraft, it can carry out its mission without putting a pilot in harm's way. Tucked in a corner of Edwards is a hangar chock-full of classified projects. We were given unprecedented access to watch these guys get the X-45 ready for a mission. The workings of the mission were classified, but we got as close as we could without being manhandled by the MPs!

Now, get this: The UCAV is not flown by remote control. The mission is preprogrammed and downloaded into the UCAV's computer. Then the plane flies itself. The mission planners just need to hit the start button. The UCAV first flew on May 22, 2002, and Boeing's lead operator Robert Horton tells us about that first mission.

• **Boeing lead operator Rob Horton:** It took off and it flew the exact profile we wanted to fly with little or no intervention by anybody on the ground. We watched the airplane fly the mission plan, come in for a descent, and make an outstanding landing—and there was nobody on stick, nobody controlling it. It did it all autonomously.•

This unmanned marvel came out swinging with specs that make it sleek, stealthy, and fast. The X-45's got a wingspan of 33.8 feet, weighs in at eight thousand pounds, and can carry three thousand pounds of high-explosive punch. And by 2008, we'll see this X-plane in action, too!

Now, I've heard a pretty good case for the unmanned aircraft. Looks to me like it's a tie, and you can expect a whole lot of knockouts by both manned and unmanned planes in the future.

Building the X-35—the manned fighter of the future.

The UCAV near its top-secret hangar.

PART FIVE:
SHIPS

"Hey, who let you
pukes on this seagoing
vessel? Stow that
sandwich and start
scrubbing!"

WHAT WAS A GREEK TRIREME AND WHY DID IT SCARE THE HELL OUT OF EVERYBODY?

"What was a Greek trireme?"
—Max, Cedar Rapids, Iowa

Modern replica of Greek tireme.

In ancient Greece, naval power was where it was at. There's a helluva lot of water around those islands, and if you had a fast, maneuverable ship, you had the advantage.

Enter the trireme, a Greek ship that was only 120 feet long—kinda puny for those days. But the genius of the trireme was its three-tiered design, sometimes stuffing 170 rowers belowdecks. This allowed the Greeks to triple their speed. These fighting ships were built low to the water—the bottom deck was only a foot or so off the waves—so they weren't made for the open ocean. Instead, these babies were suited for quick, close fighting in narrow waters. What they'd do is try to sail in close enough to ram their opponent with their bow battering rams, or sideswipe 'em to knock their oars off. Then it was close-in fighting with swords and spears. Nasty, brutish,

and short, as somebody once said.

These small, fast ships are credited with the Greek defeat of the larger, slower Persian navy at the battle of Salamis in 480 B.C. The Persian king Xerxes was looking to defeat the Greeks, so he sent twelve hundred Persian ships against them near the island of Salamis. The Greeks had only about 450 ships, but they were fast-moving triremes! They pounced on the Persian fleet in a narrow channel and sent ship after ship to the bottom. When the Persian navy tried to flee, the triremes ran 'em down!

Thousands of Persians met their maker that day—all due to that versatile ship of war called the trireme! The trireme has passed into history, but historians trace the development of today's sleek destroyers and cruisers to this noble craft.

TURTLE RULES!

> **"When was the first U.S. submarine put into action?"**
> —Gary, Norman, Oklahoma

Well, Gary, this may surprise a landlocked type like yourself, but the first U.S. submarine, called the Turtle, was used during the Revolutionary War.

You see, in 1776 the British fleet held sway over New York Harbor, which in turn made it king of the Hudson River. This split the American colonies in two. Something had to be done, so David Bushnell, a Yale grad from Saybrook, Connecticut, and fierce patriot, designed and built the Turtle. Made out of wood and held together by iron hoops, the Turtle was six feet in height and seven feet in length. It was essentially like going underwater in a large barrel. There was room for only one guy in it, and he had to be stone crazy! The pilot used brass pumps to fill or empty ballast tanks, letting the sub surface or submerge.

The Turtle had only thirty minutes of underwater time, so the submariner had to work quickly. Its only weapon, attached near the top, was a mine—another invention of the ingenious Bushnell. This was a watertight wooden keg filled with packed gunpowder, a fuse, and a clock-timer device. The Turtle was designed to sneak up on a ship so the pilot could stick a bomb under the ship's hull.

On September 6, 1776, the Turtle, piloted by Sergeant Ezra Lee, set out to attack Admiral Richard Howe's flagship, the HMS *Eagle*. Lee actually got safely under the *Eagle*, but he couldn't penetrate the vessel's copper-sheathed hull with the mine.

Heading back home, near Governors Island, Sergeant Lee thought the enemy had seen him and jettisoned the mine. An hour later, the clock-timer went off—and the Brits, thinking they were being attacked, moved their fleet away! So, while it wasn't until the Civil War that a Confederate submarine sunk a Yankee warship, already these stealthy underwater devils were proving their worth.

"What? You had enough of this old-time crap? Well, turn the page, sailor!"

Inside the Turtle.

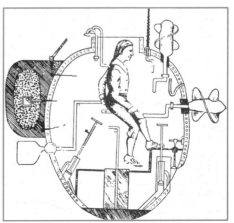

BLAZING BATTLESHIPS!

> **"Tell me more about battleship guns."**
> —Rick, Denver, Colorado

Now, here's the kind of e-mail I like. Really turns me on. All right, Rick, here we go.

The last time a battleship fired its guns in anger was in 1991, during the Gulf War. But these ironclad behemoths dominated naval warfare for more than a hundred years. Whenever you saw one of these mighty vessels coming, you knew there would be all hell to pay.

The last of the U.S. battleships commissioned were the Iowa class. Launched in 1942, the four vessels of the Iowa class were the largest and most advanced battleships that ever sailed under the U.S. flag. Each was equipped with three giant turrets that carried three devastating breach-loading, sixteen-inch Mark 7 rifles.

We visited the battleship *New Jersey*, now a museum in Camden, New Jersey, to see how her guns handled on the high seas. This ship first saw action in 1942 and was continually upgraded for battle until the early 1980s.

An Iowa-class battleship can send shells flying up to twenty-five miles.

The World War II computer that fired the USS *New Jersey's* big guns.

The firing procedure began ninety feet above the main deck in the forward main battery director. It was a long climb up, but spotters could see what was going on and what they were aiming at.

From this lofty outpost, the enemy would be sighted with radar. When a target came in range, its location was sent down to one of the first wartime computers ever made.

After that, it took seventy-seven able-bodied seamen in each turret to get the guns ready for battle. Loading began forty-five feet below the top deck in the most protected region of the ship—the powder bag loading area. This was definitely a "nonsmoking" section. Each bag weighed 110 pounds. After the charges were brought up, the shells were hoisted from the decks just above the powder storage area. Up to 168 projectiles could be stored on each level. But getting them to the hoist was a whole other challenge.

Deckhands were in constant fear of being crushed by the twenty-seven-hundred-pound shells. The poor grunts in the turrets did all the work, but it was the crew sitting way up above deck that got to pull the trigger. Once the director was on target, we'd have indicator lights that would show us that the turret was loaded and that the fire control solution was set.

Then: Fire! At the top of their game, the Iowa-class battleships could blast the enemy with a lethal barrage of up to two rounds per minute from each gun. But the introduction of aircraft carriers in World War II cut short the glory of the battleships. Today's new-fangled smart bombs have put the labor-intensive battleships out of business for good. But the thunder of the battleships will echo forever in the heads of those who found themselves on the wrong side of their guns.

DAZZLE PAINT!

These days, standard issue for military sailing vessels is battleship gray, but in World War I, ships were painted like modern art masterpieces in a wild array of colors and patterns they called dazzle paint.

You'd think these bizarre paint jobs would make the ships stand out even more. But not so. Back then, enemy submarine captains needed to plot the speed and direction of their intended target visually in order to get a direct hit with a torpedo. By using the dazzle paint job, the outline and profile of the ship was broken up; at long range it was tough to figure out the ship's speed, which end was the bow, and which end was the stern.

You could still find some dazzle paint on World War II ships, but it disappeared pretty quickly after that due to improvements in sonar and radar. This meant subs didn't need to sight targets visually anymore. Then it was back to the boring gray that we have today.

Inside a battleship's turret.

Each powder bag weighed 110 pounds.

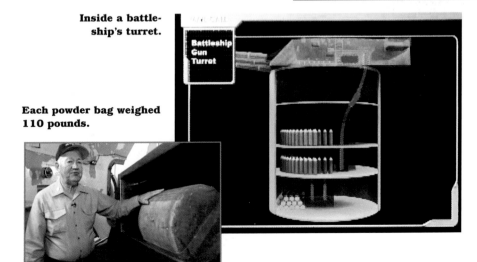

Battleship Gun Turret

DOWN INTO THE DEEP BLUE SEA: NAVY DIVERS

> **"What's the lowdown on naval deep-sea diving these days?"**
> —Dwayne, Mount Laurel, New Jersey

"The Gunny ready for the big dive!"

Listen up, landlubbers! Let there be no mistake about it! To be a Navy deep-sea diver, you need a hard hat, sturdy gear, and brass cojones, 'cause these fellows take some pretty big risks to salvage sunken vessels, retrieve lost aircraft, carry out underwater repairs, and rescue trapped submariners.

For most of their tasks, Navy divers use the Mark 21 diving rig with its superlight twenty-seven-pound helmet—or hard hat, as the Navy folks call it.

• **Petty Officer First Class J. R. Hott, USN dive instructor:** It's a demand hat, as opposed to the free-flow hats, which the Navy had used in the past. What I mean by that is it uses a scuba second-stage regulator, which is identical to what the scuba divers use. Rather than having an air supply that constantly flows through, anytime a diver takes a breath, it will give him a breath; when he stops inhaling, it stops feeding air. •

The Mark 21 has been in service for about two decades, which sounds pretty darn impressive—that is, until you hear about its predecessor, the Mark 5. For nearly seventy years Navy divers accomplished miraculous feats

in this two-hundred-pound monster suit. The suit was capped by a fifty-six-pound brain bucket.

The rig saw a lot of action after Pearl Harbor was attacked back in 1941. In the months following the surprise raid, Navy divers made more than four thousand dives and spent thousands of hours underwater in mud, muck, and oil to raise the fleet.

The Mark 5 was so good that it stayed in service until 1984, when new models, made of space-age materials, were added to the diving locker.

Even with great gear, diving is still dangerous. The biggest threat for a Navy diver doesn't come in battle. It comes from the bends—also known as decompression sickness. During a dive, nitrogen dissolves in the body tissues. When the diver ascends, the pressure on the body is reduced. If the diver surfaces too quickly, bubbles of nitrogen can form—obstructing blood flow and putting pressure on the vital nerves. The bubbles force the victim to literally bend in pain.

But for the diver inside the Navy's latest deep-diving suit, the Advanced Diving Suit (ADS) 2000, the atmosphere is the same as it is on the surface—even at two thousand feet down. You see, the atmospheric dive suit is made from one enormous chunk of aluminum, and it's built to withstand more than half a ton of pressure per square inch. So the diver inside the vacuum-sealed hard suit doesn't have to worry about "the bends."

Only a handful of divers are assigned to the Navy's deep submergence rescue unit and trained to descend to the deep in the supersuit.

• **Chief Boatswain's Mate Hugh Scully, USN, Deep Submergence Unit:** The ADS 2000, the atmospheric diving system, has thrusters that move you vertically, backward, forward; rotate you left and right and up and down. The controls are all foot-operated, and which way you're gonna go in the water depends on which way you point or touch your footpads. •

These old boys have at their fingertips tools that even old Edward Scissorhands would envy. With articulated joints that can rotate 360 degrees, divers can clamp and grip enough to attach lines, clear debris, and even open hatches. The Navy plans to use the ADS 2000 in extreme emergencies, aiding deep-sea submarine rescue efforts more than a third of a mile below the surface of the ocean.

The Mark 21: in use for more than twenty years.

A deep-diving helmet with a scuba airflow.

A Navy diver salvaging at Pearl Harbor in a Mark 5 suit.

TEST YOUR MILITARY IQ

When did the Navy first use deep-sea divers?

Answer on page 233.

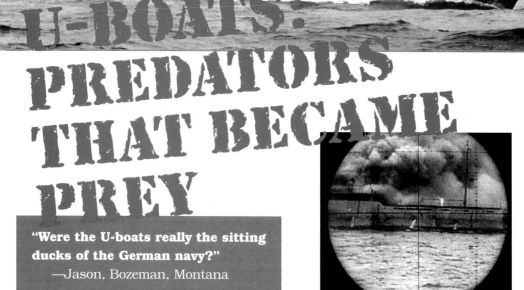

U-BOATS: PREDATORS THAT BECAME PREY

> **"Were the U-boats really the sitting ducks of the German navy?"**
> —Jason, Bozeman, Montana

Through a German periscope: death of an Allied convoy ship.

Well, we did blast most of them out of the water, Jason, but when the war started German U-boats were kicking our ass.

In the early stages of World War II, the German U-boats were the most feared predators ever seen in military combat. Allied merchant supply convoys were helpless against their cunning underwater tactics.

By the war's end, the German U-boat fleet had sunk 2,882 Allied merchant ships and 175 warships.

• **Norman Pomlar, naval historian:** Merchant sailors lived in constant fear they were gonna be torpedoed. And if you were in the North Atlantic, even in summertime, the water temperature's fifty degrees. A few hours in that, you're dead. They slept with their clothes on. The lifeboats were always rigged and ready to go with food, flares, and water. It was a very difficult period. •

U-boat is short for "unterseeboot"— the German word for submarine.

And those U-boats had the upper hand in the early part of the war because they'd broken the communications code used by Britain's Royal Navy. So that gave them a real good idea of where to hunt for the Allied convoys.

The U-boats preferred to cruise on the surface, with the ability to travel up to eighty-five hundred nautical miles. But when it came time to attack, stealth was the name of the game. The sailors on these thousand-ton steel whales were trained to submerge a boat within thirty seconds. But it was a tactic known as the "wolf pack" that gave the U-boats their teeth.

The wolf pack would start out as a great line of U-boats spread across the ocean. Once a U-boat spotted a convoy, it held its fire and radioed the others. Then they all attacked at once, using the accurate T2 torpedo. Some wolf packs were as many as forty U-boats strong.

When the Allies broke the German code, everything changed.

The Type VII C U-boat.

German U-boat captains were a tough and elite group.

The Allies were helpless against them, fighting blind with primitive depth charges set to explode at a predetermined depth.

The most common U-boat was the Type VII C, maximum speed seventeen knots on the surface, eight knots submerged. It was 217 feet long and required a crew of fifty-one sailors. They lived 24/7 in a tube filled with fuel and a maximum of fourteen torpedoes.

• **Jaurgen Oesten, captain, U-61, U-106, U-851:** In the crew's quarters there were torpedoes and potatoes and whatever stuff was hanging around in between these bunks. And there was no thing such thing as private life. Everybody knew everybody and all their bad manners and habits. •

Despite these discomforts, U-boat sailors were among the elite in the German war machine. In March 1943, the U-boats had their greatest success, sinking 120 Allied ships in a single month. Their heyday ended just two months later, in May 1943. The Allies introduced several technological advances that sent the U-boats down to Davy Jones's locker for good.

The Allies finally cracked the Germans' communications code and were able to head off an attack before it reached the good guys. An airborne radar was developed so airplanes could locate U-boats traveling on the surface of the ocean. And the Allies introduced an improved depth charge known as the hedgehog. Hedgehogs weren't set for a predetermined depth the way the old-style depth charges were. They exploded only on contact with a U-boat.

Ultimately, the U-boat crews suffered the highest casualty rate of all the branches of the German military. But at their height, the power of the U-boats and their crews seemed unstoppable.

"Stop moving your lips and turn the page, snot ball!"

LIBERTY VS VICTORY

> **"What's the difference between a Liberty ship and a Victory ship?"**
> —Russell, Elk Grove, California

The slow Liberties often convoyed together for protection from the deadly U-boats.

Interesting question, Russell. There were a lot of things that set the two apart, but they also had something very important in common—some of the bravest crews to sail the high seas!

You see, you can have the best military in the world, but you can't win if you don't keep them supplied. With fleets of Liberty ships, and later with help from Victory ships, the Allies were able to keep their forces on the go. At the beginning of World War II, the German U-boats were blowing a lot of Allied shipping out of the water. The United Kingdom was in danger of being cut off.

• **First Assistant Marine Engineer Clint Johnson (ret.):** England was in the war all by themselves. The Germans were sinking their ships faster than they could build them, and so they came up with a design that you could turn out rapidly. •

The Brits may have had the idea, but it was good ol' American muscle that cranked out the Liberty ships like cookie cutters. Once the production lines got up to speed, Liberties could be built in as little as twenty-eight

days. They were 411 feet long and 62 feet wide. And since these were civilian vessels, not Navy warships, they were crewed by members of the U.S. Merchant Marine.

At the time, Liberties were the largest class of civilian-made ships ever built. And they needed to be. Hard as it is to believe, it took more than seven tons of supplies to support one measly foot soldier for one year. Seven tons.

• **Clint Johnson:** The Liberty had an old three-cylinder steam engine that was really designed prior to World War I. They were about twenty-five hundred horsepower. They carried about ten thousand tons of cargo and they made about ten knots. •

For you landlubbers, a knot or nautical mile is about 1.15 miles. So 10 knots is 11.5 miles per hour. And that speed—or lack of it—was a big problem. You see, the Nazi subs could travel about the same speed as the Liberties. And since the first Liberties didn't have guns on them, the German subs would just surface, shoot 'em up, and sink 'em. So in early 1942, they started putting guns on the Liberties. Since these were civilian ships, they

One of the last remaining Victory ships.

added a detachment of a couple dozen U.S. Navy armed guards to each ship to handle the guns. That helped, but the German subs could still sink the ol' Liberties with their torpedoes from underwater.

That's when the Victory ships came along. The first of 534 Victory ships, the SS *United Victory*, was launched in February 1944.

Victory ships were 455 feet long. Now, that's 44 feet longer than the Liberty ships. And their hulls were reinforced to avoid fractures, a problem that often plagued Liberties. But the biggest difference between the two ships was the new steam turbine engine, which could deliver six thousand to eighty-five hundred horsepower. The Victories could reach up to seventeen knots, a six-knot increase over the Liberties. That gave them a better chance at outrunning the Nazi subs. But they still carried guns for U-boat ambushes or aerial attacks.

In total, more than three thousand Liberties and Victories were built during World War II. They carried over 75 percent of all supplies in the war. The operation of these ships came at a great cost: The Merchant Marine suffered more loss of life, by percentage of their ranks, than the four other branches of the military. Over 650 ships were sunk, and more than sixty-eight hundred seamen lost their lives.

TEST YOUR MILITARY IQ

Where does the term "deep six" come from?

Answer on page 233.

HOW MULBERRY HARBOR WAS CREATED AFTER D-DAY

"What's a Mulberry Harbor?"
—Emil, Flagstaff, Arizona

Well, Emil, Mulberry Harbor and D-Day go hand in hand, and we all know what D-Day meant to the Allied victory in World War II—and if you don't, get a freaking history book, you lowest common denominator!

A helluva lot of people contributed to the success of that operation, including the twenty thousand British dockworkers who built Mulberry Harbors.

When the Allies made the beaches of Normandy the launching point for their attempt to retake the European continent, there was still one big problem. They knew it would take weeks to recapture any of the heavily defended deepwater ports in the region. And without a constant flow of beans and bullets, the Germans would eventually push the invasion forces back into the water. So Allied leaders decided, What the hell—let's just bring an entire port with us piece by piece.

In August 1943, the Allies started building huge concrete bathtubs called caissons at British shipyards. In June 1944, they towed the nearly 150 floating structures across the English Channel and into position near Arromanches, France, and Omaha Beach.

The caissons were then filled with seawater and sunk to create piers. Then floating roadways were built from the new piers to the beaches. We also sailed in seventy badly damaged ships destined for the scrap yard and sank them outside the Mulberry Harbors to create artificial breakwaters. The Mulberry Harbor at Omaha Beach was destroyed a few weeks later by a terrible storm, but the harbor at Arromanches stood. It was more than a mile across, with thirty-three jetties.

From this harbor, thousands of tons of supplies made it to shore—until French ports were in Allied hands and the Mulberry Harbor, no longer needed, was dismantled and allowed to sink into obscurity.

These caissons were sunk to create the artificial harbor.

Mulberry Harbor contained ten miles of these floating roadways.

ANDREW JACKSON HIGGINS AND HIS BOAT

Andrew Jackson Higgins, a boat-builder with vision.

> "Can you tell me about the Higgins Landing Craft?"
>
> —Alan, Heflin, Alabama

Heck yes, I can!

Seems Alan's dad was pretty familiar with a few of those bad boys in World War II, and Alan wants the straight dope on the craft that helped his old man hit the beaches.

In 1943, the American Navy totaled 14,072 vessels. Of these boats, 12,964, or 92 percent of the entire U.S. Navy, were designed by Higgins Industries, whose founder and president was Andrew Jackson Higgins, a hot-tempered southern shipbuilder (as you can guess by his name) who hated bureaucratic red tape as much as he loved bourbon. He became famous for the landing craft that helped put our troops on the beaches on D-Day as well as all almost every other amphibious theater of the war. (In fact, he got so well known that Hitler once referred to him as "the new Noah.")

The Higgins boat was a thirty-six-foot-long wood-and-steel craft that transported troops, small vehicles, and supplies from ship to ship, or ship to shore and back again. What made the Higgins special was the fact that it could anchor very close to shore and still make a quick getaway if necessary due to its incredibly shallow draft. The Higgins boat had a unique reverse-curve hull design and so could draw only three feet of water at the stern and an amazing two feet, two inches at the bow. Add an armored ramp to that bow and you had one helluva nifty little landing craft. So nifty, in fact, that the twenty thousand Higgins boats operating during World War II landed more troops than all other types of landing craft combined.

The old Higgins boats have now been replaced by the LCU, or Landing Craft Utility. It's four times as long and can carry a hundred tons more than the old World War II workhorses. But hats off to Andrew Jackson Higgins—looks like he had the spirit of his Confederate ancestors working in him, big time!

TEST YOUR MILITARY IQ

What other small, fast World War II craft did Higgins Industries develop?

Answer on page 233.

You maggots think you know a lot about Navy stuff, but this old Marine is here to tell you you're nothin' but a bunch of sand-sucking landlubbers. Listen up!

Seeing is believing: the dirigible as aircraft carrier.

TEST YOUR NAVY IQ

Now, this is one of those squirrelly questions where there really is no set answer, but in general we're talking ten to fifteen ships centered on one big-ass flagship: the aircraft carrier.

Let's just say that this is the USS *Harry S. Truman*, a nuclear-powered aircraft carrier heading on over to the Persian Gulf to kick some butt.

The Truman's full battle group's got . . .

1 guided missile cruiser . . .
3 guided missile destroyers . . .
2 regular ol' destroyers . . .
1 guided missile frigate . . .
An ammunition ship . . .
An oiler . . .
And 2 nuclear submarines.

The other battle groups have about the same, give or take a destroyer or supply ship or two. Hope that answers your question, squid.

I've been waiting for somebody to ask me this question, Keith. Take a look at the picture. Yes, that is a dirigible, and those are airplanes dangling off it. You see, back in the 1930s the Navy was looking for ways to increase the range of their fixed-wing aircraft and provide fighter support for their airships. They killed two birds with one stone by equipping F9C Sparrowhawks with skyhooks that enabled them to be launched or recovered aboard a dirigible by means of a trapeze attached to the bottom of the airships. Then they'd haul the planes back in for safekeeping. But the 1937 *Hindenburg* disaster in New Jersey brought the Navy's airborne aircraft carrier plans to an abrupt and devastating halt.

Gunny's task force.

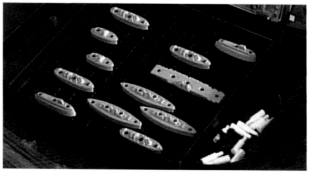

"What was America's first nuclear-powered submarine?"

—Steve, East Windsor, New Jersey

The USS *Nautilus* was actually named after the submarine in *20,000 Leagues Under the Sea.* During her twenty-year career she broke every speed and endurance record and changed naval strategy forever.

Well, I think you're just trying to fire me up, Steve! Don't tell me you haven't heard of the USS *Nautilus*, bonehead?

The USS *Nautilus* is undeniably the most famous submarine in the world because she was a record breaker in so many ways. She was the first nuclear-powered submarine when she made her maiden voyage in 1955, the first vessel of any kind to cross under the North Pole, and the first sub to circumnavigate the globe.

The USS *Nautilus* made her maiden voyage in 1955.

"What can you tell me about depth charges?"

—Corey, New Orleans, Louisiana

Couple things, Corey. They're the oldest anti-submarine weapon, going all the way back to World War I. They're basically big drums of high explosive whup-ass with a fuse slapped on so they'll detonate from the pressure of a specific depth.

If you were lucky enough to get one close, the explosion could squash a sub like a beer can. Or by dropping a lot of depth charges all around a submarine, you'd at least set up some pretty nasty pressure waves that would force the submarine to the surface—where your deck guns could score a direct hit. Launchers added some decent range to the weapons, but depth charges

"Big drums of high-explosive whup-ass!"

were never all that effective. In fact, during World War II, a German U-boat survived 678 depth charges during a single hunt.

THE PROUD COAST GUARD

> "Hey, Gunny, all this stuff about mud marines, ground-pounders, and airdales is okay—but what about the Coast Guard?"
> —Paul, Portsmouth, Virginia

The forty-seven-foot motor lifeboat is the Coast Guard's mainstay.

A force to be reckoned with in wartime.

Paul, I feel your pain. Here's your answer:

The Coast Guard has been plucking people out of the water since it was officially created back in 1915. Today the Coasties, and it's okay to call them that, do a lot. They're responsible for maritime safety, maritime mobility, protecting natural resources, and law enforcement—they're also really good at catching drug smugglers. And during wartime, Coast Guard vessels might even ship out to combat zones. On top of all that, they're now a part of the Department of Homeland Security—patrolling our harbors, coastlines, and waterways looking out for the bad guys.

To get all these jobs done, they've got a whole bunch of different vessels, from 420-foot icebreakers all the way down to small inflatable boats, along with a variety of aircraft and helicopters. To see one of their sturdiest rigs of all, the Coast Guard's Channel Islands small-boat station in Oxnard, California, invited me aboard their forty-seven-foot motor lifeboat, or MLB.

The forty-seven-foot MLB has been in the inventory since 1997, and is the Coast Guard's state-of-the-art rescue vessel. It's loaded with the latest navigational and communications gear and manned by a crew of four: the coxswain, a boat engineer, and two boat crew members. Boat Engineer Chief Kevin Brown took me belowdecks to the engine room.

• **Kevin Brown, engineer chief:** We've got twin Detroit diesel electronically controlled six-cylinder V-configuration ninety-two series turbo-charged after cool blown engines. Four hundred and thirty-five horsepower in all. •

That comes out to pretty close to nine hundred horsepower.

"Keep your hands where I can see 'em. That means you!"

Talk about doing some waterskiing! Those twin diesels can get this honey doing up to twenty-five knots. For us landlubbers, that's about twenty-eight miles an hour.

The MLB is built entirely out of aluminum. It's a tank, able to withstand the most severe conditions at sea, as long as you've got enough Dramamine. And if it capsizes, it will return to an upright position in less than eight seconds . . . Coasties say, "It's self-righting," almost unsinkable. Thirty-foot seas, no problem.

Rest assured, nothing is gonna stop the MLB and its crew from getting the job done!

CROSSING THE EQUATOR

Before a young sailor crosses the equator, he's called a polliwog. Once he crosses that line for the first time, he becomes a shellback, but not before he goes through a— let's say unique—initiation ceremony.

Back in the days before the Navy ruled that the ceremony couldn't be dangerous or demeaning, it was usually both. Polliwogs were greased up and dunked, paddled until they cried for Mommy, and dressed up to parade the decks in a pageant that can only be described as Miss Really Ugly America. In fact, I kissed King Neptune's belly. That's right, ol' Gunny's a shellback. Want to make somethin' out of it?

A Marine waits for the Coast Guard!

Rescue by air . . .

THE STORY OF THE SEABEES

"How did the Seabees build the runways that won the war?"
—Steve, Rio Ranch, New Mexico

A five-thousand-foot runway required sixty thousand Marston mats.

Can do, Steve!

That's the Seabees' slogan. And these Navy combat engineers showed that "can-do" spirit all kinds of ways during World War II, especially when they had to make a runway out of nothing in the middle of nowhere.

They'd pull out their 'dozers, clear away the brush, and start leveling out the dirt. But dirt runways, or ones made from crushed rock or crushed coral, had to be extremely level and then compacted . . . and that took time. Plus, runways made from these natural materials couldn't hold up to the pounding from heavy bomber landings and weather.

Enter a little slab of Yankee ingenuity known as the Marston mat.

Every section was ten feet long, fifteen inches wide, and had eighty-seven holes. Stamped out of sheet steel, it was also known as pierced steel planking, or PSP.

• Lara Tobias, curator, CEC-Seabee Museum: The purpose of holes in the Marston matting is to allow it to lie flat on relatively roughly graded soil. So therefore it's very useful in runways that are being built rapidly because they don't have to go through and actually compact the soil underneath. •

They fit together quickly and easily with interlocking hooks. This made it possible for a hundred men to build a 150-foot wide, 5,000-foot-long runway in just over seven days. The Seabees built Marston mat runways in Europe to provide emergency airstrips after D-Day, and throughout the Pacific.

And before you start thinking that these guys had a nice cushy job back in the rear with the gear, let me tell you that a lot of times Seabees were building these airstrips right in the middle of the action.

They came, they saw, they bulldozed.

• **Lara Tobias:** In September 1942, the Seabees began to rebuild Henderson Field, located on Guadalcanal. They could fix a bomb hit in approximately forty minutes. And they would run out there. They would fix the airfield very quickly using the Marston matting and then run back before the Japanese bombers could come back in. •

And Seabees knew how to handle a weapon. Many times Seabees would be patrolling the perimeter while the rest of the men kept building.

So I bet you're wondering what the deal is with the Marston mat name? Well, I aim to please!

• **Lara Tobias:** Marston matting is actually not named after a man named Marston. It is named after Marston, North Carolina, where it was tested. Marston matting was a very low-tech invention because it's simply a piece of steel. And so in some ways the high technology—the B-29s and all these other things that were going on—never would have been successful if it hadn't been for the so-called lowly Marston matting. •

Marston mats were used again to build the runways during the Korean War and even stuck around for the early days of Vietnam. But the rough surface of the mats tore up the tires of the faster, more powerful jets, and the steel mats were eventually replaced by smoother, lighter sections of aluminum.

So while the aircraft taking off and landing may have grabbed more of the glory, they wouldn't have gotten very far without the dependable ol' Marston mat. The Seabees' motto is "Constructumus Battamus."

For you squids out there not up on your Latin, that means "we build, we fight." And that's just what they did to help win the war. Oohrah!

The fighting combat engineers.

Laid over rough ground, the holes in the steel Marston strip evened out runways.

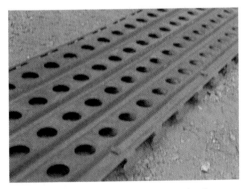

A five-thousand-foot runway required sixty thousand Marston mats.

THE NAVY'S RIVERINE PATROLS IN VIETNAM

> "What's the mission of the brown water Navy—or is that too complicated for a jarhead like you to understand?"
> —George, U.S. Navy

A member of the brown water Navy lets loose a volley.

Okay, George, I hope you're watching because I want you to read my lips! Drop down and give me twenty-five, you unorganized grabasstic piece of amphibian crap.

Now while George is eating dirt, I'm gonna show the rest of you the Navy's riverine patrol boats in action. During the Vietnam War, our troops fought hard to keep enemy forces within South Vietnam from getting resupplied. And it didn't take long to figure out that the Vietcong were using that nation's fifteen-hundred-mile-long coastline and forty-five hundred miles of rivers and canals as a liquid highway to move men and munitions.

It was up to the big men in small boats to tackle the problem. The group was called "the brown water Navy." There were three main units in the brown water Navy: Task Forces 115, 116, and 117. Each unit had a unique mission and all sorts of special boats to achieve their objective.

A few small boats had been patrolling the Vietnamese coast since 1960. But Task Force 115 officially set sail in 1965. The men of 115 were primarily charged with protecting merchant ships all along the coastline. The Navy used lots of small boats for the task, but the most versatile was a modified fifty-foot all-metal craft called a Swift boat. With twin V12 diesel engines putting out over four hundred horsepower, the swift boats could do a whopping thirty-two knots. For Navy use they were known as PCFs, or Patrol Craft Fast!

The five-man crew spent most of their time boarding and searching hundreds of sampans and junks looking for VC guerrillas and weapons. By the end of 1965, Navy commanders realized that they needed more small boats to patrol all those miles of rivers. That was when Task Force 116 was formed. The sailors of 116 were assigned the tough turf of the Mekong Delta. The boat specially designed for the mission was the PBR, or Patrol Boat River, since made famous by the movie *Apocalypse Now*. But unlike the movie, PBRs did not operate alone. As a rule, two boats patrolled the river together.

The PBR's thirty-one-foot lightweight fiberglass hull sat only two feet deep in the water—meaning this sucker could go just about anywhere. But what really made these puppies fly was the high-powered water jet propulsion system, made by our hot tub buddies at the Jacuzzi Corporation. The boats were fitted with searchlights and armed with twin .50-caliber machine guns forward, along with a single .50-cal and a mortar tube in the aft—that's the back for all you landlubbers!

But the big bad boy of the brown water Navy was Task Force 117, the mobile riverine force. Formed in 1967, this multitasking force was primarily responsible for delivering the Army's Ninth Infantry Division to the enemy's doorstep. To get that job done, they had a whole bunch of heavily armed boats, including refurbished World War II landing craft.

In the seven years these task forces operated, from 1965 to 1972, the brown water Navy proved to be a formidable fighting force in Vietnam. Their unit memorial, located in San Diego, is a fitting tribute to the men who served, and the more than two thousand who made the ultimate sacrifice, in the U.S. Navy's one-of-a-kind small-boat fleet.

Unlike in the movie *Apocalypse Now*, PBRs always patrolled together, never alone.

Task Force 115 raced these Swift boats up and down the coast.

Task Force 117 heavied up with these refurbished World War II landing craft.

MILITARY HYDROFOILS

"How fast can a hydrofoil go?"
—Martin, Rio Dell, California

Now, that's a question I just can't skim over.

The fastest military hydrofoils flew over the water at more than eighty miles an hour, but they've gone the way of the dodo bird—there aren't any left in active service. Back in the 1960s, the Navy built hydrofoil ships to improve upon the slower World War II PT boats, which could barely operate in rough seas.

Hydrofoils speed things up by attaching something like an airplane wing to the underside of a boat. The wings cut through water and lift the boat above the choppy surface. And when a ship's hull is out of the water, there's a lot less drag, which means a whole lot more speed and maneuverability.

Back in the 1960s, the Navy got serious with hydrofoils, hoping to get a leg up on the enemy with speed in the water—no matter what the conditions. They tested all kinds of configurations. Ultimately, they went with the Boeing-built *Tucumcari*, officially known as Patrol Gunboat Hydrofoil 2, or PGH-2.

As a naval lieutenant in the late 1960s, Martinn Mandles became the captain of the *Tucumcari*, one of the most seaworthy of all hydrofoils ever to sail. When they marketed a model of the *Tucumcari* in the late 1960s,

Top: The proud *Tucumcari*!

Bottom: The *Tucumcari* retracted her wings to enter harbor.

they even included a little Lieutenant Mandles.

Big deal! Call me when you get your own motivational figure, buddy!

• **Lieutenant Martinn Mandles:** The machine flies by computer control, autopilot if you will. There are three gyros in the computer and when you turn the helm—the steering wheel left or right, port or starboard—all you're doing is telling the computer that you'd like to make a turn. And the computer decides how to make the turn. •

The PGH-2 had a thirteen-man crew. She was powered by gas turbine engines and propelled by water jets placed in the aft hydrofoils. At top speed, the *Tucumcari* could cruise up to fifty miles an hour, six to eight feet above the water. At slow speeds, the hull came back down to the surface and the wings extended fourteen feet below. This might have caused trouble in shallow harbors if it weren't for the hydrofoil's innovative design. At the end of a hard day's work, the *Tucumcari*'s foils would retract, and the ship would enter and dock in ports that had as little as six or seven feet of water depth at the pier.

Built as an enforcer, the *Tucumcari* was equipped with a 40mm anti-aircraft cannon, twin .50-caliber machine guns, and an 81mm mortar aft.

The *Tucumcari* served a full tour of duty in Vietnam conducting riverine operations. Her success paved the way for a new class of hydrofoil—the Patrol Combatant Hydrofoil Missile (PHM) class.

A total of six PHM-class hydrofoils were built. The PHMs were armed with a 76mm gun mount and eight long-range harpoon missiles. But developing technologies such as high-tech radar and long-range weapons meant the speed and maneuverability of hydrofoils were no longer needed by the Navy.

• **Lieutenant Mandles:** The sad truth is that there's not one hydrofoil that remains in the U.S. Navy. But I believe that someday—just as the World War II PT boats were resurrected as the *Tucumcari*—a hydrofoil with a pedigree from the *Tucumcari* will emerge as the premier high-speed, all-weather craft of the U.S. Navy. •

When the Navy abandoned the hydrofoil program in the 1980s, all the PHM-class boats got a Coast Guard paint job and a few more years of service for drug interdiction operations.

These wings lift the vessel out of the water and make for smooth, fast sailing.

Who invented the hydrofoil?

Answer on page 233.

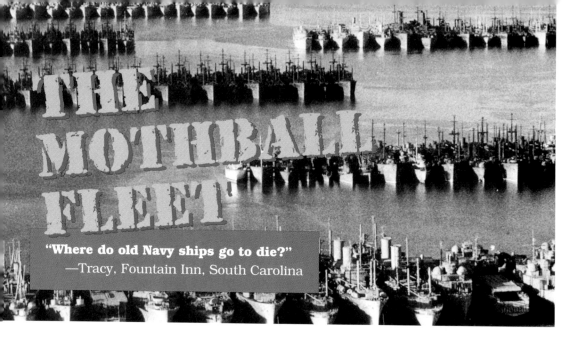

THE MOTHBALL FLEET

"Where do old Navy ships go to die?"
—Tracy, Fountain Inn, South Carolina

Well, Tracy, let's give a hint to all the geniuses out there: No actual mothballs are involved.

When a ship is retired from active duty in the U.S. Navy, she goes through a process called decommissioning. A couple of our buddies, Travis Scarborough and Mike Petronis, are managers at the inactive ship maintenance facility at Puget Sound Naval Shipyard in Bremerton, Washington. They gave us a look at what happens when a ship leaves the fleet.

One of the latest aircraft carriers to be retired is the USS *Constellation*—the Connie, as they call her. Fresh back from Operation Iraqi Freedom, she's beginning her inactive days here at the shipyard by having all her salvageable equipment removed.

• Travis Scarborough, quality assurance and inspection manager: After decommissioning, the shipyard gets her for about a year. They lay up the flight deck, take the catapult tracks off, and stow 'em down below. •

When the shipyard is finished scavenging the reusable items, the ship is taken to the inactive maintenance facility, also known as the mothball fleet. That's where the hatches are battened down. Another aircraft carrier, the USS *Ranger*, was decommissioned back in 1995 and is now in the next phase of retirement.

Travis Scarborough: We seal her up, we check her out, we put dehumidification on board that's monitored to make sure that the hull is best suited to the ocean atmosphere and to keep it from corroding.

> "Unwrap yourself from the can of suds before I put you in mothballs, meathead! This is quality time with the Gunny."

Dehumidification is the saving grace for any inactive ship. Without dry air flowing through the compartments, these beautiful ships would turn into big ol' rust buckets. Just because a ship is old doesn't mean she isn't useful, especially with nice dry air around. On average a ship is kept for about twelve years before being scrapped. That allows enough time to take parts off in case other active-duty ships in her class need replacements. And after a dozen years or so, the ship's going to be obsolete enough not be needed for any emergency reactivation. In the meantime, cavernous ships like the *Ranger* are used to store all kinds of useful items.

• **Mike Petronis, safety, health, and environmental manager:** The hangar bay of the USS *Ranger* is no longer stored for aircraft and helicopters. We use it for storage for extra mooring lines from various other ships, backup chains, and equipment that we've taken from the ship that will probably go on an existing carrier or future carriers. •

Now a part of the mothball fleet, the USS *Sailfish* served proudly from World War II on.

• **Travis Scarborough:** They cut 'em up. You'll see 'em go out of here on boxcars, on the trains. They'll have the sail on it; they have the bow planes on it and a big chunk of the hull. Just big chunks is what they haul off. •

Now, you softies out there will be happy to know that sometimes these ships do come back to life. The *Ranger* is going to be turned into a floating museum. Ships can also be purchased by the navies of other countries, assuming they're friendly, that is. And in the event of an extreme national emergency, some of these vessels can also be reinstated to active duty. But until the ultimate fate of each ship is decided, they'll stay here under the protection of the folks at the inactive shipyard.

The ghostly insides of the USS *Ranger*.

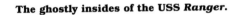

TEST YOUR MILITARY IQ

How many ships are in the mothball fleet?

Answer on page 233.

GUIDED MISSILE DESTROYERS: FAST AND DEADLY

> **"Would you please demonstrate the capabilities of today's guided missile destroyers?"**
> —Paul, Contucket, New Hampshire

Top: The USS *Preble*, a proud example of our guided missile destroyers.

Inset: All threats are diagnosed in the CIC.

Hey, Paul—get with the program, maggot! What you shoulda written was, "Hey, Gunny, get your butt out to sea and blow something up!"

I paid a visit to the Navy's newest can o' whup-ass, the USS *Preble*. The destroyer is the air defense platform for the fleet. Fast and agile, with nearly one hundred missiles at the ready, destroyers are there to protect our carriers and amphibious assault ships—heck, the whole battle group.

Known as "greyhounds of the sea," destroyers have been in the fleet since the early 1900s. In World War I and World War II, they protected merchant convoys and battle groups by chasing after submarines at high speeds, then taking them out with their deck guns,

torpedoes, or depth charges. Nowadays they let their missiles do the chasing.

On a ship like the *Preble*, the war is fought from the CIC, or Combat Information Center. Here radar and global tracking systems are combined to guide each missile all the way to the target.

• Captain Tim Batzler, USS *Preble*: The CIC is grouped in functional areas. There's an anti-surface, there's a submarine component, there's a strike warfare, electronic warfare, and then our datalinks. •

So there's a separate group to focus on each place the bad guys could come from—in the air, on the surface, or underwater. There's even a group to electronically jam enemy weapons. While at battle stations, the operators in the CIC identify all contacts as friend or foe. This information is then reported to the tactical action officer or TAO.

• **Jeff Heckert, sonar chief, USS *Preble*:** The TAO's gonna take all the information coming from all the different systems and their supervisors on board. They're gonna get their operators to feed them all the information. They're gonna make decisions, and then they're gonna pass their decisions back up to the front table for the TAO and the CO to decipher on what our priorities are gonna be. •

Once it's decided that the inbound threat is an enemy missile, called a Vampire, the TAO begins the launch sequence. The doors to the vertical launch tube fly open and the missile is on its way. The missile can be tracked and updated in flight by the computer. So now you're probably asking yourself what kinds of missiles this system can handle. The most versatile is the SM2, or standard missile, which can take out enemy aircraft and missiles; it has a range of fifty to one hundred miles.

The newest missile in the fleet is the ESSM or Evolved Sea Sparrow Missile. With the ESSM, the *Preble* can take out any incoming enemy missile from a much safer distance than its previous weapons allowed.

I'll give you one guess what the ASROC, or Anti-Sub Rocket, does.

Yeah, that's right—kills subs, even when they're submerged and at a range of more than five miles. But if you really want to reach out and touch someone, chuck a Tomahawk. Used mainly against land targets, the Tomahawk can deliver almost any type of warhead in our arsenal, high explosives, or even a nuke at a range of over a thousand miles.

What's really exciting about this ship and its weapons is the Vertical Launch System, or VLS, because it gives unprecedented flexibility to engage multiple targets simultaneously. The old rail loading system allowed the ship to fire only one or two missiles at a time. With the VLS, the *Preble* can launch all ninety-six missiles at once.

It's a pretty safe bet that anyone stupid enough to get too close to this ship is gonna wind up nothing more than a fish condo.

The *Preble* can send a missile as far as 100 miles.

HUNTING HURRICANES

"How and why does the military hunt hurricanes?"
—Bud, Campbell River, British Columbia

The devastation a hurricane brings.

The storm hunters go aloft in these WC-130H Hercules workhorses.

Well, Bud, first off, it's one helluva job. In the path of a monster storm that's six hundred miles wide with two-hundred-mile-per-hour winds, most people have just one thing on their mind: getting the hell out of Dodge.

But when everybody else is heading for the hills, the men and women of the Air Force's Fifty-third Weather Reconnaissance Squadron are moving in. They're known as the hurricane hunters and they fly directly into the eye of the storm.

"Ain't you lucky, scum bucket! Basic training starts right now!"

This dangerous duty falls to Air Force Reservists, since their top priority is to protect the community. Flying into the belly of the beast is sometimes the only way to get the critical weather data needed to predict where and when a hurricane will make landfall. It's risky, but it saves lives—tens of thousands of 'em.

Stationed at Keesler Air Force Base in Biloxi, Mississippi, the Fifty-third WRS is the only squadron of its kind in the U.S. military. These aren't your typical weekend warriors, either! One of the reasons that this mission is so unusual is that it belongs to the U.S. Air Force Reserve. There are ten full-time crews, but the other ten crews are traditional reservists. These are people who are doctors or lawyers or schoolteachers in their private lives.

The aircraft they fly is a WC-130H Hercules—a high-wing, medium-range version of the ol' C-130 workhorse that's been around since the late 1950s. Each crew is made up of six highly motivated airmen: the pilot-commander, the copilot, the navigator, a flight engineer who looks after the integrity of the aircraft, an aerial recon-naissance weather officer who tracks the storm, and the dropsonde operator, who has the best job: He gets to play bombardier by launching weather-gathering devices during the flight!

Sounds easy enough—except for that whole part about being in the middle of a friggin' hurricane!

These fliers don't even carry para-chutes—bailing out into hurricane winds would be suicide. If you can't ditch the plane and get into a raft, you're history. And the hurricane hunters have had their share of tragedy. Over the years, aircraft have been lost in the Pacific off the China coast. Rescuers flew search patterns, but all they found were pieces of the aircraft.

Despite the risks, from April to November the hurricane hunters are out there gathering information to send back to the National Hurri-cane Center. Missions can last up to eleven hours, and they can be a wild ride. The most life-threatening part of any flight is the slam dance between the eye and the rest of the hurricane, known as the eye wall.

Inside the cockpit as the hurricane hunters go to work.

• **Lieutenant Doug Rose, navigator:** It's difficult to avoid the intensity of some of these eye walls. And we will be thrown up and down two to three thousand feet pretty regularly. It's a pretty rough ride sometimes. •

• **Master Sergeant Ron Debree, dropsonde operator:** We drop the weather instruments out from a tube into the eye of a hurricane. They fall about two thousand feet a minute, and as they descend to the surface of the ocean, they send back the pressure, temperature, humidity, wind speed, and direction. That information is collected on computers, and we send it to the National Hurricane Center via satellite. •

On any given mission, hurricane hunters are confronting that eye wall up to a dozen times as they track a storm's progress. That's what I call cojones!

The "crazy canoe."

STEALTH AT SEA

"What was the British Sleeping Beauty submarine?"
—Armenia, Seattle, Washington

Get ready for a little kiss and tell, Armenia. Sleeping Beauty was the code name for the smallest operational submarine used in World War II. It was the brainchild of the SOE, Special Operations Executive—Great Britain's top-secret commando agency. The Sleeping Beauty was also used by our guys in the OSS, the World War I–era predecessor of the CIA.

This crazy canoe had a top speed of four and a half knots. It was created to sneak into enemy harbors so the operator could directly attach explosives to a ship's hull. Because the Sleeping Beauty had no navigational system on board, the operators developed a tactic called "porpoising," in which they would surface, take a visual sighting, and then dive again until the target was reached. Versions of the Sleeping Beauty were used by the Brits in France and the Aussies against the Japanese fleet in Singapore, with some success. But this one-man sub never truly lived up to its potential and was soon replaced by more practical delivery systems.

The Sea Shadow was a cool-looking vessel the Navy started using as a test platform for combat systems in 1994. When it was unveiled, the Navy brass and Lockheed-Martin—the guys who built it—called it "the next generation in waterborne stealth."

And what makes this ship so stealthy? Well, a bunch of things. Mounting the engines high above the waterline reduces the aural signature. That means it's difficult to hear on sonar. By using pontoons instead of the standard hull, there's barely any wake, so it's hard to spot visually from the air.

Because the exhaust vents inside the A-frame, there's less heat signature for infrared to get a bead on. And the angled sides make it harder to detect the craft using radar. So, James, it's pretty freaking stealthy, but you can't exactly call it invisible.

Before it was declassified, the Sea Shadow was tested only at night. It skimmed along the Northern California coast without any civvies ever knowing it was there. Makes you kind of wonder what might be cruising just off-shore tonight, huh?

The stealthy "Sea Shadow."

PART SIX:

VEHICLES

"Nobody dismissed you yet! Oohrah! Let's take these babies for a spin!"

GUNNY'S CHARIOT: THE JEEP

The classic vehicle of World War II.

I get a whole mess of questions about my beloved jeep. Is it a real World War II jeep? Yes. How fast can it go? Fast enough. Can I have a ride? No, you can't have a ride in my jeep.

It's been called all sorts of things: beetle bug, blitz buggy, peep, and puddle jumper. Officially, it's known as the "1/4 ton truck, 4 by 4." That means it can carry a five-hundred-pound payload and has four-wheel drive. Doesn't sound very exciting, but when you say jeep— now, people know what you're talking about.

By the end of World War II, automakers had built nearly 650,000 of them. Today many are still on the road, and they continue to sell like hotcakes.

My low-mileage honey is just loaded with options. A four-cylinder, inline water-cooled engine powers this baby. Delivers nearly sixty horsepower. It's a perfect second car for hauling groceries or battlefield casualties. And it makes a perfect weapons platform. Comes standard with a M1 Garand anti-theft device and rugged two-piece combat rims that will keep you advancing even after the tires have been shot off.

In the summer of 1940, the U.S. Army sent car companies a list of specifications for a new kind of scout car.

• **Jim Gilmore, restoration specialist at Combat Vehicles, Inc:** Its original purpose was to replace the motorcycle and the motorcycle and sidecar. It was to be used for dispatch work, running, hauling officers, this type of thing— not to haul freight or large amounts of equipment. It was primarily reconnaissance, and it was never considered to be a general-purpose vehicle. •

The Army tested the prototypes submitted by three automakers—the Bantam Car Company, the Willys Overland Company, and Ford—and cherry-picked the best ideas from each. Bantam was a small company and couldn't handle a really big order, so it was left to Ford and Willys to crank them out by the bushel.

So how did this four-by-four truck get the name jeep? On the War Department's numerical listing of military vehicles, it's listed as G-503.

Willys called their version of the truck the MA, for "Military Model A," and Ford called theirs the GP. So maybe that's it?

• **Jim Gilmore:** Even though the original Ford prototype and the original first four thousand or so Ford jeeps made were called GPs, that was Ford's designation for it; it did not mean "general purpose." In the Ford Motor Company, the G stands for "government vehicle," regardless of year. The P is an indicator of the type of vehicle—an eighty-inch-wheelbase reconnaissance car. No Ford documentation ever called them general purpose. •

So jeep could be from GP, as long as you don't claim that it stands for "general purpose." But here's a more likely theory: Just before the war, a mischievous little character named Jeep made its debut in Popeye cartoons. This little guy could do anything and go anywhere. Well, GIs thought the same thing about their little four-by-four trucks and started calling them jeeps.

However it got the name, the jeep

quickly became a beloved jack-of-all-trades. In one form or another, the jeep soldiered on until the mid-1980s, when it was finally overtaken by the M998 High Mobility Multi-Purpose Wheeled Vehicle—the Humvee.

I've had collectors tell me they'd give their right arm for my baby. Well, sorry, the going rate for this jeep is two arms and a leg.

In other words, dream on, buddy-boy.

The little character after whom the jeep was named?

"Nothing like a classic bike to get Gunny goin'!"

The "anything-powered" M1030M1 motorcycle of the future.

MOTORCYCLES — WAR'S GLORIOUS ANGELS

"What can you tell me about military motorcycles?"
—Jeff, Maplewood, New Jersey

Jeff, you really know how to get Gunny's heart beating faster!

Fans of *Mail Call* know that there's two things that really get the Gunny's blood pumpin'. One is annihilating watermelons with firepower. The other is test-driving the vehicles that made our military great.

So let's take a ride through military motorcycle history.

New grunts in any Marine expeditionary force take a two-week motorcycle course, and the instructors at the Combat Motorcycle School at Camp Pendleton, California, ain't just blowing smoke out their tailpipes. They've been there, done that. Chief Instructor Byron Schmidt was one of only two Marines to ride a motorcycle all the way from Kuwait to Baghdad during Operation Iraqi Freedom.

• **Gunnery Sergeant Byron Schmidt, chief instructor, USMC Combat Motorcycle School:** In a combat situation, being on a motorcycle is a little scary because you're completely exposed; it takes both hands to operate, so you have to stop doing something in order to draw your weapon. Unless you're in a whole group of other vehicles, it's a little intimidating. •

The first time motorcycles were used in combat by the U.S. military was in 1916, during General Pershing's failed pursuit of Pancho Villa. During World War I, seven- to eighteen-horsepower motorcycles were supplied by Excelsior, Indian, and a little company from Milwaukee known as Harley-Davidson. Nearly thirty-five thousand bikes were delivered for dispatch and security duty to help defeat the Germans.

But by World War II, the crafty German military had thirty different models of motorcycles, made by the likes of BMW and Zndapp. Often equipped with machine guns, the motorcycle troops were considered one of the elite units of the German army.

The baddest hog of World War II was the Harley-Davidson WLA. It was faster and more durable than anything the Germans could produce, and Harley-Davidson delivered eighty-eight thousand of them during the war. But the Allies recognized the limitations of the motorcycle, using it only for reconnaissance, dispatch, and police work.

Although the role of the combat motorcycle hasn't changed much since World War II, the machine itself is a whole new beast. The current bike ridden by the Marine Corps is the forty-two-horsepower Kawasaki KLR650. Used by the Marines since 1999, it's similar to the civilian model, with a few added modifications.

• **Sergeant Schmidt:** We've modified it with off-road tires and heavier suspension. In addition, we have a brush guard down here that protects our engine. The Marine Corps has added off-road foot pegs to the motorcycle and upgraded to an off-road shifter, which allows more room for the rider's boots. •

Topping out at more than 100 miles per hour and the ability to go for 360 miles on a single tank of gas, this vehi-cle has some serious cojones. The new Marine Corps motorcycles have been modified to run on diesel. That way they can drink from the same jug as the rest of the motor pool.

And even if diesel isn't handy, no problem. The new M1030M1, the Marines' cutting-edge experimental motorcycle, can run on just about anything, including kerosene! The old gas-burning motorcycle gets sixty miles to the gallon. But this experimental bike gets a whopping 110!

With that kind of success, nobody will be able to catch our Marine expeditionary forces! Oohrah!

The first time motorcycles were used in combat by the U.S. military was in 1916, against Mexican bandit Pancho Villa.

German World War II motorcycle troops were considered elite units.

The Kawasaki KLR650: Currently the bike of choice for the USMC.

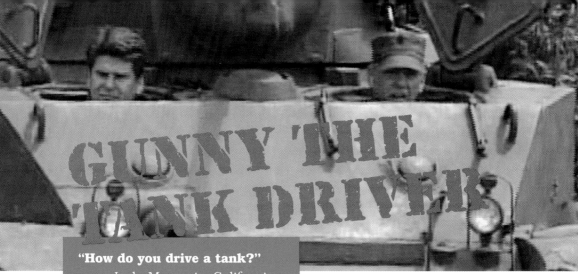

GUNNY THE TANK DRIVER

"How do you drive a tank?"
—Jack, Monrovia, California

**"Oohrah and out of the way—
here comes Gunny!"**

Well, Jack, you don't head down to the Acme Tank Driver's School, that's for darn sure!

Craig Michelson, curator of the American Society of Military History Museum, said he was gonna teach me how to drive one of these iron behemoths.

• Craig Michelson, curator of the American Society of Military History Museum: The M5A1 Stuart was produced from 1942 to 1945 by Cadillac, and they called it the Cadillac of little tanks. It had a four-man crew— a commander, a driver, an assistant driver, and a gunner. Basically a tank is just like a big bulldozer, where you're controlling the tracks to turn. The two levers on the two sides control the track. By stopping one of the tracks, that will cause you to turn. •

All tanks use the same basic principle: When both tracks are turning at the same speed, the tank goes in a straight line, but when you pull the brake and slow or stop one of the tracks, the tank will turn in that direction.

The Stuart gets its get-up-and-go from two Cadillac V8 engines. It also has a handy automatic transmission. And best of all: It has dual driving controls—a set for Craig and a set for me. Which makes this a perfect tank for driver's ed.

Weighing in at just fifteen tons, the M5 might look puny. But when it came out in 1942, this tank saw action with the Army in North Africa and in Europe, and with the U.S. Marines fighting in the Pacific. Craig told me that with a top speed of forty miles an hour, the M5 was considered fast and maneuverable.

"I am one hard-charging Gunny and I've got no time for slackers! Keep up!"

From World War II to the present day, all tanks have operated under the same basic principle.

M5 Stuart

Before I put the pedal to the metal, I decided a quick review was in order. I pulled on the right brake and the tank turned to the right; I pulled on the left brake and the tank turned to the left. To stop altogether, you pull back on both levers at the same time, but I had no intention of doing that.

Then I drove that baby right through an obstacle course filled with watermelons! Any problem? What do you think, maggothead? Piece of cake! Anyway, modern-day tanks are bigger, heavier, and they certainly deliver a heckuva lot more firepower. But believe it or not, they're still driven basically the same as they were in World War II. If it ain't broke, don't fix it.

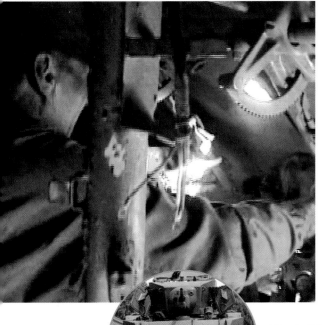

The Cadillac of light tanks.

THE HEDGECHOPPER

If you know anything about the bloody Normandy fighting in World War II, folks, you know about the hedgechopper or hedgerow cutter—or what its inventor called The Rhino—attached to the front of a tank. This simple rig was one of the unsung heroes in the summer of '44. You see, the problem was that as the Allied tanks moved in from the beaches and across the French countryside, they encountered stone and dirt berms covered with thick tangles of hedges. They were called hedgerows and had been built up over hundreds of years by French farmers. Now they were causing major headaches for our fighting men.

Sherman tanks that tried to go over them usually got a German anti-tank round in their exposed underbellies. And there was no easy way to plow through them. Luckily Sergeant Curtis Culin of the U.S. Second Armored Division came up with a solution. He took angle irons from the Nazi beach obstacles and welded them onto the front of a tank. That did the trick . . . the tank blasted through those hedgerows with no sweat.

THE FASTEST TRACKED VEHICLE IN WORLD WAR II? LET'S SETTLE IT!

> **"What was the faster, the M18 Hellcat or the M36 Jackson?"**
> —Dale, Carrington, North Dakota

Good question, Dale—both of these babies could move like hell at the time, during World War II. Which was faster? Well, Dale, I feel a visit to the racetrack coming on!

The king of the road was the M18 Hellcat. I like that name. With the pedal to the metal, the Hellcat could haul ass at nearly sixty miles an hour. That made it almost twice as fast as other World War II tanks and the fastest tracked vehicle in the war.

To see how an M18 might stack up against some competition, we paid a visit to a gearhead's ultimate garage . . . the restoration facility of an outfit called Combat Vehicles.

• **Michael Moss, president, Combat Vehicles:** Our goal is to be able to find these pieces of equipment around the world that are in derelict condition and bring them back into our shop and rebuild and restore them to the way they were used between 1941 and 1945. •

It can take these guys two thousand hours of knuckle-busting wrench turning to bring a beat-up old rust bucket back to showroom condition.

• **Bob Rubino, chief mechanic:** It's nice to have a vehicle come in that most people would write off as junk . . . something that would go to the scrap yard, and when you are done with it, it looks as good as it did the day it left the factory. •

From 1943 to 1945, twenty-five hundred M18 Hellcats rolled off the assembly line at Buick. But this ain't your daddy's Buick. Nohow. It's powered by a four-hundred-horsepower, nine-cylinder radial aircraft engine. The M18 we decided to race came from Bosnia—turns out, at the end of World War II the United States gave Yugoslavia a bunch of tanks. The folks at Combat Vehicles bought this one from Bosnian army surplus after their recent civil war.

• **Bob Rubino:** Very responsive in the steering, but you have to be careful because it is so agile. And the torsion bar suspension is like flying on a cloud. You don't feel any bumps . . . the thing doesn't rock, it doesn't pitch, it just keeps a nice steady ride. It really is a pleasure. I can see why the guys liked them. •

All that performance is there for one reason: to get its high-velocity 76mm gun pointed at bad guys fast. You see, the M18 really isn't a tank—technically it's a gun motor carrier, but it's better known as a tank destroyer. The Army's tank destroyer command wanted a fast tracked vehicle that could move in quickly, fire, and get the hell out of Dodge before the enemy knew what hit him. Mobility and firepower were its main attributes. It's a trade-off. For that, it gave up armor protection—the armor is only five-eighths of an inch thick, compared to the Sherman, which is two and a half inches.

• **Jim Gilmore, restoration specialist:** The M18 was really the zenith of tank destroyer doctrine and technology at the time. It was exactly what the tank destroyer service wanted. The later tanks we were given had larger-caliber guns, and more power and more punch, but they were not as maneuverable and they weren't as fast . . . and the doctrine of the time stressed speed, a quick strike. •

We put the M18 up against another American tank destroyer . . . the M36 Jackson. The M36 sports a 90mm gun. So it's better armed than the M18, and it's a little bigger. And the M36 kicked some serious butt in combat in World War II. The M18 lived up to its reputation as the fastest tank of its era, however: It pulled ahead with ease, leaving the M36 in the dust.

The official motto of the tank destroyer command was "Seek, Strike and Destroy." But I like the unofficial motto that the guys came up with themselves: "Shoot and Scoot." Oohrah!

The M36 saw some fierce combat in World War II.

The M18 drove at speeds up to sixty miles an hour.

And the winner and still champ . . . the M18.

THE DEUCE AND A HALF—THE TRUCK THAT WON WORLD WAR II

"What's the dope on the deuce and a half?"
—John, Bend, Oregon

A restored deuce and a half, in all its glory.

For you squids out there who don't get the lingo, John's asking about the six-by-six, two-and-a-half-ton trucks that were crucial in winning World War II. Back then, the whole U.S. war machine would have ground to a halt and had its tail kicked if it hadn't been for that unsung hero, the deuce and a half!

First off, two and a half tons doesn't mean the weight of the truck; it refers to the weight of the payload the truck can carry or tow. Six-by-six means six-wheel drive. The vehicle has a standard cab, front-wheel drive, and rear-wheel drive with a long wheelbase. But the GIs called it the deuce and a half 'cause deuce and a half is a cool way to say the number two and a half.

• **Juan Gonzales, president, WW II Impressions:** The heart of the truck is the two axles and the main bogey going through the center of the two, which holds up the entire two and a half tons of cargo that this truck can carry. There are levers and controls in the cab of the truck that will engage all the axles at once. It's a very versatile truck. The power plant of the two-and-a-half-ton cargo truck is an inline six-cylinder engine, 270-cubic-inch displacement. And it offers ninety horsepower at two thousand rpm. •

The first deuce and a half rolled off the assembly line of GMC's Yellow Truck and Coach Division in 1941. They were also built by International Harvester, Studebaker, and REO. The deuce had a top speed of forty-five miles an hour. Its wheels were fitted with special newly developed tires that had the same traction no matter what direction they were moving in; they were called NDT, or nondirectional tread.

Now, the deuce and a half got a chance to really strut its stuff when the American Army raced across France in 1944. Generals like Patton were screaming for more fuel and more ammo for their hard-chargin' armies.

The only way to get enough supplies from the beaches at Normandy, across France, and to the front line, would be with a nonstop convoy . . . so the Army set up a delivery system called the Red Ball Express.

They enlisted the support of many different quartermaster truck companies, service companies, and other units, then had trucks form a "conveyor belt." Nonstop all day long, twenty-four hours a day, continuous operation of military vehicles bringing supplies from the beach all the way up to the front lines.

During the height of the Red Ball, from August to November 1944,

The Red Ball Express brought supplies from the beaches of Normandy right to the fighting men up front.

drivers and their trucks delivered more than half a million tons of ammo, fuel, food, weapons, toilet paper—you name it. In the process, they wore out more than fifty thousand tires. The Red Ball brought fame to the deuce and a half, and it shone the spotlight on the drivers, too . . . mainly African Americans relegated to supply and service jobs by the then segregated Army.

The end of World War II certainly didn't mean the end of the deuce and a half; it's still around today. They've been trying to phase the damn thing out, but it's just too reliable to give up on. The old deuce and half can do just about anything you ask of it. But it's not perfect, is it, puke—it doesn't have a cupholder for your Big Gulp!

RED BALL CONVOYS ONLY

Expert Juan Gonzales points out the deuce's twin axles.

The deuce and a halfs on the Red Ball were mainly driven by African Americans, in the then segregated military.

How was the deuce and a half used in Vietnam?

TEST YOUR MILITARY IQ

Answer on page 233.

THE ARMORED SCOUT CARS OF WORLD WAR II

"How effective were armored scout cars back in World War II?"
—Hugo, West Palm Beach, Florida

The M3 Scout is great for a Sunday drive.

It's no secret I love my jeep, but the M3A1 Scout car ain't chopped liver, either. Hell, I love anything on wheels, especially when it comes equipped with a little firepower. But how effective was it? Well, here's the story.

The short answer is "kinda sorta."

In the late 1930s, the U.S. Army was looking for a vehicle that was fast and agile to patrol out ahead of the main force. At the time, the M3A1 seemed like the right tool for the job. It could do about fifty-five miles an hour. It was armed with a couple of machine guns and could carry six soldiers into combat. Its armor was up to half an inch thick, and the big roller thing in front was there to keep the M3 from getting its nose stuck in a ditch.

But once the war got going, it wasn't long before this baby was outclassed by the bad boys. The idea of arming cars with weapons and protecting the occupants with steel plates goes back to before World War I.

Back then, wheeled vehicles were way faster than the slow, clunky tanks of the time. So armored cars could be pretty handy when it came to scouting for the enemy and reconnaissance missions . . . as long as they stayed on the roads. Plus, wheeled vehicles were cheaper to build and easier to maintain than tracked vehicles. By the 1930s, many countries were working on a bunch of armored cars.

In 1938, the White Truck Company of Cleveland, Ohio, took one of their standard truck frames and covered the whole thing with armor plate. The M3 Scout car was born. It was powered by a six-cylinder Hercules gasoline engine. It worked great on the roads and did okay cross-country, but the armor

In wartime, though, the lightly armored Scout had its problems.

The new, improved M8 Scout reached battlefields in 1944.

made it much heavier than a regular truck. And back in the old days, in rough terrain, even with four-wheel drive, the M3 got stuck too easy. Not a good thing to do in combat.

Now, the German armored cars could really knock your socks off. These babies were really maneuverable, and really agile. Some had eight wheels and twelve-cylinder engines that could get 'em just about anyplace. The M3 was no match for these monsters. It had a tough time when it saw action in North Africa in 1942, and it spent the rest of the war on rear-echelon duty, running convoy security and the like.

In 1943 a new American armored car, the M8 Greyhound, picked up where the M3 left off. I'd say the M8

was the best armored car we had in the war. It was built by Ford. It had six wheels, so it could get into and out of places that the M3 couldn't dream of. The M8 sported a 37mm gun, and its armored skin encased the crew like a tank. And with that nice little cannon, recon units didn't have to worry so much if they ran into trouble.

Armored car development didn't end with World War II. Lots of countries, particularly Russia, saw the value of fast, wheeled vehicles.

Today our Army and Marine Corps get a lot of mileage out of their wheeled vehicles like the LAV and the Army's brand-new Stryker—'cause on the modern battlefield, they'll tell ya that speed is life.

Some German armored cars had eight wheels and twelve-cylinder engines that could take you anywhere.

THE GLORIOUS HISTORY OF THE HALFTRACK

Gunny in a vintage 1941 M2 halftrack.

Just like my beloved jeep, the Sherman tank, or the B-17 Flying Fortress, the halftrack is one of those familiar machines that screams out World War II.

Back then you would find these honeys doing all sorts of things all over the place. And the guys just loved them.

• **Gary Harper, military vehicle collector:** The halftrack is probably one of the most versatile military land vehicles that came out in World War II. Not only did the GIs come up with myriad uses for them, the government loved these big armored boxes, too. •

During the 1920s and '30s, the U.S. War Department was experimenting with a vehicle that was a cross between a truck and a tractor. They wanted something that could carry a heavy load, but still move fast and make its way over rough terrain. In 1940, the Army found what it was looking for and

standardized two base designs of an armored halftrack: the M2 and the slightly longer M3. A fully loaded halftrack can tip the scale at ten tons, but it can reach forty-five miles an hour, thanks to a 386-cubic-inch, inline six-cylinder gasoline engine.

• **Gary Harper:** It's made out of nickel chrome alloy. It even says it on the block in raised letters. A lot of people think that was to make the engine literally bulletproof, but that's not the case. The idea was to make a rugged engine that would last and last and last. •

Now, it may seem obvious how the halftrack got its name, but how the track is put together is more clever than you may think. The track is one continuous band that goes around. There's no junction, no joint, no pins, nothing. It is essentially a rubber band. The rubber is molded over steel plates held together by steel cables. The halftrack was the only vehicle of the war with this simple and reliable design.

• **Gary Harper:** These tracks were made by Goodyear, over sixty years ago. And we're still driving them on a daily basis. That should attest to the quality of what we were able to produce in 1941. •

The basic version of the halftrack was the personnel carrier, and it did a real good job of getting troops into combat. But the quarter-inch-thick armor on the sides protected the guys inside only from small-arms fire, and the open top left the occupants vulnerable to overhead artillery bursts and grenades. So it wasn't perfect. But what the halftrack lacked in armor, it made up for in versatility. The Army took that base design and modified it into all sorts of fighting vehicles, like the M15, which had two .50-caliber machine guns and a 37mm cannon to blast enemy dive-bombers out of the sky.

But my favorite version of the halftrack has gotta be the M16, better known as the quad fifty. Sporting four .50-caliber machine guns in an electric-powered turret, the quad fifty was an awesome anti-aircraft and anti-personnel weapon. Boy, I'd love to squeeze off some rounds with one of those. Get some!

It was a cross between a truck and a tractor.

A thing of beauty: the halftrack with quad .50s.

The track is one continuous band of rubber over steel plate.

TEST YOUR MILITARY IQ

How many halftracks were built during World War II?

Answer on page 233.

HEAVY HAULERS

Well, Jeff, you can't exactly call a tow truck, so let me introduce you to the guys who'll ride to the rescue!

I headed on out to Fort Irwin in the California desert, home of the Army's national training center. It's a thousand-square-mile dustbowl where hard-hitting combat vehicles have plenty of room to roam. And when they run into trouble, they turn to the Army's heavy-metal beasts of burden. Staff Sergeant Scott Molle, a driver from the 1158th Transportation Company of the Wisconsin National Guard, helps crew this biggest of rigs—the Heavy Equipment Transport, or HET. It doesn't just haul away broken tanks, but also saves wear-and-tear on combat vehicles by taking them right to the fight.

• **Staff Sergeant Scott Molle:** The main thing the Army likes to use HET for is to haul equipment after it comes in on the ships. We'll take it to wherever they want it to go. But we also use HET in case there is a broken-down vehicle out there. We will go back and recover that vehicle and bring it back to our area and fix it. •

Top: The Heavy Equipment Transport, or HET, can haul anything on any battlefield.

Inset: The HET's two winches can pull up to sixty tons.

The M1070 tractor and the M1000 trailer weigh in at forty-five tons. The tractor is powered by a five-hundred-horsepower, V8 Detroit diesel engine. It's got an eight-wheel axle where you can lock in all four axles. And you can deflate the tires so that they can spread out and get better traction.

• **Sergeant Molle:** We have a central tire inflation system called the CTIS. You can change the setting to Snow or Sand, which deflates the tires for better traction. And it also has Highway, for highway speed, which brings it back up to its normal operating pressure so you get better mileage with the truck. •

The truck also has two winches, each of which is capable of pulling thirty tons—together we're looking at sixty tons of pull! The winches pull vehicles straight onto the trailer. And that trailer can hold up to seventy tons, which means that even a combat-loaded Abrams tank can hitch a ride. The trailer's got forty tires and two spares up in the rack. And they tell me they can run with a flat tire if they have to. When I was over in Kuwait and Iraq, I saw plenty of HETs pulling their weight. They were hauling right up to the front from day one.

HETs have been around since 1993, so they weren't available for Operation Desert Storm. Back then in 1991, the Army used M746 or M911 tractors, but they were having a hard time carrying the heavy Abrams tanks. When HET came along, that all changed, big time!

THE DRAGON WAGON

Now, the HET is a hit, but it wasn't our first heavy hauler. Ever hear of a World War II monster called the Dragon Wagon? This big boy entered service in 1943 and weighed in at thirty-eight tons. A 240-horsepower engine powered the M25 tractor, which was also equipped with six-wheel drive. The cab was armored to protect the seven-man crew from small-arms fire and shrapnel. The Dragon Wagon came with three winches, one in front and two in back, capable of dragging a combined seventy-eight tons' worth of equipment. And the M15 trailer had no problem carrying vehicles weighing up to forty tons, like the Sherman tank. The M25 had such a catchy nickname that even today some HET crews still call their rigs Dragon Wagons.

World War II's famous "Dragon Wagon" hauled a pretty good load.

The Sno-Cat

The Rollagon

The Snow Scout

The Snow Train

HOT VEHICLES FOR A "COLD" WAR

"What kind of vehicles does the military have for extreme arctic conditions?"

—Zia, Pittsburgh, Pennsylvania

Over the years, the U.S. military has experimented with all kinds of transport for what I guess you could call the ultimate Cold War. Motivated by the potential for a Cold War conflict in Siberia or North Korea or even a surprise Commie invasion of Alaska, the U.S. Army experimented with all kinds of tires, tracks, and sleds to move troops and gear across snow and ice. Here's a little pictorial for you folks who move your lips while reading— which is all of you!

The Sno-Cat

In the 1960s, they came up with the Sno-Cat, which delivered independent power to each of its four huge tracks. The Cats were so popular that there's quite a market for vintage ones these days, if you've got one stashed behind your doghouse . . .

The Rollagon

The Rollagon had oversized low-pressure rollers, which is where the name comes from. They were originally designed in the 1960s, went through a redesign in the 1980s, and are now used for transportation around the Alaska pipeline.

The Snow Scout

My personal favorite was the Snow Scout, a weird combination of sled and aircraft that could skim over the frozen north at forty miles per hour; some thought it looked like a giant frozen beetle out there. But compared to the Rollagon's fifteen-mile-per-hour speed, it could move!

The Snow Train

The real incredible hulk of the era was the Snow Train, a behemoth that could transport huge amounts of gear and still have room left over for a rolling barracks and chow hall. The Snow Train still holds the record for the longest truck in the world. The final version was 572 feet long, with fifty-four wheels and a gross weight—unloaded— of more than four hundred tons.

We ain't fighting too many battles up in the Arctic these days, but if we ever do run up against a polar bear with an attitude, the U.S. Army is ready. Now, that Snow Train is pretty awesome, but I wouldn't want to have to parallel-park the sucker.

THE STORY OF THE LCAC

For those of you nitwits out there who don't know what the hell Ray is talking about, let me translate. LCAC equals "Landing Craft Air Cushioned." It's a U.S. Navy hovercraft. The reason we've got it here instead of over in the "Ships" section is that the LCAC seems to magically hover over both land and sea. Even with heavy payloads of vehicles, cargo, and personnel, it skims over the surface at high speeds.

LCACs saw action in the Persian Gulf and Somalia and proved just how critical they are to quick-strike amphibious operations.

It's quite a craft: Approximately forty feet wide by eighty feet long, it travels at speeds of fifty knots, with a two-hundred-mile nautical range. It carries a payload of approximately seventy tons. It's got four diesel turbine engines.

As they say, "No beach out of reach!" Oohrah!

These humongous engines have two jobs: They power the rear propellers and drive a fan that inflates the air cushion. The fan pumps air down into the black flexible skirt, and that's the secret to lifting the craft off the ground.

And since it's floating, it doesn't really matter if the LCAC is traveling over ground or water, although the LCAC driver we talked with compared it to riding a roller coaster for two hours!

In a combat situation, the LCAC can pack twenty-four fully equipped combat-ready Marines into the port cabin. On the cargo deck, it can carry all kinds of fighting vehicles, artillery, and even the messy M1 Abrams tank. Since they were first deployed back in 1982, the Navy's LCACs have effectively quadrupled the number of beaches we can hit. And since these babies are bringing in around seventy tons of fighting vehicles and artillery at a time, it's all run and gun.

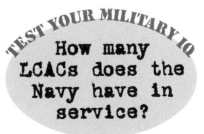

TEST YOUR MILITARY IQ

How many LCACs does the Navy have in service?

Answer on page 233.

STRYKER: COMBAT VEHICLE OF THE FUTURE

"Can you give me any details on the new Stryker Wheeled Armored Vehicle?"
—Pete, Staten Island, New York

The Stryker: rapid response in a powerful package.

Inset: The Stryker provides a quick exit for its nine-infantryman cargo.

Pete, when the 82nd Airborne Division landed in Saudi Arabia in 1990 as the first response to Iraq's invasion of Kuwait, they stood a good chance of becoming speed bumps for Saddam Hussein's tanks, because these paratroopers didn't have armored vehicles. But they were the only force the Army could get to Saudi Arabia quickly enough to discourage Iraq's forces from rolling through the rest of the Middle East.

The 82nd held its breath. And it got lucky—Saddam's mechanized forces stopped at the Kuwaiti border. Even so, the incident showed Army brass that they had a serious problem.

• **Colonel Mike Rounds, Stryker Brigade commander:** We have light forces, and we can pick them up and move them very quickly. But if you're going up against an enemy that has heavy forces, they don't have the lethality. On the other end of the spectrum we have heavy forces that have a phenomenal capability to go toe-to-toe with any other army in the world. The problem is that it takes a long time and a lot of lift to get them to where we need to fight, because they're heavy. How do we fill the gap between the light forces and the heavy forces? •

The answer is now taking shape in the form of the Stryker Brigade—a medium-weight armored force that can reach any hot spot in the world within ninety-six hours. The quick-response Stryker Brigade takes it name from its new ride, a cutting-edge armored fighting vehicle called, you guessed it, the Stryker.

The Stryker can fit a nine-person infantry squad, along with a driver and vehicle commander, but it's small enough and light enough to fit in a C-130 cargo plane. The Stryker rolls off the aircraft ready to fight. And it's built for speed—seventy miles an hour, and forty miles an hour over semi-rough terrain. Instead of using tracks, eight rubber tires—linked to a central tire inflation system—help the Stryker speed over any terrain and avoid flat tires.

Weighing in at just under twenty tons—ten tons lighter than the current Bradley Fighting Vehicle—the Stryker still has fairly thick skin. It can stop heavy machine-gun fire. With added bolt-on plates, it can deflect rocket-propelled grenades. And it's no slouch at delivering firepower of its own.

• **Staff Sergeant Kenneth Lethcoe, Stryker Training Team:** Currently it has a Remote Weapons Station on top, mounted on a pedestal that has 360-degree rotation. It can mount either a .50-caliber machine gun or a Mark 19 40mm grenade launcher. •

A camera mounted below the gun barrel shows the vehicle commander what he's aiming at. It also helps him navigate. But the most outstanding feature of this new warhorse is an onboard computer that's linked to brigade headquarters. The vehicle commander can see a map of the battlefield that's constantly updated with information about the fight.

Strykers have already gotten a chance to strut their stuff in war games. And the units that faced off against these vehicles didn't know what hit 'em. The Stryker is probably never going to completely replace the Bradley. But with its ability to go almost anywhere—fast—and to keep the soldiers it carries up to date about the battle, I have a feeling that the Stryker just might catch some bad guys with their pants down. Remember, that's Stryker with a *y*. The vehicle gets its name from two Medal of Honor recipients—one in World War II and the other in Vietnam, both named Stryker. Betcha didn't know that.

The onboard computer helps the Stryker commander plot a course and aim fire.

The Remote Weapons System is mounted above and features a camera and either a .50-caliber machine gun or a Mark 19 40mm grenade launcher.

LET'S NOT FORGET FLYER 21

Going places other vehicles can only dream about!

"What's the Flyer 21 used for, and by whom?"
—Ken, Myrtle Beach, North Carolina

Ken, good question! There's a new breed of combat vehicle that's a cross between a jeep and a dune buggy. It's called the Flyer 21!

There's no doubt about it, the Flyer 21 is a kick-ass, multipurpose vehicle. It can make mincemeat out of any terrain and go places that other vehicles can only dream about. That way the U.S. Special Forces can sneak up and scare the snot out of the bad guys. The Flyer is the brainchild of Oded Nechushtan, who helped design vehicles while in the Israeli military. He came to the States to do high-speed off-road racing, then combined that with his military background to create the Flyer.

• **Oded Nechushtan, Flyer 21 designer:** It is the only military vehicle in service with unique off-road racing technology incorporated into the vehicle. There's no other military vehicle like it today. •

But the Flyer's more than just a souped-up dune buggy. This demon can pack a big punch, with either a .50-caliber machine gun, a 40mm grenade launcher, or anti-tank missiles—no wonder airborne units and the Marines are also checking it out. The first version used by the Special Forces was a go-anywhere ambulance able to carry six stretchers. There was also a stretched-out troop carrier that could fit seventeen people. The latest version of the Flyer is modular so it can quickly switch from a weapons platform to a six-person troop carrier or ambulance.

The Flyer weighs only half as much as the Humvee while still carrying nearly the same size payload. This should give fast-moving outfits like Special Forces, paratroopers, and Marines a lot more flexibility. And to top it all off, they fit inside helicopters—the preferred mode of transportation for these quick-strike forces.

And one of the coolest features is the ability to stack one Flyer on top of another inside transports. You can even drive two at a time into the cargo hold. Stacking allows some aircraft to carry and air-drop two or even three times as many Flyers as Humvees.

Besides incredible mobility and easy transportability, another secret to the Flyer's success is its tubular frame. That's what makes it light but also strong and durable. There's also a lot of redundancy—which in this case is a good thing.

• **Oded Nechushtan:** There are three spring systems in one corner of each vehicle. So if something goes wrong and one system fails, you can

continue to run the second one. And if the second one fails, you can continue to run on the third one, which is very important for a military application. •

Now, maybe you're looking at the big fat tires and thinking, Those suckers are gonna get flattened by enemy gunfire—well, think again, pal. The tire pressure is so low that you can still drive to safety with bullet-riddled tires and even make a getaway on three wheels if one of the front two gets completely blown away. That's because the engine is mounted in the back. That takes weight off the front tires and gives the driver great visibility with a short front end. The Flyer has a low center of gravity but still has sixteen inches of ground clearance, twice as much as most other military vehicles.

The Flyer 21 is one helluvan awesome ride, but I told my little jeep, don't worry—you're still the only one for the old Gunny, baby!

Stacking the Flyer for easy delivery!

The Flyer boasts Ma Deuce mounted on top.

GENTLEMEN START YOUR ENGINES!

The winner and still champ.

"What is the fastest vehicle used by the Army today?"
—Jason, Colorado Springs, Colorado

W ell, I hate to disillusion you, Jason, seeing as how you're only twelve years old and all, but it ain't my trusty jeep here.

At least, not yet.

The straight answer to Jason's question is the new Stryker Wheeled Armored Vehicle, which we just talked about a few pages back. It can reach speeds of up to seventy miles an hour, making it the Army's fastest general-issue vehicle. But I've got an even better response to Jason's question that goes way beyond the official answer.

"What? This is the first book you've finished since *Black Beauty*? Drop and give me fifty, puke!"

Meet the Sarge—a nitro-methane-powered beast that can move out at 330 miles an hour! Now, I know some of you out there are saying to yourselves, Hey, Gunny! You ain't playin' fair here. This isn't a combat military vehicle—it's a top fuel dragster.

Well, you're right, but pay attention, dirtballs: Jason's question was "What is the fastest vehicle used by the Army?" Now, technically, the Army doesn't own Sarge. The crew and mechanics aren't soldiers, and it doesn't pack any firepower, but the Army uses the Sarge very effectively in its new recruiting campaign. It's a great way to reach the thousands of fans of National Hot Rod Association drag racing!

So the Army is this dragster's chief sponsor, but the Sarge is owned by Schumacher Racing, based outta Indianapolis.

I met up with the team at the Firebird International Raceway outside Phoenix, Arizona. Tony Schumacher is the lucky fella who gets to put the pedal to the metal.

• **Tony Schumacher:** This is the fastest-accelerating vehicle on the planet. We go 330 mph in four seconds. So when you're trying to relate to that and you're talking about the U.S. Army, it's very easy to explain

The challenger and its intrepid driver.

teamwork, honor, duty, self-discipline, and all that—it fits perfectly with an Army program. •

Tony has zoomed the Sarge up to 333.08 miles an hour—the fastest speed ever recorded on a National Hot Rod Association track. Underneath the hood, we're talkin' a seven-thousand-horsepower Hemi. When Tony hits the throttle, Sarge registers a 2.5 on the earthquake Richter scale!

Now, here's a little Drag Racing 101. Basically, it's an acceleration contest between two cars startin' from a standing start over a straight quarter-mile course. The drivers' reaction time is critical. They keep their eyes on a set of starting lights called a Christmas tree. When the lights blink down from amber to green, they're off!

Tony Schumacher: When that light turns green and you hit that accelerator it's like bein' shot. It's painful. You're stuck to that seat like Velcro. We do a lot of training for that, 'cause it's a lot of G's on your body. But equally, when you hit the parachutes at the end you go from 330 mph to 230 in one second, so you're decelerating at six G's. And that's an incredible range there—from a plus 5.5 to a minus 6.

Now, boys and girls, I did something you maggots might consider stupid—I challenged Tony to a race. My trusty jeep against Sarge. You guys just don't know the meaning of loyalty!

It's a tradition with Tony that he pack his own brake chute on the Sarge. Well, with all the horses I got under my hood . . . I thought it was best to pack a chute, too. I got all ready on the firing line, there was a thumbs-up from my crew chief—and I took off. My eye was on the speedometer and I thought my honey was hauling butt. But then I realized that the Sarge was nowhere in sight—and he wasn't eating my dust, either.

Ladies and gentlemen, I lost, but the ol' jeep ran a valiant race. And while Sarge might be able to beat us on pure speed—highly overrated, if you ask me—we've got 'em beat hands down on firepower and endurance.

Still, I gotta admit, that dragster is the coolest recruiting gimmick since Uncle Sam started giving the finger!

Semper fi. Carry on!

And—they're off!

PART 1: WEAPONS

How much did the average medieval weapon weigh?

Answer: Between two and three pounds.

When was the longbow replaced by firearms?

Answer: By the end of the sixteenth century.

Why did pirates call their flag the Jolly Roger?

Answer: The origin is mainly unknown . . . but for one tantalizing clue: Roger was eighteenth-century slang for having sex!

During the Civil War, soldiers of which army carried the bowie knife?

Answer: The Confederates.

Who was the minie ball named after? Think, maggots---it ain't Minnie Mouse.

Answer: Its inventor was French army Captain Claude Etienne Minie.

True or false: Okay, birdbrain---was there really a special carrier pigeon Medal of Honor?

Answer: True. It was called the Dickin Medal.

Name two other big guns of World War II. Hint: They sound like your grannies, maggots!

Answer: Big Bertha and Anzio Annie.

What's M1 thumb?

Answer: That's what happens when you don't pull your thumb out fast enough and the bolt smashes it. Ouch!

Who else besides the military got a lot of use out of BAR?

Answer: Believe it or not, the gangs of the Roaring Twenties added it to their arsenal of weapons, and the police did the same.

How much does the M18A1 Claymore weigh?

Answer: It weighs 3.5 pounds.

What does a fist pumped twice mean? No, numbskull, we're not asking for the check!

Answer: Move out, double-time!

Where did the word sniper come from?

Answer: The word sniper comes from the British, who used to hunt a fast little game bird called the snipe.

Today one target point can be destroyed with one smart bomb. How many did it take during World War II?

Answer: 648 bombs.

PART TWO: GEAR

When was the last mounted cavalry charge the U.S. Army made?

Answer: Against Pancho Villa in Mexico in 1916.

What was the jetpack's maximum flight time?

Answer: 20 seconds.

Okay, Dr. Atkins---how many calories in each C-Ration?

Answer: 1,100 calories.

PART 3: GRUNTS

Why is a grunt called a grunt?

Answer: The phrase grunt work began as a railroad term for unskilled labor.

How far could an M109 self-propelled gun blast its projectiles?

Answer: 11.2 miles.

What's the range of a MILES laser?

Answer: 800 meters.

Who were the first military smoke jumpers?

Answer: The men of the Army's courageous 555th unit were not only the first smoke jumpers but the first all-black parachute unit in American history.

PART FOUR: AIRPLANES

Oswald Boelcke's second in command was Max Immelman. What did he become famous for?

Answer: The Immelman Turn, a half loop, half roll, was quite useful in shaking off enemy planes.

Has anyone ever ejected at supersonic speed?

Answer: One airman, George Smith, ejected from an F-100 Saber in a dive. Witnesses heard a sonic boom as he did so.

What was a "blood chit"?

Answer: World War II pilots sewed little flags into their jackets. If they were shot down, this would let the locals know they'd get a reward for helping.

What's the heaviest vehicle that can currently be airdropped?

Answer: A 38,000-pound front-end loader.

PART 5: SHIPS

When did the Navy first use deep-sea divers?

Answer: In the 1880s to recover valuable torpedoes.

Where does the term "deep six" come from?

Answer: From the centuries-old nautical phrase "by the deep six," meaning the water is six fathoms deep.

What other small, fast World War II craft did Higgins Industries develop?

Answer: The PT boat.

Who invented the first hydrofoil?

Answer: Alexander Graham Bell's last invention, back in 1919, was the hydrofoil. The HD-4m, as he called it, set a 71 mph record on open water that wasn't broken until 1963.

How many ships are in the mothball fleet?

Answer: About 120.

PART 6: VEHICLES

How was the deuce and a half used in Vietnam?

Answer: As a gun truck with a heavy-caliber machine gun mount.

How many halftracks were built during World War II?

Answer: 40,000.

How many LCACs does the Navy have in service?

Answer: 91.

PHOTO CREDITS

INDEX

In addition to hosting *Mail Call*, **R. Lee Ermey** is a retired Marine Corps Drill Instructor, Vietnam veteran, and actor. He has appeared in more than sixty movies, including *Apocalypse Now, Full Metal Jacket, Dead Man Walking,* and *Leaving Las Vegas.* He lives in California. Visit www.thehistorychannel.com/mailcall and www.rleeermey.com.